ABOUT THE PUBLISHER

New York Institute of Finance

. . . *more than just books.*

NYIF offers practical, applied training and education in a wide range of format and topics:

* *Classroom training:* evenings, mornings, noon-hours
* *Seminars and conferences:* one-, two-, and three-day introductory, intermediate-, and professional-level programs
* *Customized training:* need-specific programs conducted on your site or ours; in New York City, throughout the United States, anywhere in the world
* *Independent study:* self-paced learning—basic, intermediate, or advanced
* *Exam preparation:* NASD licensing (including Series 3, 6, 7, 24, 27, 63); C.F.A.; state life and health insurance

Subjects of books and training programs include the following:

* Account Executive Training
* Brokerage Operations
* Currency Trading
* Futures Trading
* International Corporate Finance
* Investment Analysis
* Options Trading
* Securities Transfer
* Selling Securities
* Technical Analysis
* Treasury Management
* Yield Curve Analysis

When Wall Street professionals think **training**, *they think NYIF.*

For further information, please call or write to us. Please specify your areas of interest—classroom training, custom programs, independent-study courses, exam preparation, or books—so that we can respond promptly to your inquiry.

New York Institute of Finance
70 Pine Street
New York, NY 10270-0003
212 / 344-2900
FAX: 212 / 514-8423
TELEX: 238790

Simon & Schuster, Inc.   A Gulf + Western Company
"Where Wall Street Goes to School" tm

Managing international treasury transactions:

Accounting, taxation, and risk control

John I. Tiner

Joe M. Conneely

(Chapter 9 entitled "United States Taxation" by David F. Windish.)

New York Institute of Finance

Library of Congress Cataloging in Publication Data

Tiner, John I.
  Managing international treasury transactions : accounting, taxation, and risk control / John I. Tiner and Joe M. Conneely.
    p. cm.
  Rev. ed. of: Accounting for treasury products. 1987.
  Includes index.
  ISBN 0-13-551474-6 : $65.00 (U.S.)
  1. Banks and banking—Great Britain—Accounting. 2. Banks and banking—Taxation—Great Britain. 3. Financial futures—Great Britain—Accounting. 4. Financial futures—Taxation—Great Britain.
  I. Conneely, Joe M. II. Tiner, John I. Accounting for treasury products. III. Title.
HG1708.T56 1988   87-34765
657'.833—dc19   CIP

© Arthur Andersen & Co. 1987, 1989. © Chapter 9, David F. Windish, 1988

Published in the United Kingdom under the title Accounting for Treasury Products: A Practical Guide in Accounting, Tax & Risk Control (2nd edition).

Published in the United States and Canada by NYIF Corp. A Division of Simon & Schuster Inc, 70 Pine Street, New York, New York 10270-003.

English language edition except the United States and Canada, published by Woodhead-Faulkner (Publishers) Limited, Simon & Schuster International Group, Fitzwilliam House, 32 Trumpington Street, Cambridge CB2 1QY, England

British Library Cataloging in Publication Data
Tiner, John I.
  Accounting for treasury product: a practical guide to accounting, tax and risk control. 2nd ed.
  1. Financial institutions—Accounting
  2. Risk
  I. Title.   II. Conneely, Joe M.
  657'.48   HG1708

ISBN 0-85941-590-2
All rights reserved. No part of this book may be reproduced in any form or by any means without permission in writing from the publisher.

Printed in the United States of America

10 9 8 7 6 5 4 3 2 1

This publication is designed to provide accurate and authoritative information in regard to the subject matter covered. It is sold with the understanding that the publisher is not engaged in rendering legal, accounting, or other professional service. If legal advice or other expert assistance is required, the services of a competent professional person should be sought.

From a Declaration of Principles Jointly Adopted by
a Committee of the American Bar Association and a
Committee of Publishers and Associations

New York Institute of Finance
(NYIF Corp.)
70 Pine Street
New York, New York 10270-0003

Contents

Introduction, xiii

Risk patterns xv
Accounting framework xvi
Corporate users xviii
Taxation xix

CHAPTER ONE
The accounting environment, 1

Accounting background 3
Accounting objectives 4
Existing accounting framework 5
Accounting issues 6
Profit-and-loss recognition 8
Corporate users 10
Institutional users 11
Summary 13

CHAPTER TWO
Financial futures, 15

The product	17
Short-term interest-rate contracts	18
Long-term interest-rate contracts	19
Foreign-exchange contracts	19
Stock index contracts	19
Delivery	20
Markets	20
The exchange and the clearinghouse	21
The exchange	21
The clearinghouse	21
Margining	22
Uses	23
Hedging	23
Speculating	25
Arbitraging	26
Accounting for financial futures	26
Overall basis of accounting	26
Hedging	28
Currency futures	40
Stock index futures	40
Speculation	40
Disclosure	42

CHAPTER THREE
Forward-rate agreements, 43

The product	45
Uses	47
Assets	49
Liabilities	49
Interest spreads	49
Markets	49
Accounting for forward-rate agreements	49
Overall considerations	50
Hedge accounting	50
Speculation	57
Management information	59
Disclosure	60

CHAPTER FOUR
Swaps, 61

The product	63
Users	65
Interest-rate swaps	65
Currency swaps	67
Cross-currency swaps	68
Asset-based swaps	69
Accounting for swaps	70
Corporate users	72
Financial institutions	94
Matched intermediaries	95
Swap traders	98
How are swaps revalued?	99
Asset-based swaps	103

CHAPTER FIVE
Currency and interest-rate options, 105

The product	107
Basic terminology	107
Valuation	108
Uses	109
Speculators	109
Hedgers	109
Traders	110
Income enhancers	111
Trading strategies	111
Sell futures contract/buy call option	112
Sell futures contract/write put option	112
Write a put-call straddle	112
Traded stock options	113
Margining	113
Accounting for foreign currency and interest-rate options	114
Background	114
Professional standards	115
Accounting entries	115

Contents

CHAPTER SIX
Interest-rate caps, collars, and floors, 135

The product 137
    Interest-rate cap 137
    Interest-rate floor 138
    Interest-rate collar 138
Uses 140
Markets 141
Accounting for interest-rate caps, collars, and floors 141
    Accounting 143
    Interest-rate caps 143
    Interest-rate floor 149
    Interest-rate collar 152

CHAPTER SEVEN
Risk control, 153

Discussion of general risks 155
    Financial system risk 156
    Market pricing of financial risks in the long run 157
    Risk concentration 158
    Risk assessment and risk taking by individual firms 159
    Growth of multinational portfolios 160
    The volatility of markets 161
    Market or price risk 162
    Credit risk 163
    Technology risk 165
    Settlement or delivery risk 165
    Market liquidity risk 167
    Country and transfer risk 167
    Transaction-type risk 167
    Other risks 168
Risks by financial instrument 169
    Currency and interest-rate options 169
    Interest-rate and currency swaps 171
    Interest-rate caps, collars, and floors 175
    Interest-rate futures 176
    Forward-rate agreements 177

Contents

NIFs/RUFs	178
Repurchase agreements	179
Synopsis of general internal controls applicable to trading operations	182
Procedure and policy manuals	183
Credit limits	183
Trading limits	185
Trade tickets	185
Accounting records	185
Reporting	186
EDP support	187

CHAPTER EIGHT
United Kingdom taxation, 189

Introduction	191
Types of users	192
Banks and financial institutions	192
Trading activities	192
Investment activities	193
Exempt organizations	193
General U.K. tax principles	193
Income versus capital	194
Income tax schedules	195
Deductibility of expenses	196
Deductibility of interest	197
General concepts	197
Banking activities	198
Trading company	198
Investment management companies	199
U.K. branches of nonresident companies	199
Discount versus interest	199
Costs of finance	200
Critical issues for treasury instruments	200
Capital gains tax	201
Currency gains and losses	203
Revenue versus capital	203
Marine Midland and the Inland Revenue Statement of Practice	206

Taxation of specific treasury instruments 210
    Interest-rate treasury instruments 210
    Exchange-traded instruments 211
    Amendments to U.K. tax treatment 212
    Over-the-counter (OTC) instruments 214
Swaps (interest and currency) 222
    General aspects of swaps 222
    Commencement of swap-arrangement fees 222
    Periodic payments under swap 223
    Currency swaps—exchange gains and losses 226
Currency options 234
    Banks/other financial concerns 234
    Commercial users 234
    U.K. value added tax 235

CHAPTER NINE
United States taxation, 239

Introduction 241
General principles of U.S. taxation 242
    The ordinary income/capital gain distinction 243
    Tax treatment of capital gain or loss 244
    Interest and discount 246
    Currency gains and losses 250
Users of treasury instruments 254
    Banks and financial institutions 254
    Regulated investment companies (mutual funds) 255
    Tax-exempt organizations 256
Taxation of specific treasury instruments 256
    Interest-rate swaps 257
    Options, straddles, and Section 1092 258
    Section 1256 contracts 262
    Section 988 transactions 265
    Qualified Section 988 hedges 270

Glossary of terms, 293

APPENDIX ONE
Comparative risk table, 307

x

APPENDIX TWO
Inland Revenue Statement of Practice on exchange rate fluctuations, 311

Introduction	313
Marine Midland—a summary	313
Definitions	314
The recognition of exchange differences: Accounts treatment and tax consequences	315
Translation and conversion	315
The Inland Revenue view	315
Application of conversion bases	316
Capital and current liabilities	316
Matched assets and liabilities	317
Same currency	317
Matching of capital assets in foreign currency with current liabilities	318
Assets and liabilities not matched	318
A practical approach	319
More than one currency	323
Hedging transactions	324
Overseas branches and trades	326
Assets held on the "realization" basis	327
Roundabout loan arrangements	329
Nontrading companies	329
Groups of companies	330
Capital gains	330
Assessments open for earlier years	330

APPENDIX THREE
The London International Financial Futures Exchange limited taxation guidelines (issued 1982), 331

Method of assessment	333
Timing of assessment	334
Exchange conversion	335
Nonresidents	335
Capital gains—delivery	335

Contents

APPENDIX FOUR
Inland Revenue tax treatment of transactions in futures, 337

APPENDIX FIVE
Extract from Banker's Association letter to members of October 2, 1979, 341

APPENDIX SIX
U.K. Inland Revenue recognized overseas exchanges, 345

APPENDIX SEVEN
Inland Revenue Statement of Practice on tax treatment of transactions in financial futures and options (issued July 1988), 349

Introduction

Over the last ten years, commodity prices, foreign-exchange rates, and interest rates have become increasingly volatile and, accordingly, a need has arisen for a method to manage the commercial risks arising from the instability of these markets. Not surprisingly, financial instruments have been developed and established quickly to manage these risks, and over the last five years there has been an exponential growth in the use of these instruments.

This period has also seen the end of rapid balance sheet growth for many banks and the beginning of an era in which banks are placing greater emphasis on financial instruments as a means of improving return on assets. Banks are becoming far more involved as intermediaries in the capital markets and to a great degree this has been achieved through what has come to be known as the "securitization of lending," which to some extent has replaced traditional forms of lending. This development has been accompanied and accelerated by innovations in the capital markets. These innovations have enabled the needs of investors in different markets to be linked or arbitraged and also have contributed to the growth in the bond market as they provide ready access, through the swap mechanism, to a number of markets. Accordingly, the financial markets available to borrowers have increased significantly and this has been accompanied by increased competition among financial institutions to service the needs of these borrowers.

While these new financial instruments are to some degree an extension of traditional lending and risk management activities, their attributes differ significantly from those used in the past. These new instruments (i.e., futures, forward-rate agreements, options, interest-rate caps, and swaps) are complex from a legal, economic, accounting, and control perspective. They have the ability to transform assets, liabilities, and income and expense streams and can pose significant risks to the institutions that trade in them. Furthermore, the majority of these financial instruments are, in accounting terminology, "off-balance sheet," as they give rise to contingent assets and liabilities rather than the more traditional forms of assets and liabilities.

Growth in the use of these instruments should continue as they gain wider acceptance among corporate treasurers and as more combinations and permutations are derived from the initial instruments. In view of current volumes, the use of these instruments has gone beyond that of providing a customer service and has expanded to that of a trading nature.

Although the driving force for financial product innovation may have come from the demands of the major multinational corporations, there have been good reasons why the banks should want to get involved. During the 1970s, most banks experienced a massive growth in the size of their balance sheets. This brought many of them close to the capital ratios imposed by the bank regulators and hence they looked for other means of achieving profitable growth. Accordingly, banks are becoming far more involved as intermediaries in the international capital markets generating fee income and trading profits from taking short-term positions. Their role is to link lenders and borrowers rather than taking long-term positions themselves. They are identifying arbitrage opportunities for their customers and are arranging transactions to enable their customers to access markets not otherwise available to them. The essential features of this new era are that most of these new financial products are off-balance sheet and so have not currently required capital cover. Furthermore, most of the risks and rewards of customer exposure have frequently been passed to the nonbanking sector.

Risk patterns

Perhaps one of the most interesting features of this new product development is that the risks attached to many of the instruments, such as options and caps, are asymmetrical, unlike traditional methods of treasury management, such as those used in the forward foreign-exchange market, in that if one party gains, the other loses. This can pose major risk control issues for the writers or sellers of these instruments: the commercial and investment banks. Although these banks have been competing fiercely for corporate business as writer or seller, they very often find themselves in an extremely difficult risk management environment. This can be illustrated by the writer of a five-year interest-rate cap. Once interest rates start to exceed the cap rate, the writer has potential exposure extending out five years. A prudent risk manager will hedge at least part of that exposure as interest rates start to approach the cap rate, so that if interest rates do in fact rise to above the capped rate, the bank has some protection against losses under the cap agreement. Such prudent management can, however, turn against the writer if, say, interest rates were suddenly to fall so that the current interest rate is less than the capped rate. If the risk manager has been unable to remove the hedge in anticipation of the drop in rates, then by definition the hedging contract will represent a loss-making open position as there is no current exposure under the cap that requires protection.

This very simple example highlights the problems of risk management, and also demonstrates many of the problems associated with the traditional accounting distinction drawn between a hedging transaction and a speculative transaction. In the above example, if the interest-rate cap had been hedged using a deposit mismatch in the bank's money book, traditional accounting would provide that the interest payable and receivable on the deposits would be accrued over the life of the related deposits, while the premium received on the interest-rate cap would either be revalued or amortized over the cap life. Either way, the profit-and-loss recognition of first the hedged position and then, following a fall in interest rates, the interest-rate position on the deposits would not agree with the economic factors underlying the risk manager's decisions. This specific problem and other similar problems are covered in detail in the product chapters of this book.

While those responsible for initiating transactions in these instruments understand the commercial implications, it is unclear whether those responsible for accounting, supervision, and taxation have a clear understanding of the business rationale and the associated risks. It is this lack of understanding that causes much of the confusion that surrounds the current accounting environment for these instruments.

Accounting framework

There are no accounting standards either in the United Kingdom or internationally covering these instruments and the regulatory authorities have not finalized their proposals on the method of accounting for prudential supervision purposes. In the absence of accounting or other requirements, specific industries tend to develop a "best practice" that most participants in that industry tend to follow.

Because of the rapid development and complexity of these new financial instruments, the banking community has not developed a standard practice applicable to each individual instrument. Many banks treat the same instruments in different ways, in respect of both profit-and-loss recognition and balance sheet treatment. This is far from satisfactory, since the published accounts of banks are a key source of information for setting limits on, say, interbank deposit lines. Comparability is essential if sensible judgments and recommendations are to be made. In the absence of standard accounting practices, there is no doubt that disclosure of accounting policies and the size of commitments or contingencies, covering each new instrument traded, is fundamental for the reader being able to make rational conclusions from a set of bank financial statements.

In establishing the appropriate accounting treatment for a particular instrument, the underlying philosophy should be that the accounting treatment properly reflects the economic risks inherent in the transaction, both actual and contingent. In certain situations, this philosophy will apply to a group of transactions where, for example, a dealer has entered into four or five different transactions to exploit an arbitrage opportunity.

Care needs to be exercised in applying this concept for U.K. financial reporting purposes. Companies' statutory accounts are required to comply with the Companies Act of 1985 and Statements of Standard Accounting Practice. It is therefore important to ensure that in establishing accounting policies that reflect the economic substance of a transaction there is no breach of the Companies Act nor of Statements of Standard Accounting Practice. In most cases, it is possible to formulate policies that do not conflict with these requirements. If such a conflict arises, it may be necessary to adopt the policies reflecting the economic risks for management accounting and reporting purposes, and appropriate adjustments made for financial or statutory reporting purposes.

This leads to the next key accounting issue concerning new financial instruments: What are the implications for management information purposes? It is obvious that the amounts reflected in the reports from which strategic or dealing decisions are taken must accurately reflect the economic and commercial factors underlying the transactions. In practice, this is often difficult to apply effectively. For example, although a fixed against floating interest-rate swap may have been correctly reflected in the swap accounting and reporting system, there may be an equal and opposite position in financial futures, which if the two systems are not integrated or combined, will not show up in assessing the entities' overall risk position. Again, the pace of product innovation has caused some problems in this area as financial institutions are continually seeking to ensure that integrated systems meet all the requirements of the deal initiators and of general management.

Corporate users

Most of the foregoing issues concern the financial institutions that are responsible for developing the new instruments and for selling them to their corporate customers. These customers also should consider carefully the accounting, reporting, and tax implications of a transaction before committing themselves. The corporate users are generally involved with new instruments for one of two reasons:

1. To protect against adverse currency or interest-rate movements on exposures arising on their normal business.
2. To exploit an opportunity to raise funds in a currency or at an interest rate not otherwise available.

The new instruments often appear highly complex to the corporate user and are marketed by the banks on the "what-we-can-do-for-you" basis. Quite rightly, the banks concentrate on the commercial advantages of the product. However, the timing of any profit-and-loss impact arising from the transaction and the related impact on earnings per share, the presentation in the statutory accounts, and the impact of the entities' tax position are key issues for the corporate user, that may not be always fully addressed before entering into the transactions. The incidence of withholding taxes could render the transaction unprofitable, or immediate recognition of costs on transactions that will generate benefits in future years could harm short-term profitability. These are only two of the many pitfalls arising if the corporate user gives inadequate consideration to the accounting, reporting, and tax implications of a transaction.

Because the risks are not always symmetrical between the buyer and the seller, neither is the accounting treatment. Hence, it is important to consider the accounting treatment for the buyer separately from that applicable to the seller.

Taxation

It is perhaps not surprising that the recently developed financial instruments very often do not easily fit into existing U.K. tax legislation and tax case law. Tax advisers could be excused for thinking that failure to obtain reasonable and rational tax treatment for such products will at best restrict the size of the potential market, if not wipe out any commercial potential of a prospective new product before any transactions are consummated.

Taxation is and could continue to be one of the essential factors that any potential user of the new instrument market should consider. Because of the uncertainty of tax treatment that exists for many of the new financial instruments, all users and potential users would be well advised to seek appropriate professional advice before undertaking a particular type of transaction.

The purpose of this book is to provide a basis for accounting for the major new financial instruments that reflects both underlying economic factors and fundamental accounting standards. The book also analyzes the various tax consequences of the products and examines some of the risk control considerations.

Because currently none of the industrialized countries of the world has specific accounting standards covering new financial instruments, it is highly likely that the sections on accounting and on risk control will be applicable throughout the world. In this wider context, it is desirable that there is some consistency of accounting treatment between the major financial centers where most of the new instruments are traded. It is hoped that this book will assist in achieving such consistency.

CHAPTER 1

The accounting environment

Accounting background

To date, the accounting, regulatory, and banking communities have yet to establish an accounting and reporting framework for new financial instruments and, while in the United States limited guidance has been given through various Financial Accounting and Standards Board (FASB) statements, there are no current pronouncements in the United Kingdom for these instruments. Accordingly, the situation has arisen where accounting and reporting standards have been and are being developed in an *ad hoc* manner. As a result, significant segments of financial institutions' activities are not being included—or are at best only partly included—in the traditional balance sheet. Furthermore, the measurement of income flows and risks and disclosures is not being performed in a uniform and consistent manner.

In summary, these new financial instruments and the associated contingent risks now form a significant part of a financial institution's business and a need exists for sound accounting, regulatory, and control standards to be developed and implemented. The remainder of this chapter explores the accounting objectives and frameworks needed for these instruments, and the chapters that follow cover the accounting implications on an instrument-by-instrument basis.

Accounting objectives

The accountant's objective is to reflect the economic substance of past business transactions in the accounts. Typically, the accountant will look first to published standards as a primary reference for minimum standards of presentation and disclosure. From there, the application of those guidelines in particular circumstances becomes a matter of professional judgment and best practice. However, current pronouncements in the United Kingdom covering these instruments are limited to what constitutes a "true and fair view," and these assessments have been left largely to professional judgment.

The problems and issues identified above are similar to those experienced during the rapid expansion of the commodities futures markets, and to a great degree the accounting for new instruments has been based on principles underlying commodity futures accounting—namely, the basic premise has been adopted that the objective of any accounting principle is to ensure that the accounting reflects, as closely as possible, the economic effects and objectives of the transaction. Building on the accounting for commodity futures and straightforward deposit swaps, the principle of differentiating between speculative and hedging transactions have evolved. As the economic effects and objectives attributable to a speculative position may differ significantly from those relating to a hedge position, the accounting should likewise differ. Furthermore, the accounting for a hedge position should be consistent with the accounting followed for the actual cash market transaction.

It is not surprising, therefore, that this traditional approach has been applied in the accounting for new financial instruments. Current "best practice" and any related accounting standards stress continually the importance of defining whether a transaction constitutes a hedged or a speculative position.

Furthermore, accountants, to some degree, have also differentiated between corporate and financial institutional users, as the economic effects, underlying rationale, and objectives differ significantly. Applying these concepts together with the hedging/speculative criteria, one can arrive at the following "transaction types":

1. Speculation.
2. Hedging.
3. Trading.

The underlying liquidity of the instrument must be considered as this will also affect the accounting measurement.

The accountant then simply applies the appropriate measurement techniques to assess the evaluation of assets and liabilities. In a similar fashion, the measurement of income flows is performed. While this approach may sound straightforward, the issues the accountant must consider (i.e., hedging versus speculating, corporate versus institutional users, and liquid versus illiquid instruments) are not.

This—in conjunction with the instruments' complexity and evolving use—results in the application of accounting measurement techniques being a matter of judgment at best.

Existing accounting framework

Notwithstanding the wide range of differing accounting practices throughout the world, the following four fundamental concepts are generally accepted everywhere:

1. *Going concern.* Accounts are prepared on the assumption that unless there is evidence to the contrary, the entity to which they relate will continue in business for the foreseeable future.
2. *Accruals.* Revenues and costs are recognized as they arise rather than when they result in cash movements. There is a "matching" of costs and revenues.
3. *Prudence.* Revenues should not be recorded before their ultimate realization is reasonably certain. Provision is made for all known costs.
4. *Consistency.* Any accounting method adopted should be applied consistently from one period to the next.

These concepts are applied somewhat differently in individual countries—with prudence in particular being interpreted far more strictly in some countries than it is in the United Kingdom or the United States. Furthermore, most countries involved in these new markets now have a reasonably sophisticated structure of accounting standards that have been propounded by their various professional accounting bodies. There are also a limited number of international accounting standards that attempt to draw the various national approaches closer together. The relevant accounting standards may be summarized as follows:

1. *United Kingdom*
   Statements of Standard Accounting Practice (SSAP):
   SSAP 18–Accounting for Contingencies
   SSAP 20–Foreign Currency Translation
2. *United States*
   Statements of Financial Accounting Standards (SFAS):
   SFAS 5–Accounting for Contingencies
   SFAS 52–Foreign Currency Translation
   SFAS 80–Interest Rate Futures
3. *International*
   International Accounting Standards (IAS):
   IAS 10–Contingencies and Events Occurring After the Balance Sheet Date
   IAS 21–Accounting for the Effects of Changes in Foreign Exchange Rates

This chapter does not attempt to provide a complete review of the above standards and it is important to recognize that with the exception of SFAS 52, covering forward foreign-exchange contracts, and SFAS 80, covering interest-rate futures, these standards do not refer specifically to the kinds of transaction under discussion in this book.

Accounting issues

Having considered the objectives and the broad framework, the accountant is then in a position to apply accounting measurement and disclosure techniques. In order to do this, the following issues should be addressed:

1. Should an asset or liability be retained in the balance sheet, and if so what value should be attributed to it?
2. How should gains or losses, costs or benefits arising from the transaction be reflected in the profit and loss account?
3. To what extent should details be disclosed in an entity's financial statements?
4. To what extent can there be a setting off of assets and liabilities in an entity's balance sheet and profit and income and expense in the loss account?

The diversity of the financial instruments under consideration is such that it is unlikely that authoritative accounting standards can be developed. Instead, it is suggested that accounting standards be developed within the following framework:

1. There should be complete disclosure of the contractual commitments that arise from these instruments; namely, an entity's accounting policies for these instruments should be disclosed fully, together with the details of the contingent assets, liabilities, and the commitments that arise from dealing in these instruments. Given the problems that these instruments pose for accounting measurement, there is a clear need for stringent disclosures.
2. Where appropriate, the effects of the instruments should be placed on the balance sheet. Where this is not appropriate, the underlying commitments should be carefully analyzed and in line with standard accounting practices, and provisions should be made for losses, where appropriate.
3. In most instances, the question of balance sheet and profit and loss account set-off will be a matter of fact and will involve a careful evaluation of the legal documentation. Clearly, the question of substance over form is a difficult issue and the application of such a principle will have to be supported through full disclosure where appropriate.

The next issue that must be resolved is determining the value of the asset or liability, whether on- or off-balance-sheet, which has arisen from the transaction. In the absence of other overriding considerations, balance sheet valuation should be based on a mark-to-market approach as this reflects underlying liquidity. In cases where it may not be possible to accurately determine a market value (long-term currency contracts), it may be appropriate to carry the instrument at cost, although provision should be made for any perceived impairment in value. It should be noted that as instruments become more accepted, there will be an increase in their liquidity and thus more of a basis to use a mark-to-market approach.

The determination of market value is straightforward for instruments traded on an organized exchange, since there is usually continuity of quoted bid and offer prices. For certain instruments, such as forward-rate agreements, which are traded on a dealer-to-dealer basis (usually through a money broker), there is also a liquid market through which prices can be obtained. The market value of other instruments traded on a dealer-to-dealer basis but for which there is not a continuous flow of prices, could be determined by performing a theoretical valuation either by reference to original pricing formulae or by computing the cost/benefits arising from closing the position being revalued.

Particular care should be taken when using the latest dealt price in respect to an instrument for which there is limited marketability, or prices supplied by in-house dealers when the institution is not a market maker, to ensure that the prices used are appropriate.

Profit and loss recognition

Having determined the basis of valuation for the balance sheet, the question that then arises is how to treat the change in valuation in the profit and loss account. The traditional approach has been to determine whether the underlying economics of the transaction represent a hedged or a speculative position. While this approach can have serious flaws, it does have the following advantages:

1. It embraces the concepts of accrual accounting, going-concern, and,

to a lesser degree, prudence, all of which are fundamental accounting principles.
2. It attempts to achieve a symmetry between the underlying asset, liability, or contingent risk being hedged and the financial instrument being used.
3. It is an approach generally well understood by accountants and is widely used for accounting for risk transfer instruments.
4. To a great degree, existing control systems are based on this method of accounting.

While the hedge or "accruals" approach discussed above may appear to be relatively straightforward, it may not always be workable in practice because it assumes that one can readily identify hedged transactions.

Attempting to apply the "hedging" criteria to new financial instruments may not be appropriate in all circumstances as it may fail to recognize certain unique characteristics of the instruments.

In order to apply a hedge or accruals approach, one must understand the objectives and users behind the transaction. In order to do this, the following should be considered:

1. Corporate versus institutional user.
2. Hedging versus speculative versus trading objectives.
3. Liquid versus illiquid instruments.

If this is developed into a matrix, the framework can be set as in Table 1.1.

Table 1.1

	Corporate		Institutional	
	Liquid	Illiquid	Liquid	Illiquid
Speculative	LCM	LCM	MM	MM or LCM
Hedging	AA or LCM	AA or LCM	MM or LCM or AA	MM or LCM or AA
Trading	N/A	N/A	MM	MM or LCM

LCM = Lower of cost and market value
MM = Market-to-market value
AA = Accruals accounting

Corporate users

The framework for corporate users assumes relatively low volumes and the ability to identify whether a transaction is speculative or a hedge. If corporate users were actively trading, one would look to the institutional side of the matrix. The lower of cost or market approach for corporate users who are engaged in speculative activities reflects the prudence concept and the hedging section of the matrix assumes that the usual criteria for hedge accounting have been met, as follows:

1. The price behavior of the hedging medium and the item being hedged should be closely correlated.
2. The instrument and the related asset or liability should correspond both in terms of maturity and amount.
3. If the instrument has been taken in anticipation of a commitment, that commitment should reasonably be expected to be fulfilled.

In the United States, designation as a hedge is also required. This restricts the ability to wait until the outcome is known before deciding whether to follow hedge or speculative accounting. This would also be the recommended practice outside the United States.

When transactions qualify as hedges, the accounting treatment for them should conform with the accounting treatment of the underlying transaction being hedged as follows:

1. *Existing asset or liability.* If a position is taken against an existing asset or liability, then, where the hedged asset or liability is being revalued to market, unrealized profit or losses on the position should also be credited or debited to the profit or loss account. If the hedged asset (long position) is being carried at the lower of cost or market value, or a hedged liability (short position) is being carried at the higher of cost or market value, then the opposing treatment should be applied to the hedging transactions. If the hedged asset or liability is being carried at amortized cost, unrealized profits or losses on the position should be amortized over the remaining life of the hedged item.
2. *Trade commitment.* Unrealized differences on hedging a firm trade

commitment should be deferred until the commitment matures. It is necessary, however, to monitor the position of the underlying commitment throughout the life of the contract. If the commitment is cancelled before the contract is exercised, the previously deferred gains or losses should be taken to profit and loss, together with any subsequent differences.

3. *Potential commitment.* The situation regarding potential commitments requires further examination. An example might be a manufacturer who believes he may order goods for delivery next December but is unsure whether or not he will place a firm order and buys a number of currency option contracts. Another example is a person entering into a tender for a large overseas fixed price contract who wishes to protect the foreign exchange exposure that could arise.

In the United States, forward currency transactions would not be regarded as hedges and there would be no justification for deferring mark-to-market differences. With respect to futures contracts (other than tax contracts), SFAS 80 permits hedge accounting for transactions that hedge probable potential commitments. However, in the United Kingdom, the criteria are less stringent and there is scope for treating these transactions as hedges provided that there is a reasonable likelihood that the related business commitment will crystallize.

Institutional users

The institutional user would normally include banks and other financial concerns (which could include certain corporate users) who buy and sell financial instruments as part of an overall trading activity. This activity would involve positions in different instruments on different exchanges and, possibly, positions in over-the-counter (OTC) as well as exchange-traded instruments.

The matrix assumes that a market-to-market approach should be always used for profit and loss recognition for liquid instruments. For illiquid instruments, a market-to-market approach should be used if the activity is that of a market maker with the caveat that a lower of cost or market approach should be used for extremely illiquid instruments.

The use of a mark-to-market approach for hedge accounting represents something of a departure from established accounting practice and reflects the following:

1. The trading volumes, the inherent and growing liquidity in the market, and the consequent transferability of the instruments makes the determination of whether a hedged transaction exists—a difficult, if not impossible task.
2. The ability of these instruments to transform the nature of assets, liabilities, and income streams—and the underlying economic risk—makes identification of the underlying economic rationale difficult.
3. The application of accrual accounting to the valuation of hedging assets and liabilities is questionable and may result in the accounting not reflecting the underlying economic rationale.
4. The increasing complexity and volume of these transactions is making it increasingly more difficult to design systems to monitor and record these transactions on a hedging or accrual basis.

Having made the important distinction between corporate and institutional users and the differing accounting methods suggested, it is worth noting that such a distinction should not always be rigidly applied. There are still many institutional users who are effectively using the financial markets as end users rather than as traders or market markers.

Finally, the question of fees and commissions related to these instruments must be addressed. Generally, such fees and commissions comprise an arrangement element and a risk management or continuing obligation element. While the principles of recognition of these elements has historically been relatively straightforward, it has become more difficult to ascertain what portion of the fee relates to continuing services. While any alloction made may be arbitrary in nature, such an allocation will often be required in order to achieve some matching of costs and revenues. Any allocation made should be determined logically by reference to the pricing, should be applied consistently, and if the effect is material, should be disclosed in the notes to the accounts.

Summary

In summary, the approach outlined above is one that incorporates fundamental accounting principles and that is tailored to the economics underlying the instrument and to its user. A broad approach or framework has been set out as it is not thought that authoritative accounting standards should be established on an instrument-by-instrument basis.

Some commentators may believe that rigorous standards can be developed on a product basis, but in the authors' opinion this may result in the development of numerous accounting standards that may be out of date when published and that in any case may not reflect the economic realities of many situations.

In short, the approach set out above avoids the development of another set of accounting standards that would be complex, difficult to implement, and may oversimplify the risks and benefits attributable to the instruments.

This approach also recognizes the specialized nature of the instruments and the needs of their users. Developing accounting standards for financial institutions that manage interest-rate and currency risks involves considerations that differ from those applicable to commercial companies.

For example, a traditional approach to hedge or accrual accounting may be appropriate for commercial companies with few interest-rate hedges but may be inappropriate for banks and financial institutions that extensively use interest-rate and currency-rate instruments to establish and manage risks.

Some accountants believe that the approach could be expanded to incorporate mark-to-market accounting for both sides of the hedge combination. Marking both sides of the hedge combination to market would reflect market value changes through the income statement and would avoid deferrals, effectiveness tests, and other complications. This alternative would, however, be a radical departure from existing standards and it is somewhat questionable as to whether accountants are ready for it yet. Such an approach would necessitate further developments in current value accounting methodology, especially in the area of the market value of short-term banking assets and liabilities. For example, if interest-rate options were being used to hedge a deposit book, the question then would arise as to how to mark to market the bank's deposit book.

Any approach to accounting for these instruments will have benefits and costs and will require significant thought. Finally, the new financial instruments market is an extremely complex area and a comprehensive analysis of the issues is necessary to ensure the development of accounting principles that will be of use and will be accepted by the business community.

The accounting sections that follow are intended to be a practical guide to the methods of accounting for the instruments covered in this book. Each section covers the underlying accounting principles applicable to the particular instrument and includes practical examples for both the corporate and institutional user.

CHAPTER 2

Financial futures

The product

A financial futures contract is an agreement to buy or sell a standard quantity of a financial instrument or foreign currency at a future date at a price decided at the time the contract is made on the floor of an exchange. The effect of such a contract and therefore its main purpose is to transfer the risk of price movements from one party to another.

The key ingredient in any futures contract is its "fungibility." That is to say, one futures contract is identical and interchangeable with another futures contract in the same financial instrument and with the same maturity date. This quality of fungibility enables the holder of an open position in a futures contract to offset ("close") his commitment against an equal and opposite commitment before actual delivery of the underlying financial instrument is required under the original contract. It is rare for a contract to remain open until its settlement date, and, as a result, only 2% of contracts are settled by actual delivery on most futures markets.

There are four basic types of financial futures traded on the various exchanges:

1. Short-term interest-rate contracts.

2. Long-term interest-rate contracts.
3. Foreign-exchange contracts.
4. Stock index contracts.

Short-term interest-rate contracts

Short-term interest-rate contracts, such as the Treasury bill, negotiable certificates of deposit (CDs), Eurocurrency, and sterling deposit contracts are based on a three-month debt instrument. These futures contracts are based on financial instruments that account for the bulk of the instruments that are traded in the money market, which is a market for short-term, heavily traded credit instruments with maturities of less than one year. The underlying market on which the futures are based is extremely active and mitigates against any significant pricing imperfections.

Each contract trades at an index price, which is typically calculated as 100 less the implied annual interest rate in that contract. This method of pricing is designed to maintain the normal inverse relationship between prices and inherent interest rates. A typical example may be as follows:

Example

If a contract (with a lot size of $1 million) has been traded at a price of $85.00, the market has agreed to purchase the instrument at a price that will yield an annualized 15% interest rate over the three-month life of the instrument. If the price of the instrument declines by a basis point (i.e., 0.01) from $85.00 to $84.99, the trader that bought the instrument at $85.00 will lose $25.00. This loss is calculated as

$$0.01\% \times \$1{,}000{,}000 \times 0.25 = \$25$$

The factor of 0.25 that is introduced into the calculation simply reflects the fact that the contract has a maturity of three months, or 0.25 of a year. This is an approximation as the actual deposit is for either 90 or 91 days. U.S. dollar contracts are on a 360-day basis, while sterling contracts are on a 365-day basis.

The popularity of these short-term interest-rate futures may be largely attributed to high and increasingly volatile interest rates. This volatility makes the long-term fixed-rate debt less appealing because the price sensitivity on these long-term instruments is higher.

Futures contracts often are preferred to the equivalent cash market transactions because they provide several of the benefits of the cash market without the related risks. Thus, futures contracts are normally listed at least two years in advance, their price is freely accessible to all interested parties, and as described later on in this chapter, there are stringent credit risk safeguards.

Long-term interest-rate contracts

Long-term interest-rate contracts, such as Treasury bonds and 20-year gilt contracts, are priced on the same discount basis as in the cash market. Thus, the 20-year gilt contract on the London International Financial Futures Exchange (LIFFE) is priced as a percentage of its face value, on the assumption of a standard 12% coupon yield and a 20-year maturity.

Foreign-exchange contracts

Foreign-exchange futures contracts are priced in terms of the underlying exchange rate. However, in contrast to the forward currency markets, all foreign-exchange futures are priced in terms of the number of dollars per unit of foreign currency.

Stock index contracts

Stock index contracts, such as the Financial Times-Stock Exchange 100 (FT-SE 100) contract and Standard and Poor's (S&P) 100 and 500 contracts, are based on the underlying stock indexes. These are weighted indexes consisting of a basket of the largest companies as defined by their market capitalization.

Delivery

Although the delivery month, price quotation, contract size, price limit, and margin are uniform for a particular interest-rate futures contract on a given exchange, the securities that may be delivered against that contract will vary.

For example, U.S. Treasury bond futures on the Chicago Board of Trade call for the delivery of nominal 8% Treasury bonds that mature or are noncallable for at least 15 years from the date of delivery. Currently, there are over 20 issues that meet those qualifications. In recognition of this fact, a conversion factor is applied to the futures settlement price in order to ensure that both the futures contract and the financial instrument that is actually delivered reflect the same inherent value. However, owing to the biases in the conversion factor and the peculiarities of the cash market, it will be more cost effective to deliver some securities than others.

Markets

There has been a spectacular growth in financial futures trading since it was started with a currency future by the International Monetary Market (IMM) in Chicago in 1972. This is largely due to an attempt by the financial markets to stabilize the volatility in interest rates, inflation, and exchange rates that has become the hallmark of the developed Western world. Financial futures markets have subsequently been established in most of the principal financial centers of the world.

Financial futures markets act as a mechanism for those wishing to shed risk (hedgers) to those wishing to assume risk (speculators). These markets also enhance liquidity in the underlying cash markets by providing detailed price information at all times. Futures markets differ from forward markets in that they are based on standardized contracts that establish quantity, type, and delivery points before trading commences. Forward contracts are tailored to the needs of specific users and are therefore not readily transferable into the market at large. The standardization of the futures contracts and the manner in which they are traded (i.e., through recognized exchanges) allow commercial and financial institutions to manage their business risks by flexible and efficient hedging techniques.

The goals of these hedgers are the same as those of the agricultural producers and consumers who first used futures in the last century: to obtain financial certainty in the conduct of future business while minimizing credit risk. Conversely, the speculators who trade for their own profit increase the volume of trading and thereby create the liquidity that is necessary to ensure an efficient market.

Two important participants in all financial markets are the exchanges through which all deals are executed and the clearinghouses that process and guarantee those deals.

The exchange and the clearinghouse

The two organizations that make up a futures market are the exchange and the clearinghouse.

The exchange

The exchange comprises the marketplace in which trades are executed on an open, "outcry" basis. They are organized to ensure the existence of a competitive and orderly marketplace. The financial futures market in London executes its trades through the London International Financial Futures Exchange (LIFFE). This is broadly similar in respect to the contracts that it offers and the method of its operation to the more established exchanges in New York and Chicago.

It will become a recognized investment exchange under the 1986 Financial Services Act, and the members of the exchange will be regulated by the Association of Futures Brokers and Dealers (AFBD), which intends to become a self-regulating organization also under this act.

Each exchange is composed of a limited number of members, each qualifying under certain financial requirements, as well as being subject to various moral and ethical requirements. These members may either act on their own behalf ("floor trader") or on the behalf of a client ("floor broker").

Chapter 2

The exchanges around the world are:

1. London International Financial Futures Exchange (LIFFE).
2. Chicago Board of Trade.
3. International Monetary Market.
4. New York Futures Exchange.
5. Singapore Money Exchange.
6. Sydney Futures Exchange.
7. The MATIF (Paris).

The clearinghouse

The clearinghouse is the organization that processes all trades executed on the floor of the exchange. It acts as counterparty to all transactions entered into on the floor of the exchange and assumes the contractual relationship between the buyer and the seller. Furthermore, as a result of the margining of all open losses (see below), the clearinghouse is able to guarantee all contracts.

The clearinghouse is also responsible for determining the profit and loss on all open positions. This is calculated by revaluing all open positions at the closing contract prices traded on the exchange ("marked to market"). This profit or loss is then used in the margining process.

Margining

The obligation of a party to fulfill its commitment under a futures contract is secured by a margin (good faith) deposit. Margins comprise cash and other securities or guarantees deposited with the clearinghouse. They are of two types:

1. *Original margin.* This is a fixed sum that is payable in respect to each open contract. It typically varies between 0.1 and 6% of the face value of the contract.
2. *Variation margin.* Open financial futures contracts are marked to market at the end of each business day by the clearinghouse, and any

unrealized gains or losses that arise as a result of this revaluation are added to or deducted from the original margin.

A variation margin will only be called if the loss on revaluation causes the margin to fall below the "maintenance margin" level, which will usually be less than the original margin. The variation margin is settled daily by a cash transfer between the member and the clearinghouse.

The margining procedures described here apply to the members of the exchange. It is likely that when a transaction is performed through a broker, the broker will have its own margining procedure that will depend on its assessment of the creditworthiness of the client. It is therefore important for any corporate client to consider the brokers' various margining procedures before selecting a particular broker to act on its behalf.

Uses

The uses of financial futures are conventionally divided into three categories:

1. Hedging.
2. Speculating.
3. Arbitraging.

Hedging

Hedging is used to reduce risk of loss through adverse price movements in currency rates, interest rates, or share prices by taking a position that is equal and opposite to an existing or anticipated position in the cash market. In practice, no hedge is perfect because the relationship between the price of the futures contract and the price of the underlying financial instrument, which is known as the "basis," is never constant. The reasons for the volatility of the basis are complex, but this volatility is one of the key factors to be considered when deciding which futures contract is appropriate for hedging a particular

Chapter 2

risk (the volatility of the basis is one of the attributes of the futures markets that is of interest to the arbitrageurs). For example, if the value of the underlying instrument declines in value in response to a particular market phenomenon, and the futures contract rises in respect to the same phenomenon, the futures contract would be of little use as a hedging strategy for that underlying instrument.

Thus, if a company considered that interest rates might rise, and knew that it would need to borrow a certain amount of money in a specified currency in three months' time, it could hedge its interest-rate risk by selling financial futures contracts maturing on that date. If rates did rise, any additional borrowing costs would be substantially offset by the profits arising on the short futures contract position. The extent to which the profits on the futures contract exactly offset the additional borrowing costs would again partly depend on the basis.

This type of hedging strategy, which is known as a "short hedge," may be illustrated by an example.

Example—Short hedge

A developer is currently financing an 18-month construction contract with a floating-rate loan from his bank. The loan is for 100 points (1%) above the three-month CD rate and is fixed every three months.

The developer is currently paying 13.05% interest and is concerned that the interest rate will rise. All other things being equal, the project will only remain profitable so long as the interest rate remains below 14% over the remaining nine months of the contract period.

The developer could secure the profitability of the contract by selling short a series of the appropriate amount of three-month CDs over the remaining life of the loan. At the completion of the contract in June, the relative interest expense under the hedged and unhedged positions may have been as shown in Table 2.1.

It is clear from this example that if the developer had not embarked on this short-term hedging strategy, the contract would not have been profitable. It should however be re-emphasized that the interest rates could also have fallen substantially, in which case the developer would have lost an opportunity to profit from the hedging strategy.

Table 2.1 Actual interest expense

Contract Date	Amount Financed ($)	CD Rate (%)	Loan Rate (%)	3-Month Interest Expense ($)
December 15	30,000,000	12.05	13.05	989,625
March 15	40,000,000	14.05	15.05	1,521,722
June 15	50,000,000	13.80	14.80	1,870,556
Total			14.45	4,381,903

Contract Date	Sold	Bought	Gain	Number of Contracts	Futures Gain	Net Hedged Expense ($)
December 15	88.27	88.04	0.20	30	15,000	974,625
March 15	88.20	85.92	2.28	40	228,000	1,293,722
June 15	87.95	86.23	1.72	50	215,000	1,655,556
Total					458,000	3,923,903

3-Month Period Beginning	Comparative Unhedged	Interest Rate Hedged
December 15	13.05	12.85
March 15	15.05	12.77
June 15	14.80	13.08
Annualized	14.45	12.94

Note: The interest rates are based on 360-day years and 91-day quarters. The hedged interest rates are the interest rates implicit in the above futures contracts and may be derived therefrom using the above periods.

Speculating

The speculators provide the liquidity to the market that enables the hedgers to buy or sell in volume without difficulty. Futures enable the speculator to profit from movements in the financial markets without actually having to purchase the underlying financial instrument. However, this does require that the speculator assume a considerable price risk.

Arbitraging

Arbitrage in financial futures involves the use of futures contracts to profit at minimal risk from any anomalies in the pricing of futures contracts. These anomalies may typically arise in two ways:

1. Pricing anomalies between cash instruments and financial futures.
2. Pricing anomalies between financial futures *per se*.

Arbitraging strategies are typically extremely complex and may involve the use of multiple combinations of futures and financial instruments in order to maximize the risk/return ratio. One form of arbitraging these perceived market imperfections is to establish a "spread," whereby a square position is maintained for a particular contract but with a built-in delivery gap. For example, a March contract may be purchased and a June contract sold. A further benefit of this type of strategy is that there is a reduced margin payable to the clearinghouse.

Accounting for financial futures

There have been no accounting pronouncements produced in the United Kingdom on the accounting for financial futures.

In the United States, the Financial Accounting Standards Board (FASB) has issued statement number 80, which applies to all exchange-traded futures contracts except foreign currency futures that are covered by FASB 52. The accounting requirements of these FASBs are similar to the principles generally applied by entities reporting in the United Kingdom and that are recommended in this chapter.

Overall basis of accounting

The objective of an accounting policy is to ensure that the accounting for a transaction reflects, as closely as possible, the economic effects and the objectives of the transaction. Thus, accounting for speculative and hedge positions will differ. Furthermore, the accounting for a hedge position should be consistent with the accounting followed for the actual or anticipated cash market transaction.

To trade in financial futures, the trading concern must deposit margin with its broker, who will in turn deposit margin with the clearinghouse. This margin may be either the deposit of funds or the pledging of a security acceptable to the market. Funds deposited as margin should be recorded as a "deposit."

In common with the accounting for forward foreign-exchange contracts, the gross amount of securities deliverable represents commitments and should not be dealt with on the balance sheet.

In general, unrealized gains and losses arising from the change in quoted market values of futures contracts should be recognized in the profit and loss account currently, as should realized gains and losses. This basis of accounting (usually referred to as "mark to market") should be followed under the following circumstances:

1. When the futures positions are speculative.
2. When futures positions represent hedges of asset positions or short positions that are stated at market value.
3. When criteria to qualify as a hedge are not met.

However, futures contracts should be valued at the lower of cost or market when a reporting entity uses the lower of cost or market method for its short-term or other trading positions.

In establishing detailed accounting policies and procedures, it is important that entities have clearly defined criteria that must be satisfied if a futures trade is to be classified as a hedging transaction for accounting purposes. Such criteria would typically be:

1. At the time the futures contract is entered into, its purpose should be specifically identified and documented.
2. The price of the futures contract and the hedged asset or liability should have a high degree of positive correlation.
3. For an anticipatory hedge, the anticipated cash market transaction should reasonably be expected to be fulfilled in the ordinary course of business.

Hedging

If the hedge criteria are satisfied, the accounting treatment applied to the futures trade will depend on the type of position being hedged and the basis on which that position is carried in the accounts.

Short hedge of an asset carried at cost. A short hedge of an asset carried at cost represents the sale of futures contracts to hedge against the decline in market value of a holding of a fixed-interest asset.

This hedge may be used by the holder of a fixed-interest security or by a financial institution to protect the value of fixed-rate loans made to customers. Gains and losses on the futures contract should be deferred and recognized as income when the asset is sold, or recorded as an adjustment to the carrying value of the asset if the futures contract is closed out prior to sale of the asset.

However, the carrying amount of an asset should not be adjusted to an amount above its fair market value at the date the hedge position is closed. Any premium resulting from the adjustment to the carrying value of the asset should be amortized to income over the remaining life of the asset as an adjustment to interest income, so that on maturity of the asset, the carrying value is equivalent to redemption value.

Example—Short hedge of an asset carried at cost

On August 15, 19X0, a company purchases a £1,000,000, 25-year, 11% bond with semiannual interest, at par. By August 15, 19X1, interest rates have fallen and the bonds are quoted at £107 10/32, or £1,073,125. The purchase is funded by fixed-rate debt maturing on August 15, 19X2.

The company does not wish to sell the bond but wants to protect the value of the bond against a rise in interest rates. The company decides to hedge by selling December 19X2 long gilt contracts at the current market price of £84. From a study of the relative movements of the bond price and the futures contract price, the company determines that if the value of the bond falls to £99 31/32 (yield 11%) by August 15, 19X2, the futures contract price will fall to £77 25/32 (yield 10.93%).

Therefore, the loss on the bond would be

$$£1,000,000 \frac{(107\ 10/32 - 99\ 31/32)}{100} = \underline{\underline{£73,438}}$$

Financial Futures

The gain on the futures contract would be

$$£50,000 \frac{(84 - 77\ 25/32)}{100} = £3,109$$

and the number of contracts needed to hedge is

$$\frac{73,438}{3,109} = 23.62$$

The number of contracts sold is thus 24.

Assume that on August 15, 19X2 the bonds have fallen to £88 2/32 (yield 12.5%) and the December long gilt contract price has fallen to £68 17/32 (yield 12.4%). The results are:

Date	Cash Market	Futures Market
August 15, 19X1	Company holds bond with market value of £1,073,125 and decides to hedge (£1,000,000 × 107 10/32)	Sell December 24, 19X2 long gilt contracts at £84 (lot size is £50,000)
August 15, 19X2	Sell £1,000,000 bond at £88 2/32	Buy December 24, 19X2 long gilt contracts at £84 (lot size is £50,000)
	Realized loss based on *original* cost:	Gain:
	£1,000,000 $\frac{(100 - 88\ 2/32)}{100}$	£50,000 × 24 $\frac{(84 - 68\ 17/32)}{100}$
	= £119,375	= £185,625

If the company marked its bonds to market, the loss that the company would have suffered in 19X2, had it not hedged the bond at August 15, 19X1, can be calculated as follows, using market values at both dates:

$$£1,000,000 \frac{(107\ 10/32 - 88\ 2/32)}{100} = £192,500$$

This assumes that the unrealized profit of £73,125 arising from the increase in market value of the bond from a cost of £1,000,000 to the

August 15, 19X1 value of £1,073,125 has been recorded in the company's accounts at August 15, 19X1.

The accounting entries for the foregoing transactions are:

August 15, 19X0

(i) To record purchase of bonds

Dr Investment in bonds		£1,000,000
Cr Cash		£1,000,000

August 15, 19X1

(ii) To record payment of margin on the futures contracts at £1,000 per contract to broker

Dr Original margin (balance sheet account)	£	24,000
Cr Cash	£	24,000

August 15, 19X1 to August 15, 19X2 (cumulative)

(iii) To record open gains on the futures contracts

Dr Variation margin (balance sheet account)	£	185,625
Cr Deferred gain on hedge (balance sheet account)	£	185,625

August 15, 19X2

(iv) To record return of margin on the closing of the futures position

Dr Cash	£	209,625
Cr Original margin	£	24,000
Cr Variation margin	£	185,625

(v) To transfer deferred gain on hedge on the sale of the futures contracts to show the effective reduced cost of the bonds

Dr Deferred gain on hedge	£	185,625
Cr Cost of investment in bonds	£	185,625

(vi) To record gain on sale of bonds

Dr Cash	£	880,625
Cr Profit on sale of bonds	£	66,250
Cr Cost of investment in bonds (£1,000,000 − £185,625)	£	814,375

The profit on the transaction is

Gain on the futures contracts	£	185,625
Loss on the bond (carried at cost)	£	119,375
	£	66,250

In summary:

Debit (Credit)		Balance Sheet				Profit and Loss Account
	Cash	Investment in Bonds	Original Margin	Variation Margin	Deferred Gain on Hedge	Profit on Sale of Bonds
August 15, 19X0 (i)	(1,000,000)	1,000,000				
August 15, 19X1 (ii)	(24,000)		24,000			
August 15, 19X1 to August 15, 19X2 (cumulative) (iii)				185,625	(185,625)	
August 15, 19X2						
(iv)	209,625		(24,000)	(185,625)		
(v)		(185,625)			185,625	
(vi)	880,625	(814,375)				(66,250)
At y/e December 31, 19X2	66,250	—	—	—	—	(66,250)

If the bonds are not sold, then the entry to record the profit on sale is not required and the entry to transfer the deferred gain would be to the unamortized discount account, rather than cost of investment in bonds.

Hedges of assets carried at lower of cost or market value. Unrealized gains and losses arising on futures contracts used to hedge assets carried at the lower of cost or market value should be included when determining the necessary adjustment at the end of each reporting period. For example, where the yield on a fixed-rate bond is protected by going short of the relevant futures contract and following a fall in interest rates the price of the bond falls to below cost, the bond will be written down to market value. The futures contract should be revalued and the unrealized gain recognized in the profit and loss account to offset the loss in the cash market bond. If, at a reporting date, the price of the bond has increased to above cost (the unrealized gain would not be recognized in the profit and loss account), the futures contract will show a loss that should be deferred. However, if the loss on the futures contract exceeds the gain of the bond, the excess loss should be taken to the profit and loss account immediately.

The deferred losses should be taken to the *profit and loss account* when the hedged position (or commitment) is sold (or honored). If the hedged asset is held after the futures position is closed out, the deferred gain or loss should be included in the carrying amount of the asset being hedged. The asset (at its adjusted cost) will then be compared with market value at the end of each reporting period to evaluate any required write-down to market.

Long hedge of a liability carried at cost. A long hedge of a liability carried at cost is the purchase of futures contracts to protect against the risk of falling interest rates.

An example of such a hedge includes buying interest-rate futures contracts against fixed-interest rate deposits that are used to fund floating interest-rate loans—that is, interest-rate "spread hedge." Gains and losses on futures contracts bought to hedge against falling interest rates for existing fixed-interest rate liabilities should be deferred and treated as an adjustment to the carrying amount of the liability. Any premium or discount resulting from the adjustment to the carrying amount of the liability should be amortized to income over the expected remaining life of the liability as an adjustment to interest expense.

Example—Hedge of a liability carried at cost

A bank issues £100 million six-month certificates of deposit (CDs) on September 1 at an interest rate of 11%. This interest rate is equal to the discount rate on 180-day Treasury bills. The CDs are used to fund floating interest rate loans currently yielding 13%.

The bank is satisfied with its 2% spread between the interest income on the loans and the interest expense on the CDs, and wants to protect against any reduction in this spread if interest rates fall in the near future.

The bank hedges the risk by buying 200 December 90-day Treasury bill contracts (£1,000,000 per contract) at a price of £89 6/32 (i.e., at an interest rate of 10 15/32%) and the December Treasury bill futures contracts are trading at duration and are to be used to hedge 180-day CDs.

Assume that on December 1, 19X0, the 90-day Treasury bill rate has

Financial Futures

dropped to 10 15/32% and the December Treasury bill futures contracts are trading at 89 26/32% (i.e., at an interest rate of 10 6/32%). The results are:

Date	Cash Market	Futures Market
September 1	Issue £100 million CDs at 11%	Buy 200 December 90-day Treasury bill contracts (£1,000,000 per contract) at £89 6/32% (interest rate of 10 26/32%)
December 1	The interest rate has fallen to 10 15/32%	Sell 200 December Treasury bill contracts at £89 26/32 (i.e., interest rate of 10 6/32%)
	Interest cost: £1,000,000 × 11% × 6/12 = £5,500,000	Gain: $200 \times £1,000,000 \times \frac{89\ 26/32 - 89\ 6/32}{100} \times 3/12$ = £312,000
	Effective cost of funds: £5,500,000 − £312,500 = £5,187,500	
	which is equivalent to 10.36% annualized.	

The accounting entries for the foregoing transactions are:

September 1, 19X0

(i) To record issue of the CDs

Dr Cash	£100,000,000	
Cr Certificates of deposit issued		£100,000,000

(ii) To record payment of margin on the futures contracts at £1,000 per contract

Dr Original margin	£ 200,000	
Cr Cash		£ 200,000

September 1, 19X0 to December 1, 19X0 (cumulative)

(iii) To record open gains on the futures contracts

Dr Variation margin	£ 312,500	
Cr Deferred gain on hedge		£ 312,500

Chapter 2

December 1, 19X0

(iv) To record return of margin on the closing of the futures position

Dr	Cash	£	512,500
Cr	Original margin	£	200,000
Cr	Variation margin	£	312,500

The deferred gain should be shown as an adjustment to the carrying value of the deposit and amortized to the profit and loss account over the remaining life of the CDs, which is three months from December 1, 19X0. Hence, on December 31 one-third of the gain should be accrued as follows:

(v)	Dr	Deferred gain on hedge	£	104,167
	Cr	Interest expense	£	104,167

In summary:

Debit (Credit)	Cash	Certificate of Deposit Issued	Original Margin	Variation Margin	Deferred Gain on Hedge	Interest Expense
		Balance Sheet			Profit and Loss Account	
September 1, 19X0 (i) (ii)	(100,000,000) (200,000)	(100,000,000)	200,000			
September 1, 19X0 to December 1, 19X0 (cumulative) (iii)				312,500	(312,500)	
December 1, 19X0 (iv) (v)	512,500		(200,000)	(312,500)	104,167	(104,167)
At y/e December 31, 19X2	100,312,500	(100,000,000)	—	—	(208,333)	(104,167)

The interest cost of the CDs has been excluded from this table. If the interest expense had been included in the profit and loss account the effective cost of funding for the month of December would have been (£100,000,000 × 11% × 1/12) − £104,167 = £812,500, which is equivalent to 9.75% annualised.

Anticipatory long hedge of an asset to be carried at cost. An anticipatory long hedge of an asset to be carried at cost is the purchase of futures contracts to secure current yields on planned purchases of fixed-interest-rate assets which, when acquired, will be carried at cost.

In the case of an anticipatory long hedge, gains or losses on futures contracts should be deferred and then amortized over the period to maturity of the asset as an adjustment to interest income.

Example

On May 1, a company expects to receive £1,000,000 on August 15 that will be invested in three-month CDs and is satisfied with current yields of 11%. The current September futures price is 90. The company wishes to hedge against the possibility of interest rates falling before August 15 by buying September short interest-rate contracts. On August 15, when the company receives £1,000,000, the CD rate has fallen to 10% and the September future is trading at 90.5. The results are:

Date	Cash Market	Futures Market
May 1	Current rate is 11%	Buy 4 September sterling short interest-rate contracts at 90 (£250,000 per contract)
August 15	Buy £1,000,000 90-day CDs at 10%	Sell 4 September sterling short interest-rate contracts at 90.5
	Interest earned:	Gain:
	£1,000,000 × 10% × 3/12	$4 \times £250,000 \times \frac{(90.5 - 90)}{100} \times 3/12$
	= £25,000	= £1,250

Effective income on the investment:

£25,000 + £1,250 = £26,250

which is equivalent to 10.5% annualized.

May 1

(i) To record margin paid to broker at £1,000 per contract
  Dr Original margin   £   4,000
  Cr Cash   £   4,000

May 1 to August 15 (cumulative)

(ii) To record open gains on hedge
  Dr Variation margin   £   1,250
  Cr Deferred gain on hedge   £   1,250

August 15

(iii) To record return of margin
  Dr Cash   £   5,250
  Cr Original margin   £   4,000
  Cr Variation margin   £   1,250

(iv) To record purchase of CD
  Dr Cost of investment   £1,000,000
  Cr Cash   £1,000,000

Interest on the CD is then accrued at the rate of £25,000 over the three months and the deferred gain of £1,250 is amortized over the same period. At any interim reporting date, the CD is shown at cost less the unamortized balance on the deferred gain on hedge account. Hence, on September 15 one month's interest is accrued on the CD and one-third of the deferred gain on the hedge is amortized to give the following accounting entries:

(v) To record one month's accrued interest
  Dr Interest receivable   £8,333
  Cr Interest income   £8,333

(vi) To amortize one month's gain on the futures hedge
  Dr Deferred gain on hedge   £   417
  Cr Interest income   £   417

Financial Futures

In summary:

Debit (Credit)	Cash	Investment in CDs	Balance Sheet Original Margin	Variation Margin	Deferred Gain on Hedge	Interest Receivable	Profit and Loss Account Interest Income
May 1 (i)	(4,000)		4,000				
May 2 to August 15 (cumulative) (ii)				1,250	(1,250)		
August 15 (iii) (iv)	5,250 (1,000,000)	1,000,000	(4,000)	(1,250)			
September 15 (v) (vi)					417	8,333	(8,333) (417)
at September 15	(998,750)	1,000,000	—	—	(833)	8,333	(8,750)

Anticipatory short hedge of a liability. An anticipatory short hedge of a liability is the sale of futures contracts to protect against the risk of rising interest rates when a fixed interest liability is to be incurred.

Examples of short anticipatory hedges include the sale of futures contracts pending the issue of fixed-interest-rate debt or, in the case of a deposit-taking institution, the rollover of deposits taken at, say, three-month intervals. Gains or losses on futures contracts sold as an anticipatory hedge of a liability should be deferred and included in the measurement of the liability incurred. The gains or losses should then be amortized to income over the period to maturity of the liability.

Example—Anticipatory short hedge of a liability

A financial institution is currently funding some long-term fixed-rate loans yielding 13% with 180-day deposits costing 10.25% per annum. On June 1, the institution identifies £10,000,000 of the 180-day deposits that will be maturing on November 15. It is anticipated that these deposits will be rolled-over.

Interest rates for 180-day deposits stand at 11% on June 1, giving a spread of 2%. The institution wishes to hedge against a rise in short-

Chapter 2

term rates so as to protect the 2% spread. The hedge is established by selling 40 December three-month sterling interest-rate contracts of £500,000 at 88.75. The total value of these futures is £20,000,000 (twice that of the liability to be hedged) because the futures contract is for a 90-day instrument, whereas the liability to be hedged is a 180-day instrument.

Assume that on November 15 rates have fallen and the deposits are rolled-over at 10%. The December three-month sterling interest-rate contract is trading at 89.50. The results are:

Date	Cash Market	Futures Market
June 1	Current interest rate is 11% Objective is to lock in to a 2% spread as from November 15	Sell 40 December three-month sterling interest-rate contracts at 88.75
November 15	Take £10,000,000 of 180-day deposits at 10%	Buy 40 December three-month sterling interest-rate contracts at 89.50
	Interest cost:	Loss:
	£10,000,000 × 10% × 180/360	$40 \times £500,000 \times \frac{(89.5 - 88.75)}{100} \times 3/12$
	= £493,150	= £ 37,500
	Interest cost (net):	
	£493,150 + £37,500	= £530,650
	which is equivalent to 10.61% annualized.	

The accounting entries for the foregoing transactions are:

June 1

(i) To record margin deposit of £1,000 per contract

Dr Original margin	£40,000	
Cr Cash		£40,000

June 2 to November 15 (cumulative)

(ii) To record open loss on futures hedge

Dr Deferred loss on hedge	£37,500	
Cr Variation margin		£37,500

Financial Futures

November 15

(iii) To record payment of variation margin
    Dr   Variation margin   £37,500
    Cr   Cash   £37,500

(iv) To record recovery of original margin on closing out the futures contracts
    Dr   Cash   £40,000
    Cr   Original margin   £40,000

The deferred loss on the hedge is amortized to interest expense over the period to maturity of the deposit (180 days). At any interim reporting date, the deposit will be shown net of the unamortized balance on the deferred loss account.

Thus, for example, on December 31, 19X0, 45 days of this deferred loss will have been amortized by making the following journal entry:

(v) Dr   Interest expense (37,500 × 45/180)   £9,375
    Cr   Deferred loss on hedge   £9,375

In summary:

Debit (Credit)	Cash	Original Margin	Variation Margin	Deferred Loss on Hedge	Interest Expense
		Balance Sheet			Profit and Loss Account
June 1 (i)	(40,000)	40,000			
June 1 to November 15 (cumulative) (ii)			(37,500)	37,500	
November 15 (iii)	(37,500)		37,500		
(iv)	(40,000)	(40,000)			
(v)				(9,375)	9,375
At y/e December 31, 19X0	(37,500)	—	—	28,125	9,375

The impact of hedging in this example has been to reduce the spread that the institution would have obtained. This is because the hedge was designed to protect the institution if interest rates rose, whereas in fact they fell. The hedge prevented the institution from benefiting from the fall in rates. Thus, by not hedging the spread in the futures market, the institution would have obtained a higher spread.

Currency futures

A currency futures contract represents the sale of a futures contract in anticipation of a change in foreign-exchange rates. Currency futures contracts are similar in their uses to the interest-rate futures described earlier. The contracts may be used for both speculative or hedging purposes and are used in the same way as forward foreign-exchange contracts.

Where currency futures are used to hedge against changes in foreign-exchange rates in respect of foreign currency assets or liabilities and such assets and liabilities are translated into the reporting currency at closing spot rates, then the futures contracts should be revalued and any gains or losses reflected in the profit and loss account as they arise. This is the same accounting treatment as if the balance sheet currency exposures had been hedged in the forward foreign-exchange market.

Where currency futures are used to hedge income or expense streams in foreign currencies, the gain or loss arising on the futures transaction should be deferred and released to the profit and loss account to match the related income or expense.

If the futures transaction is speculative the contract should be marked to market with losses being recognized immediately.

Stock index futures

These futures are used and accounted for in the same manner as other futures contracts that give rise to a deliverable commodity.

Speculation

In many instances, organizations may find themselves in a situation whereby they enter into a futures contract without having an underlying asset or liability hedge. Where this occurs, the futures contract must be treated as being for speculative purposes. This requires that the contract be marked to market—that is, all unrealized and realized gains and losses arising from a change in quoted values for the

Financial Futures

contract are recognized currently in the profit and loss account, although nonfinancial companies may defer the recognition of unrealized gains until they have been realized.

Example

During November, a dealer in a bank considers that U.K. interest rates are likely to fall in the very near future given recent economic indications. Hence, the price of the U.K. long gilt future should increase since they are fixed-interest instruments.

The dealer went long by buying 20 of the £50,000 March 30-year 12% notional gilt contracts at £110 14/32.

Assume that during December a sterling crisis led to an increase in U.K. interest rates. This caused a weakening in the price of the long dated gilt futures contract. On December 31, the March 20-year 12% notional gilt features price stood at £106 9/32.

The cost of the acquisition was
November 1, 19X0

$$20 \times \frac{£50,000}{100} \times 110 \ 14/32 = £1,104,375$$

The value of the contract at
December 31, 19X0

$$20 \times \frac{£50,000}{100} \times 106 \ 9/32 = £1,062,813$$

Unrealized loss at
December 31, 19X0 £ 41,562

The accounting entries are:

November 19X0

(i) To record payment of margin of £1,000 per contract
    Dr Original margin   £ 20,000
    Cr Cash   £ 20,000

December 31, 19X0

(ii) To record open loss on the futures contracts
    Dr Loss on futures contracts   £ 41,562
    Cr Variation margin   £ 41,562

This journal takes the unrealized loss to the current period's profit and loss account and sets up a liability account.

In summary:

Debit (Credit)	Balance Sheet			Profit and Loss Account
	Cash	Original Margin	Variation Margin	Loss on Futures Contracts
November 19X0 (i)	(20,000)	20,000		
December 31, 19X0 (ii)			(41,562)	41,562
At y/e December 31, 19X0	(20,000)	20,000	(41,562)	41,562

Disclosure

The recommended level of disclosure for financial futures contracts is:

1. A description of the accounting policies or practices followed for futures contracts, noting in particular the method of recognizing unrealized and realized gains and losses.
2. The contracted amount of all long and short positions at the balance-sheet date.
3. The amounts of any unrealized gains and unrealized losses on open contracts at the balance-sheet date that have not been recognized in income.

CHAPTER 3

Forward-rate agreements

The product

A forward- (or future-) rate agreement (FRA) is a contract whereby two parties agree on a fixed-interest rate that is to be paid on a notional deposit of specified maturity commencing at a specific future time. It is used primarily by banks to alter their exposure to interest-rate movements, while maintaining their liquidity profile. Typically, the buyer of an FRA wishes to minimize exposure to rising interest rates, and the seller is seeking to limit exposure to falling interest rates.

An example of an FRA where the buyer wishes to protect him- or herself from interest rates above 8 1/2% and the seller from interest rates below 8 1/2% is typically expressed as:

8 1/2% on £10,000,000 for 6 against 9 months

This expression can be analyzed in three parts:

1. The 8 1/2% represents the "reference interest rate." This rate will be compared with the relevant LIBOR (London Inter Bank Offer Rate), and the difference between these two rates will then be used to calculate an amount of interest payable on the relevant principal.

Chapter 3

This amount is known as a "compensatory payment." For example, if the relevant LIBOR is greater than 8 1/2%, the buyer will receive a compensatory payment from the seller. The relevant LIBOR is the prevailing rate on the settlement date.

2. The £10,000,000 represents the relevant principal used in the calculation of the compensatory payment. Under no circumstances will the relevant principal change hands between the counterparties, and it is therefore a notional deposit.
3. The "6 against 9 months" defines the start date (settlement date) and the maturity date of the notional deposit. In this case, the notional deposit commences six months from the date on which the agreement was signed, and matures nine months after the agreement was signed. By implication, the notional deposit will last for three months.

The compensatory payment is usually made on the settlement date of the agreement. This payment must be discounted since it is being paid in advance of the maturity of the notional deposit. The formula for calculating this compensatory payment is as follows:

$$ND \times \frac{(L - R) \times DP}{365 \text{ days*}} \times \frac{1}{1 + \frac{(L \times DR)}{365 \text{ days}}}$$

where
ND = notional deposit
DP = number of days for which the notional deposit runs
L = LIBOR on the settlement date
R = reference interest rate
  *There will only be 360 "interest" days where the contract currency is U.S. dollars.

Thus, if in the above example the prevailing LIBOR on settlement date was 8%, the compensatory payment would be calculated as follows:

$$£10,000,000 \times \frac{(8\% - 8 \ 1/2\%) \times 90 \text{ days}}{365 \text{ days}} \times \frac{1}{1 + \frac{(8\% \times 90 \text{ days})}{365 \text{ days}}}$$

$$= £12,000$$

The direction of this payment is a function of two things:

(a) Whether the party to the agreement was the buyer (long hedge) or the seller (short hedge) of the FRA
(b) Whether the LIBOR on the settlement date is greater or less than the reference interest rate

Table 3.1 may assist for this purpose:

Table 3.1

	$L>R$	$L<K$
Buyer	Receiver	Payer
Seller	Payer	Receiver

In summary, the major points to note about FRAs are as follows:

1. No principal amount changes hands.
2. No premium is payable at the outset of the agreement.
3. The compensatory payment is made on the settlement date of the FRA.

In the United Kingdom, in order to avoid violating the gaming laws, and thereby becoming unenforceable, it is important that the FRA is used in a specific hedging operation as part of the normal business activities of both parties to the agreement (a speculative FRA would amount to no more than a gamble on the future movement of interest rates). However, it is possible that speculative positions may arise as a result of FRAs purchased or sold. For example, if the underlying financial instrument that generated the original interest-rate exposure is disposed of, the FRA will no longer form part of a hedging strategy but will become a purely speculative interest-rate position.

Uses

The sole theoretical use of FRAs is to hedge against interest-rate exposure, although in practice it is probably true to say that a number of users actually create interest-rate positions by dealing in FRAs.

The FRA developed out of the forward deposit market, where one party contracts to make a deposit with the other party on a date in the future at a predetermined rate. The particular attraction of an FRA compared with a forward deposit is that on settlement date no principal changes hands and hence the "deposit" does not appear on the entity's balance sheet.

The FRA is in effect an "over-the-counter" financial future that enables a party to the transaction to adjust its interest-rate profile without prejudicing its liquidity position or exposing itself to the credit risks involved in transferring principal sums. The major advantages of FRAs as compared with exchange-traded financial futures are as follows:

1. FRAs are nonstandard contracts and, as such, may be tailored to the demands of the individual counterparties. This is particularly relevant when considering an interest-rate strategy relating to a currency for which there are no interest-rate futures contracts.
2. No margin is required.

The major disadvantages of FRAs as compared with standard financial futures are as follows:

1. FRAs are not transferable and, consequently, may only be cancelled by reversal with another equal and opposite FRA. Financial futures on the other hand are freely transferable on the relevant futures exchanges.
2. The credit risk on FRAs, which is confined to the compensatory payment, will vary with each counterparty. The credit risk relating to futures is uniform and perceived to be small because the clearinghouse assumes the contractual relationship between the buyer and the seller, and acts as the counterparty to both.

There are a number of FRA hedging strategies that may be adopted depending on the nature of the principal involved. Following are some examples.

Assets

1. Buy an FRA to protect against a fall in the market value of fixed-interest securities due to rising interest rates.
2. Sell an FRA to protect against a fall in the interest income of floating-rate investments.

Liabilities

Buy an FRA to cushion the effect of anticipated increases in interest rates when floating-rate debt has been issued.

Interest spreads

1. Buy an FRA to protect spreads during a period of rising interest rates, where fixed-interest assets are funded by floating-rate debt.
2. Sell an FRA to protect spreads during a period of falling interest rates, where variable-rate assets are funded by fixed-interest debt.

Markets

The FRA market is predominantly a U.S. dollar market, with London as the main activity center. The counterparties to the agreements are typically banks brought together through an intermediary broker, which receives a commission.

Accounting for forward-rate agreements

Forward-rate agreements are relatively new to the financial marketplace. Hence, like most other new financial instruments, there have been no formal announcements as to the accounting requirements for them, either in the United Kingdom or in the United States. Thus, one must look to the economic substance of each transaction.

Chapter 3

Overall considerations

An FRA does not call for an exchange of the principal amount upon which the transaction is based, at any time during the life of the contract. The principal is only a notional sum used for calculating the interest differential that is to be paid or collected to or from the counterparty to the agreement. This principal does not, therefore, represent an asset or a liability in the balance sheets of either of the parties in the relationship.

For the following reasons, it is usually only appropriate to account for an FRA on the settlement date of the transaction:

1. The value of an FRA is only known at the settlement date (i.e., the strike date on the agreement, not at the date of signing the agreement).
2. FRAs are not tradeable commodities such as interest-rate futures; hence, there is not a liquid market from which to ascertain a market value.
3. Most FRAs are purchased or sold for hedging purposes.

Hedge accounting

The primary use of FRAs is for hedging purposes, whereby any gains or losses on the FRA agreement should be offset by opposite gains and losses on the initial position.

On this basis, the following basic rules apply:

(a) Net receipt under FRA—gain
(b) Net payment under FRA—loss

The gain or loss generated on settlement date should be amortized evenly over the period of the notional deposit. Since the most common application of the FRA is to hedge deposit maturity gaps, the amortization method of accounting will provide the same results as if the gap had been hedged by a forward deposit.

The following example demonstrates the accounting for an FRA

Forward-Rate Agreements

sold to protect a floating-rate asset against adverse interest-rate movements, while at the same time maintaining an interest-rate spread between the asset and the fixed-rate liability that is providing the funding.

Example

A bank has taken a six-month deposit from May 1 to November 1 of £10,000,000 at an interest rate of 12.5%. This deposit is being used to fund a rollover loan (three-month loan, May 1 to August 1) at an interest rate of 12.3%.

The bank is funding a 12.3% loan with a 12.5% deposit because it will receive the 12.3% interest after three months and thus can then be reinvested with the principal at a rate to ensure that the total interest received will, at the minimum level, cover the interest payable on the deposit.

To hedge against a drop in interest rates for the period August 1 to November 1, the bank sold a 3 against 6 FRA at 12.4%.

The selection of the FRA rate has to be above the break-even requirement, given the differential rates being used between the funding of the loan and the deposit. This break-even rate is 12.318%, calculated as follows:

Interest payable on the deposit:
£10,000,000 @ 12.5% × 184/365 = £630,137

Interest receivable on the loan:
Initial 3-month period
£100,000,000 @ 12.3% × 92/365 = £310,027
Final 3-month period
£10,310,027 @ 12.318% × 92/365 = £320,107
Total interest receivable = £630,134

(The difference between the interest payable and receivable figures arises from the rounding-up of the rates.)

On this basis, the FRA interest rate has been set at 12.4%, i.e., above the break-even figure of 12.318%.

Settlement day (August 1)
Consider two potential scenarios:

Chapter 3

I. *Three-month LIBOR = 11.5%*

The LIBOR rate is lower than the FRA rate (this is the risk that the bank wished to cover itself against).
  Settlement is calculated in accordance with the discounting formula:

$$ND \times \frac{(L - R) \times DP}{365 \text{ days}} \times \frac{1}{1 + \frac{(L \times DP)}{365 \text{ days}}}$$

where
ND = notional principal
DP = number of days for which the notional deposit runs
L = LIBOR on the settlement date
R = reference interest rate

This gives a receivable due from the counterparty of

£10,310,027 × (11.5% − 12.4%) × 92/365
× 1/(1 + (11.5% × 92/365))   = £22,729

The overall impact of this is as follows:

Interest expense (£10,000,000 × 12.5% × 184/365)   = (630,136)
Interest income
Initial 3-month period
− £10,000,000 × 12.3% × 92/365 = £310,027
Final 3-month period (where the funds are rolled-over
at the lower LIBOR rate)
− (£10,310,027 + £22,729) × 11.5% × 92/365 = £299,568
                                               = 609,535
Interest receivable from FRA   = 22,729
Net gain on the transaction   £ 2,128

Accounting entries
No accounting entries are recorded upon entering into the agreement since, as noted above, the principal amounts are purely notional and do not represent assets or liabilities. On settlement day (August 1), the LIBOR rate is known for the duration of the FRA agreement. Hence the outcome of the transaction is quantified and the following entries made:

Forward-Rate Agreements

August 1

(i) To record the receipt from the FRA counterparty and hold in a deferral account until fully amortized

Dr	Cash	£22,729
Cr	Deferred gain on FRA (balance sheet account)	£22,729

The FRA is effective over a three-month period, hence the FRA receipt needs to be amortized over the period August 1 to November 1.

August 31

(ii) To record the first month's amortization of the amount received on settlement date

Dr	Deferred gain on FRA	£ 7,576
Cr	Interest income (FRA)	£ 7,576

In summary:

Debit (Credit)	Balance Sheet		Profit and Loss Account
	Cash	Deferred Gain on FRA	Interest Income—FRA
August 1 (i)	22,729	(22,729)	—
August 31 (ii)	—	7,576	(7,576)
At month-end	22,729	(15,153)	(7,576)

Similar entries are made during September and October such that the account "deferred gain on FRA" clears to zero by November 1, the date on which the notional deposit matures.

Note that the accounting entries for the deposit, loan, and associated accrued interest is not shown above. However, the effect of amortizing the FRA receipt evenly over the life of the notional deposit is to produce a constant yield throughout the period August 1 to November 1.

Chapter 3

II. *Three-month LIBOR = 13%*

In this instance, the LIBOR rate is higher than the FRA interest rate. This will give rise to a net payment on settlement date to the counterparty to the agreement.

Using the discounting formula, the settlement amount is

£10,310,027 × (13.0% − 12.4%) × 92/365
× 1/(1 + (13.0% × 92/365))   = £ 15,097

The overall impact of this is as follows:

Interest expense (£10,000,000 × 12.5% × 184/365)	= (630,136)
Interest income	
—£10,000,000 × 12.3% × 92/365 = £310,027	
—(£10,310,027 − £15,097)	
× 13.0% × 92/365 = £337,335	
	= 647,362
Interest payable arising from the FRA	= (15,097)
Net gain on the transaction	£ 2,129

Accounting entries
The following entries arise:

August 1

(i) To record the payment of interest to the counterparty and to hold the expense in a deferral account until amortized

    Dr Deferred loss on FRA   £15,097
    Cr Cash   £15,097

August 31

(ii) To record the first month's amortization

    Dr Interest expense (FRA)   £ 5,032
    Cr Deferred loss on FRA   £ 5,032

The amortization adjustment has to be performed each month. The second entry enables identification of the actual funding cost for each month (i.e., by adding the amortized FRA payable amount to the monthly accrued interest on the deposit) and, by comparison with the income generated from the loan, the effectiveness of the hedge is determinable.

Forward-Rate Agreements

In summary:

	Balance Sheet		Profit and Loss Account
	Cash	Deferred Loss on FRA	Interest Expense –FRA
August 1 (i)	(15,097)	15,097	—
August 31 (ii)	—	(5,032)	5,032
At month end	(15,097)	(10,065)	5,032

Note that the accounting entries for the deposit, loan, and associated accrued interest are not shown.

One of the major issues in accounting for FRAs is whether the amortization of payments and receipts on different transactions are netted, by being taken to a single FRA account in the profit and loss account, or whether receipts and payments should be treated separately. The resolution of this turns on whether the user accounts for interest on a gross or a net basis. If, as in the above example, the user attempts to identify separately interest income on deposits placed and interest expense on deposits taken and makes appropriate adjustments for hedging interest rates on either side through the use of FRAs, the payments and receipts from FRAs would need to be individually allocated.

However, most banks account for interest on a net basis, being more interested in the spread than in the gross values. In such cases, the amortization of all FRA payments and receipts should be taken to a single profit and loss account, which would serve to adjust the actual interest spread on the underlying deposits taken and placed.

The foregoing example shows the accounting treatment where the FRA is used to hedge an actual balance-sheet position. FRAs are also frequently used to hedge against anticipated future cash flows. An example of the accounting for an anticipatory liability hedge is as follows.

Chapter 3

Example

A bank is expecting to receive a $10 million six-month deposit in three months' time on November 1, 19X0. The bank's management is concerned that interest rates may rise in the intervening period. Hence to minimize its exposure the bank decides to buy a 3 against 9 FRA at a rate of 6.75%. The current six-month LIBOR is 6.5%.

On November 1, the deposit is received and interest on it is payable at 7.25%. Six months' LIBOR at the same date is 7.5%.

Date	Cash Market	FRA
August 1, 19X0	—	Buy a $10 million 3 against 9 FRA at 6.75%
November 1, 19X0	Receive $10 million for 6 months at a rate of 7.25%	LIBOR = 7.5% Hence, settlement on FRA
	Interest payable = $10m × 7.25% × 180/360 = $362,500	$10m × (7.5% − 6.75%) $\times \dfrac{180}{365} \times \dfrac{1}{1 + (7.5\% \times 180)/360} =$ $36,144 Thus, interest receivable from the FRA = $36,144

The effective interest rate on the deposit is therefore as follows:

$$\frac{(\$362{,}500 - \$36{,}144) \times 360/180}{\$10{,}000{,}000} = 6.52\%$$

Without the hedge, the interest rate would have been 7.25%.

Accounting entries
November 1

(i) Dr Cash $10,000,000
    Cr Deposits $10,000,000
    Being receipt of deposit.

Forward-Rate Agreements

(ii) Dr Cash $36,144
    Cr Deferred gain on FRA $36,144

Being receipt from the counterparty on the FRA held in a deferral account until fully amortized.

November 30

(iii) The FRA is effective over a six-month period, hence the FRA receipt needs to be amortized over the period November 1, 19X0 to May 1, 19X1.

Dr Deferred gain on FRA $6,024
Cr Interest expense (FRA) $6,024

Being the first month's amortization of the deferred interest expense.

In summary:

Debit (Credit)	Balance Sheet			Profit and Loss Account
	Cash	Deposits	Deferred Gain on FRA	Interest Expense —FRA
November 1, 19X0				
(i)	10,000,000	(10,000,000)		
(ii)	36,144		36,144	
November 30, 19X0				
(iii)			6,024	6,024
At month-end	10,036,144	(10,000,000)	(30,120)	(6,024)

Note that the entries in this example do not show the accounting entries for the accrued interest payable on the deposit. However, the effect of amortizing the FRA receipt evenly over the six-month period is to reflect a level cost of funding of 6.52%.

Speculation

A speculative position may arise in two ways:

Chapter 3

1. An FRA is purchased or sold with the intention of taking a view on the future movements in interest rates.
2. An FRA agreement is entered into for the purposes of a hedge but the underlying position changes leaving only the FRA agreement, which therefore becomes speculative.

In such cases, the FRA should be marked to market to reflect changes in future interest rates and gains and losses taken to the profit-and-loss account as they arise (although for certain users, notably nonfinancial institutions, it would be prudent to defer the recognition of unrealized gains until they are realized). The marked value of an FRA position could be determined by reference to quoted FRA rates (obtainable from money brokers) for the relevant start date and contract period. As an alternative, a valuation using the FRA discounting formula and the appropriate forward forward rate in the cash market could be used to determine the market value of an FRA position.

An example of how a speculative FRA could be treated using the FRA formula approach is as follows:

Example

On November 1, 19X0, a dealer in a bank assumes that U.K. interest rates will fall in the near future. He therefore decides to sell a £1 million 3 against 6 FRA at a rate of 10.25%.

By December 31, 19X0, U.K. interest rates have increased. Although the period of the notional deposit does not start until February 1 (also the settlement date), since the FRA is a speculative venture it should be marked to market between the period from deal date to settlement date. The market value can be calculated by using the FRA formula and the latest available 3 against 6 forward forward rate of 11.5%. Hence on December 31, 19X0 the calculation would be as follows:

$$£1m \times (11.5\% - 10.25\%) \times \frac{92}{365} \times \frac{1}{1 + \left[11.5\% \times \frac{92}{365}\right]} = \underline{\underline{£3,062}}$$

The £3,062 represents an unrealized loss on the agreement because if LIBOR on February 1 is at 11.5% then this sum will become payable to the counterparty. Following the mark-to-market requirements this unrealized loss should be reflected in the 19X0 profit and loss account.

Hence the following accounting entry is required to reflect the loss and to set up a balance sheet account that might be called "unrealized loss on FRA" until the agreement matures.

Dr	Loss on FRAs—profit and loss account	£3,062
Cr	Unrealized loss on FRA—balance sheet account	£3,062

In summary:

	Balance Sheet	Profit and Loss Account
	Unrealized Loss on FRA	Unrealized Loss
December 31, 19X0	3,062	3,062
Year-end	3,062	3,062

If on December 31, 19X0 interest rates had fallen to 9% in line with the dealer's expectations, then there would have been an unrealized profit of £3,062. The bank would need to consider whether such a profit should be recognized on an unrealized basis. If it is active in a range of interest-rate products it would not seem unreasonable to take credit for unrealized gains on open FRAs.

Management information

The accounting treatment considered above is valid for both management and financial accounting purposes. It is essential, however, that all management reports showing current and future interest-rate exposures should include the full principal value of all open FRAs. Otherwise incorrect interest positions will be reported. Where management information forms an integral part of the accounting system, it may be necessary to set up a series of "dummy" entries in order to ensure that the principal value of FRAs is excluded from the management and financial statements but is included in reports of interest exposures provided to dealers.

Disclosure

The recommended level of disclosure for forward-rate agreements is as follows:

1. A description of the accounting policies for FRAs including commentary on the method of recognizing gains and losses.
2. Where the amounts are material, it may be appropriate to disclose the level of open forward-rate agreements. However, for banks that are actively engaged in a range of short-term instruments, it may be sufficient to state that as of the balance-sheet date there were open forward-rate agreements entered into in the normal course of business.

    It should be remembered that the principal amount under an FRA is not a commitment; it is a notional amount to which interest-rate differentials are applied.
3. Deferred gains and losses in respect of matured agreements should, where material, be separately disclosed.

CHAPTER 4

Swaps

A swap is a financial transaction in which two counterparties agree to exchange streams of payments over time. An interest-rate swap involves no exchange of principal either at inception or on maturity, but involves the periodic exchange of streams of interest payments, of differing characters in accordance with predetermined rules, arising on an underlying notional principal amount.

A currency swap is a transaction whereby two counterparties agree to exchange specific amounts of two different currencies at the outset, and make periodic repayments over time in accordance with a predetermined rule to reflect differences in interest rates between the two currencies concerned. These interest-rate differentials will usually be fixed by reference to the interest rates prevailing at the inception of swap, although they could be variable throughout the term of the agreement as the currency interest rates change.

The product

Perhaps the most significant development in the capital markets in recent years is the evolution of the swap product. The particular significance of the swap product within the capital markets is that borrowers can now fund their requirements in a variety of ways, but economically change the interest-rate or currency exposure from the basic terms of the initial funding to a basis that more closely accords with their needs.

The interest swap is in effect a form of credit arbitrage in which, in theory, no party loses. It exploits the differences in perception of a borrower's creditworthiness for fixed as opposed to floating-rate funds or vice versa.

The currency swap finds its roots in the back-to-back and parallel loan product of the 1970s. These loan arrangements, which evolved primarily to avoid exchange control regulations, were recorded on each of the entities' balance sheets and therefore became less attractive as constraints on balance-sheet growth were imposed either by regulators or the market, or both. The currency swap enables the parties to achieve the same objective as the back-to-back loan—that is, to access a currency market not otherwise accessible, but without having to put the principal amounts involved on their balance sheets.

The interest-swap market is now very substantial, with estimated outstandings of some $300 billion of which approximately $50 billion is believed to have been written in 1986. A secondary market has now been developed in interest-rate swaps and liquidity has been further enhanced by the standard documentation now available in the London and New York markets. In London, the British Bankers Association Interest Rate Swap (BBAIRS) standard terms and conditions are now widely used for interbank swaps traded in the wholesale market and also frequently form a basis for the longer dated "capital markets" agreements. In New York, the International Swap Dealers Association (ISDA) has also issued standard terms and conditions for interest-rate swaps and the Association is also working on preparing similar documentation for currency swaps.

The so-called "plain-vanilla" swaps are at present the most dominant kind of swap transaction. However, as more players have entered the market the margins on these swaps have been driven down and many of the market participants are now researching other swap opportunities that are hybrids of the basic products, in order to earn larger fees.

Both the interest-rate swap and the currency swap are liability management products. Currently, the fastest developing product within the swap market is the asset-based swap. This enables the holders of debt investments to transform either the interest rate (from fixed to floating or vice versa) or the currency, or both. This is believed to be a particularly effective tool for the portfolio manager.

Users

There are two main users of the swap markets:

1. The end user.
2. The intermediary.

The end user engages in the swap market in order to alter his or her interest-rate or currency exposure for some economic or financial reason. The intermediary, on the other hand, engages in the swap market in order to generate fees or, exceptionally, to earn trading profits from establishing an open position in the swap.

End users cover the entire commercial sphere including banks, corporations, and sovereign states.

There are broadly five main reasons why an end user will engage in the swap markets:

1. To obtain low-cost financing.
2. To obtain high-yield assets.
3. To hedge interest and currency exposure arising in the normal course of business.
4. To implement short-run asset/liability management strategies.
5. To speculate.

Interest-rate swaps

In the international capital markets, fixed-income investors are more credit-sensitive than investors in floating-rate instruments. Consequently, a greater premium is demanded from lower-rate companies in the fixed-rated debt markets as compared with the floating-rate markets. This relative arbitrage enables both the highly rated company (AAA) and the less highly rated company (BBB) to profit from participating in an interest-rate swap. A simple example will help to clarify this proposition.

Let us assume that the companies have access to funds at the rates listed in Table 4.1. It is clear that while the AAA company may obtain cheaper funds in both instances, as one would expect, it has a greater relative advantage in fixed-rate funds. The two companies may both take advantage of this situation if the AAA company issues fixed-rate debt and the BBB company issues floating-rate debt.

Table 4.1

	Fixed	*Floating*
AAA company	11.0%	LIBOR + 1/4%
BBB company	12.5%	LIBOR + 3/4%
Differential	1.5%	0.5%

While the two companies will remain responsible for servicing their own debt throughout its life, they may agree to exchange income streams in such a way as to assume the other company's interest liabilities. Figure 4.1 illustrates the point. At first sight, it appears as though only the AAA company benefits from the swap since it receives 0.2% (11.2% − 11.0%) more from the BBB borrower than it pays in interest, whereas the BBB borrower receives 3/4% ((LIBOR − (LIBOR + 3/4%)) less from the AAA borrower than it pays in interest. However, Table 4.2 illustrates that both companies benefit from the swap.

Interest-rate swaps are used both to hedge outstanding interest commitments and to obtain cheap funds.

Figure 4.1

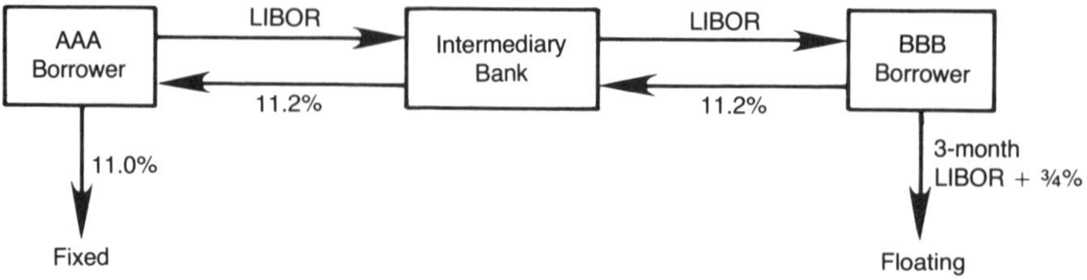

```
                LIBOR              LIBOR
   ┌─────────┐ ──────→ ┌──────────┐ ──────→ ┌─────────┐
   │  AAA    │         │Intermediary│        │  BBB    │
   │Borrower │         │   Bank    │         │Borrower │
   └─────────┘ ←────── └──────────┘ ←────── └─────────┘
                11.2%                  11.2%
        │                                          │ 3-month
        │ 11.0%                                    │ LIBOR + 3/4%
        ▼                                          ▼
      Fixed                                     Floating
```

Swaps

Table 4.2

	AAA Company	BBB Company
Interest	11.0%	LIBOR + 3/4%
Swap receipt	(11.2%)	(LIBOR)
Swap payment	LIBOR	11.2%
Net payments	LIBOR − 0.2%	11.95%
Direct financing (see above)	LIBOR + 0.25%	12.5%
Net benefit from swap	0.45%	0.55%

Currency swaps

A currency swap is simply an exchange of liabilities denominated in different currencies. In contrast to interest-rate swaps, a currency swap involves an initial exchange of the principal that is then reexchanged at a predetermined rate on the maturity of the swap.

Swaps are all about the counterparties using the markets in which they have a comparative advantage and exchanging their obligations to their mutual benefit. In the case of a currency swap, the counterparties take advantage of the credit arbitrage that exists between two markets where the counterparties hold a relative position of preeminence.

A typical currency swap will involve three basic steps:

1. Equivalent amounts in different currencies will be exchanged.
2. Interest payments will be exchanged periodically during the life of the swap.
3. The principal sum will be reexchanged at a predetermined rate on the maturity of the swap agreement.

Since the exchange rate for the reexchange of the principal on the maturity of the swap is predetermined, the final liability is fully hedged, guaranteeing that each party will receive the exact sum needed to satisfy its obligations.

At this point, it may be beneficial to illustrate the point with an example.

Example

Let us suppose that the World Bank wishes to raise Swiss francs but does not feel that it has the market presence to raise these funds at a reasonable rate, or, alternatively, that it has already saturated the Swiss market with its straight bonds. It may enter into a swap with a Swiss-based company seeking U.S. dollar funds as in Figure 4.2. This flow of funds at the outset of the swap and relating to the principal will be exactly reversed on the maturity of the swap. The periodic exchange of interest (see Figure 4.3) will continue during the life of the currency swap, thus completing the effective exchange of the currency and funding cost for the life of the swap.

Figure 4.2 Currency swap

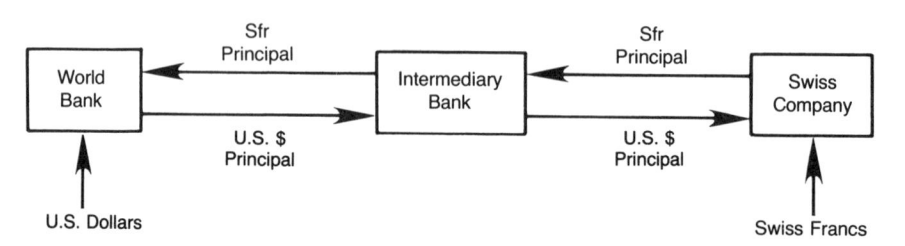

Like interest-rate swaps, currency swaps may be used to hedge foreign-exchange exposure from existing debt, although more commonly they are used to exchange fixed-rate funds raised on a new bond issue.

Figure 4.3 Periodic exchange of interest

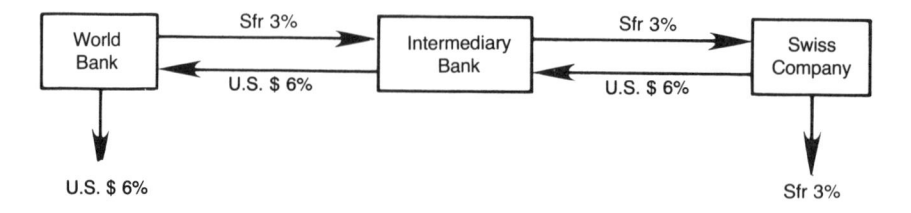

Cross-currency swaps

A cross-currency swap is in effect a combination of an interest swap and a currency swap. Two parties with borrowings in different currencies and different interest-rate profiles (fixed or floating) agree to service the principal and interest of the other party's external funding. However, there is no swapping of credit obligations, both parties remaining responsible for their debt to the third-party creditors.

Payments are made between the parties to match the servicing and amortizations of principal of the other party's "real-world" borrowing.

Asset-based swaps

Asset-based swaps are now widely considered to be the fastest growth area in the swap market. Currently the main users of the asset-based swaps are investment banks that may use this mechanism to convert a security that is paying a fixed-rate return into a floating-rate investment. Alternatively, a floating-rate investment may be converted into a fixed-rate investment, or, to take the process to its logical conclusion, a fixed-rate investment may be converted into a floating-rate investment in another currency.

This conversion process effectively repackages an investment portfolio either into a form that is more consistent with the bank's funding structure or into a form that will represent a more attractive package to be sold to investors. Furthermore, in converting the yield of an asset into another currency, the asset swap could be used effectively as a currency hedge.

There are a number of reasons why the asset-based swap may be preferable to other interest-rate hedging devices, such as interest-rate futures or options.

First, futures and options with the necessary characteristics may not be available on the market and, even to the extent that they are, will involve fairly substantial dealing costs both in terms of commission and the market maker's spread. Second, while the portfolio may be sold, the size of the investment portfolio may militate against its successful absorption into the market.

The asset-based swap on the other hand has the advantage that the peripheral costs are minimized and the interest flow will complement the capital value of the portfolio.

Chapter 4

Accounting for swaps

As with most of the new financial instruments, there are no rules, regulations, standards, or guidelines either in the United Kingdom or internationally covering the accounting for swap transactions. While this may imply that there is some flexibility in the method of accounting for swaps (and indeed the users of the market adopt a variety of principles), it is nevertheless important to pay attention to the fundamental principles underlying the preparation of financial accounts. These have been summarized in Chapter 1. For the purposes of swap accounting, the most important underlying principles are as follows:

1. Prudence in the recognition of profits and losses.
2. Matching of income and expense.
3. Consistency in accounting between like items and from one year to the next.
4. Appropriate provision for or disclosure of contingencies.
5. Translation of foreign currency transactions and currency assets and liabilities.

Within the framework of these principles, it is possible to design accounting policies and procedures that ensure that the financial accounts properly reflect the economic substance of the particular swap transaction or portfolio of swap transactions. This should be considered the primary objective of the accounting policies applied to swap deals, remembering, of course, that for statutory reporting purposes the accounts will be required to give a true and fair view of the affairs of the company.

The swap market has developed in such a way that certain markets now reflect reasonable liquidity, while other segments of the market are less liquid and mainly comprise hybrid transactions, which are not traded outside the primary market. The liquidity of a market is an essential consideration in establishing whether unrealized gains on open swap positions should be reflected in the profit and loss account or deferred until realized. This is consistent with the objective of reflecting the economic substance of a transaction or group of transactions, and also the market in which such transactions are written.

Before constructing the accounting procedures and policies for any swap deal, the economic risks and consequences of the deal should be analyzed. For straight interest-rate and currency swaps, these are reasonably well formulated and the accounting practices being developed by many participants in these markets are at last showing some consistency. This is probably due to the maturity of these products and the desire to develop some industry standards for transactions that have common features.

This is not the case with specifically designed transactions that may be hybrids of the more traditional types of deal such as interest-rate swaps, currency swaps, and asset-based swaps. These hybrids require careful analysis, and hence it is crucial that the accountant is able to analyze and interpret the economic risks of a complex transaction in formulating the appropriate accounting treatment.

In addition to analyzing the economic risks it is also necessary to consider the reasons for undertaking the transaction. From an accounting point of view, there are typically five reasons for entering into a swap deal:

1. To obtain access to funding of the desired nature at interest rates that are less than those available in the open market.
2. To obtain access to funding in a currency at a rate that is less than that available in the open market.
3. To hedge against known or planned cash flows.
4. To speculate on the future movement of interest rates or currency rates.
5. To exploit arbitrage opportunities between the swap market and other financial markets.

The swap market tends to comprise financial institutions that act as either intermediary or principal in swap deals, and end users that may be other financial institutions, corporations, supranational bodies, or governments. Usually, the objective of the financial institution and the end user will be different. The financial institution will typically carry out a swap deal to provide a swap opportunity for its customers. These financial institutions may operate the swap activity either by hedging or warehousing each open swap position, until a matching or near-matching swap is identified or by running a swap portfolio with no specific hedging of individual transactions.

An end user will normally use the swap market to obtain cheaper access to a particular currency or interest-rate profile, or to hedge against known or planned cash flows.

Because the economic objectives of the financial institutions quoting swap prices are usually different from the objectives of the end users, the accounting considerations should be considered separately.

Corporate users

Interest-rate swap. The corporate sector principally utilizes the interest-rate swap market to obtain access to either fixed- or floating-rate borrowings at a rate that is cheaper than that available in the market.

In forming the appropriate accounting treatment for the corporate sector it is essential to remember that the purpose of the swap is to reduce the cost of funding underlying borrowings, and hence the funding rate reflected in the accounts of the corporate should be the actual rate on the borrowings as adjusted for the net payment or receipt under the interest-rate swap agreement.

The swap payments and receipts should therefore be accrued evenly over the period to which the payment relates. The charge to the profit and loss account should be made to adjust the interest cost of the entities' borrowings, which will also have been accrued on a straight-line basis over the relevant rollover periods. No entries are required in the accounts in respect of the interest principal amount of interest-rate swaps, since it is a purely notional figure and represents neither an asset, a liability, nor a contingency.

Example

On January 1, 19X6, B Limited—a BBB-rated manufacturing company—wishes to raise $20 million of fixed-rate funding for five years. It has been quoted by its bankers interest rates of 11% fixed or a floating rate of LIBOR + 1%. B Limited's bankers have another customer, A Limited, an AAA-rated computer services company that is interested in raising $20 million of floating-rate funds for five years. The rate available

Swaps

to A Limited is LIBOR + 1/4%. A Limited can obtain five-year fixed rate funds for 9 1/4%.

With the bankers acting as intermediary, A and B enter into an interest-rate swap, as illustrated in Figure 4.4.

Figure 4.4

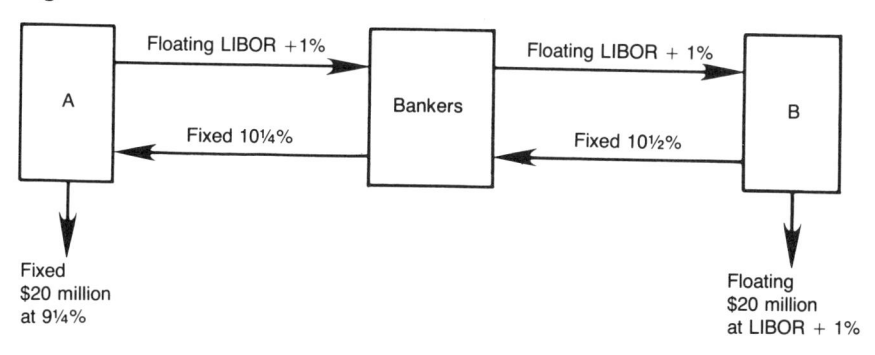

```
              Floating LIBOR +1%              Floating LIBOR + 1%
   ┌───┐ ──────────────────────► ┌───────┐ ──────────────────────► ┌───┐
   │ A │                         │Bankers│                         │ B │
   │   │ ◄──────────────────────  │       │ ◄──────────────────────  │   │
   └─┬─┘       Fixed 10¼%        └───────┘       Fixed 10½%         └─┬─┘
     │                                                                │
     ▼                                                                ▼
   Fixed                                                            Floating
   $20 million                                                      $20 million
   at 9¼%                                                           at LIBOR + 1%
```

A Limited borrows fixed-rate funds in the open market at 9 1/4% and B Limited borrows floating-rate funds at LIBOR + 1%. They then agree to swap their funding profile based on a notional amount of $20 million. To compensate A Limited for entering into the swap, B pays A 10 1/4%, 1% more than the cost of A's borrowings. It should be noted that B actually pays 10 1/2%, but 1/4% is retained by the bank as an arrangement fee. (The position of the intermediary bank is considered in detail later in this chapter, and is not considered further in this example.)

The periodic payments between A and B are made every six months on June 30 and December 31. Company B's financial year ends on March 31.

A summary of the overall cash flow of the transaction is as follows:

	A	B
Fixed-rate borrowing	− 9 1/4%	
Floating-rate borrowing		− LIBOR + 1%
Swap payments	− LIBOR + 1%	+ LIBOR + 1%
	+ 10 1/4%	− 10 1/2%
	LIBOR	10 1/2%

Accounting treatment

The accounting treatment for company B is as follows:

The loan of $20 million should be shown on B Limited's balance sheet in the normal way. No amounts are shown on the balance sheet in respect to the principal amount of the swap. The $20 million to which the swap payments relate is purely notional and in a single-currency interest-rate swap will never be exchanged.

The periodic payments under the swap should be accrued over the relevant six-month periods. These accruals will be made on a straight-line basis and will represent an adjustment to funding costs.

Company B makes up management accounts each quarter. LIBOR for each relevant period is as follows:

3-Month Period	Average LIBOR (%)
March 31, 19X6	8
June 30, 19X6	8 1/4
September 30, 19X6	9 3/4
December 31, 19X6	9 1/2
March 31, 19X7	8 1/2

The accounting entries for the first two years of the swap, for company B, appear in Table 4.3. Using the method of accruals illustrated in this table, company B reports an effective funding cost of 10 1/2% at each management and financial reporting date. This is demonstrated in respect to the financial years ending on March 31, 19X6 and March 31, 19X7:

March 31, 19X6
Average balance outstanding in period $ 5,000,000
($20,000,000 × 3/12)
Actual interest accruals on loans $ 450,000
Net accrual under interest-rate swap   75,000
                                                 $ 525,000
          Funding rate   10 1/2%

March 31, 19X7
Average balance outstanding in period	$20,000,000
Actual interest on loans	$ 2,000,000
Net cost under interest-rate swap	100,000
	$ 2,100,000
Funding rate	10 1/2%

Other issues. There are a number of other issues that need to be considered for the corporate user of the type of plain-vanilla interest swap illustrated above.

FEES. In the example above the swap payment/receipt was determined by computing the difference between the fixed rate of 10 1/2% and the relevant floating rate.

It could be argued that the 1/4% retained by the intermediary bank should be treated as fees charged by the bank for setting up the swap, and hence should be charged to the profit and loss account at the inception of the swap. However, as far as the borrower is concerned the 10 1/2% fixed rate is simply the cost of the swap quoted by the bank and has been assessed by company B on that basis. Indeed it is unlikely that company B will be aware of the percentage retained by the bank. It would therefore seem reasonable and accord with the matching concept to accrue all elements of the swap as illustrated in the above example. If in exceptional circumstances separate identifiable arrangement fees are paid at inception of the swap, it would seem prudent to charge them to the profit and loss account on a cash basis.

FOREIGN CURRENCY TRANSLATION. If the swap is denominated in a currency other than the entities' reporting or base currency, then the assets, liabilities, and profit and loss account items arising therefrom should be translated into the base currency in accordance with the entities' foreign currency translation policy. This will usually mean assets and liabilities being translated at the spot rates of exchange ruling at the balance sheet date and the profit and loss account items being translated at average spot rates for the period. If the net currency position has been specifically hedged, the hedged rate should be used for translation purposes.

Table 4.3

Debit (Credit)	Balance Sheet				Profit and Loss Account
	Bank Loans	Debtors	Creditors	Cash	Interest Expense
January 1, 19X6					
$20,000,000 borrowed at LIBOR + 1%	(20,000,000)			20,000,000	
Interest-rate swap—no balance sheet effect					
March 31, 19X6					
Accrue for interest on loan:					
$20,000,000 × 9% × 3/12			(450,000)		450,000
Accrue for net payment under swap:					
$20,000,000 × 10 1/2% × 3/12 = (525,000)					
$20,000,000 × 9% × 3/12 = 450,000			(75,000)		75,000
End of 19X5/X6 financial year	(20,000,000)	—	(525,000)	20,000,000	525,000
June 30, 19X6					
Pay interest on bank loan:					
($20,000,000 × 9 1/4% × 3/12) + $450,000 = $912,500			450,000	(912,500)	462,500
Net payment made under swap:					
$20,000,000 × 10 1/2% × 6/12 = (1,050,000)					
$20,000,000 × 9% × 3/12 = 450,000					
$20,000,000 × 9 1/4% × 3/12 = 462,500			75,000	(132,500)	62,500
(137,500)					
Total c/f	(20,000,000)	—	—	18,950,000	1,050,000

September 30, 19X6
Accrue for interest on loan:
$20,000,000 × 10 3/4% × 3/12
  = 525,000   (537,500)
Accrue for net payment under swap:
$20,000,000 × 10 1/2% × 3/12
  = 537,500
$20,000,000 × 10 3/4% × 3/12
  = 525,000
    12,500   12,500   537,500

December 31, 19X6
Pay interest on bank loan:
($20,000,000 × 10 1/2% × 3/12)
  + $537,500 = $1,062,500   (1,062,500)
Net payment made under swap:
$20,000,000 × 10 1/2% × 6/12
  = (1,050,000)
$20,000,000 × 10 3/4% × 3/12
  = 527,500
$20,000,000 × 10 1/2% × 3/12
  = 525,000
    12,500   (12,500)   525,000

March 31, 19X7
Accrue for interest on loan:
$20,000,000 × 9 1/2% × 3/12   (475,000)
Accrue for net payment under swap:
$20,000,000 × 10 1/2% × 3/12
  = (525,000)
$20,000,000 × 9 1/2% × 3/12
  = 475,000
  (50,000)   (50,000)   475,000
                                                                                       12,500   50,000

End of 19X6/X7 financial year   20,000,000   —   17,900,000   2,625,000

77

TERMINATION. Some swap agreements permit either party to close out a swap upon settlement of a fee. The fee will reflect the present value of interest differentials between the fixed rate under the swap and the fixed rate from termination date to the maturity of the swap. It is also possible that the swap may be assigned to a third party, also in settlement for a fee calculated on the same basis.

The accounting treatment in respect of any fees paid or received (sometimes referred to as premiums and discounts) will depend on the specific circumstances prevailing.

By way of illustration, if in the last example, at the end of the second year of the swap agreement (December 31, 19X7), party A wished to terminate the agreement and rates of interest for three-year funds were 13% fixed, then A would have to pay B the present value of 13% less 10 1/2% applied to $20,000,000 for each of the six periodic payments remaining (ignoring the intermediary bank):

$$(13\% - 10\ 1/2\%) \times \$20,000,000 \times 1/2 \times 6/1 \times \frac{1}{(1 + 0.065)6}$$

$$= \$1,028,000$$

Note: An annual rate of 13% has been used to discount the future flows.

This would represent the cost to B of having to find a new counterparty at current fixed rates of interest. B would still be paying LIBOR + 1% on the actual borrowings and be matching this through the swap, but would be paying 13% fixed to the new swap counterparty.

If B maintains the floating-rate borrowings and enters into the swap with company C, then the amount settled should be expressed as future interest differentials that should be accrued over the relevant future periods. B will then reflect the same funding costs as if the original swap had not been terminated. It is also possible that company B would pass the settlement direct to C as an inducement to enter into the swap on the same terms as A. In this case, B is acting purely as a paying agent for the settlement and would record the receipt and payment that would net out, and then continue to account for the swap as if no change had taken place.

This accrual treatment will normally be appropriate for corporates that are transforming underlying borrowings. Such a treatment very often will not be appropriate for banks that trade in swaps. This situation is covered later in this chapter.

Currency swaps. The currency swap involves an exchange of currencies at the inception of the swap and a reexchange, at the same spot rate, on maturity. During the life of the swap, periodic payments are made between the parties to reflect differences in interest rates applicable to the two swapped currencies. The main reasons for the corporate sector using the currency swap market are as follows:

1. To hedge against currency exposures.
2. To obtain foreign currency loans at an acceptable price.
3. To use surplus funds effectively in a blocked currency.
4. To minimize interest costs.
5. To avoid problems with exchange control regulations.

Although the Accounting Standards Committee has issued a Statement of Standard Accounting Practice on foreign currency translation (SSAP 20), it does not refer to the accounting for currency swaps. This is unlike the equivalent standard in the United States (Financial Accounting Standard 52), which specifically covers currency swaps.

FAS 52 requires currency swaps to be treated as foreign-exchange transactions and be valued according to the intent on entering into the deal. The way in which gains and losses are treated also depends on the purpose of the transactions, and again these are stated in the standard. Four methods of valuation are identified in FAS 52 (see Table 4.4).

Table 4.4

Purpose	*Treatment of Gains and Losses*
1. Hedge of a net investment in a foreign subsidiary/affiliate	Adjustment to shareholders' equity
2. Hedge of a foreign currency position (including foreign currency debt)	Reported in net income
3. Hedge of a foreign currency commitment (including interest on foreign currency debt)	Deferred and included in the measurement of the foreign currency transaction
4. Speculation	Reported in net income

Chapter 4

Currency swaps result in a balance-sheet currency position with an equal and opposite position off the balance sheet (this being the commitment to reexchange the currencies at the same initial spot rate).

In most cases, both the foreign currency balances reported in the balance sheet and the financial commitment to reexchange should be revalued at closing spot rates of exchange.

This will ensure that there is no profit and loss account effect from the translation of a fully hedged position. To the extent that the exchanged currencies have been purchased/sold spot for other currencies, a spot revaluation of the balance sheet will ensure that this change in currency exposure is properly reflected in the profit and loss account. In certain circumstances, it may be that the required treatment of the balance-sheet position is not to revalue but to carry at the original rate. This scenario is covered later in this chapter.

The periodic payments, which represent differences in the interest rates of the two currencies concerned, should be accrued evenly over the period to which the payment/receipt relates. As for interest-rate swaps, the periodic payment should be treated as an adjustment to interest expense.

Example

On June 30, 19X6, company X, a U.K. company, wishes to borrow Deutschmarks for three years in order to fund an investment in its German subsidiary. It is uncertain when it will need the funds and so wishes to raise them immediately. Company X has not tapped the German market previously and has been quoted a prohibitive rate on the DM9 million required. Through its bankers, it has identified a currency swap opportunity with a German company that is investing in the United Kingdom and requires sterling funding for a similar period. The U.K. and German companies currently have surplus sterling and Deutschmark funds, respectively. They therefore enter into a swap; the details are illustrated in Figures 4.5 and 4.6.

The annual fee represents the difference in interest rates between sterling and Deutschmarks and compensates company X for holding a currency that is at a premium in the forward market, but for which the forward reexchange is to be at spot rates.

The fee is computed as follows:

Swaps

One-year sterling interest rates	10 %
One-year Deutschmark interest rates	4 1/2%
Difference	5 1/2%

$$£3,000,000 \times 5\ 1/2\% = £165,000$$

Assume the following:

1. That company X holds the Deutschmark funds in liquid form until January 1, 19X7 when it makes its additional investment in its German subsidiary.
2. That its financial year ends on December 31.
3. That it prepares management accounts each quarter.
4. That on July 1, 19X9 the investment is liquidated at original cost.

Figure 4.5a Inception (July 1, 19X6)

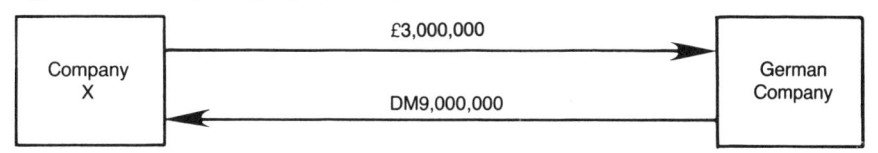

```
                    £3,000,000
Company X  ──────────────────────────▶  German Company
           ◀──────────────────────────
                    DM9,000,000
```

Being the spot exchange of currencies at a sterling/Deutschmark rate of 1:3.00.

Figure 4.5b At each annual anniversary (July 1, 19X7–19X9)

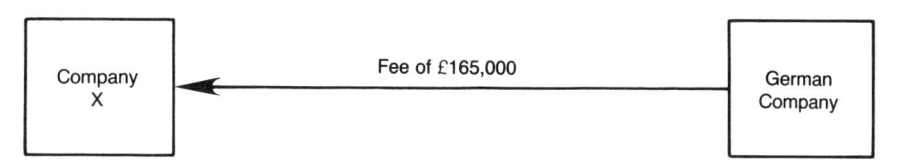

```
                  Fee of £165,000
Company X  ◀──────────────────────────  German Company
```

Figure 4.6 Maturity (July 1, 19X9)

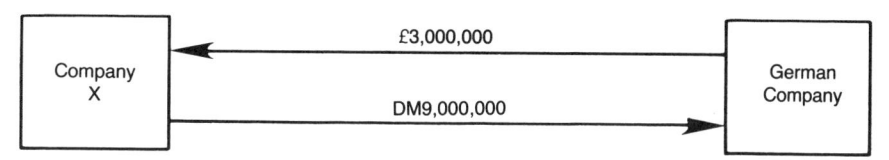

```
                    £3,000,000
Company X  ◀──────────────────────────  German Company
           ──────────────────────────▶
                    DM9,000,000
```

Being the reexchange of currencies at the original spot rate of 1:3.00.

Spot exchange rates applicable to the periods illustrated in Table 4.5 are as follows:

	£/DM
September 30, 1986	2.80
December 31, 1986	2.85
December 31, 1987	3.10
June 30, 1988	3.15

The accounting entries and presentation for company X appear in Table 4.5.

The above example illustrates a number of important points in accounting for currency swaps:

1. If the funds received are invested in short-term assets that are translated into the reporting currency at spot rates, then by revaluing the commitment to reexchange at the prevailing spot rate, any foreign-exchange gains and losses will be completely offset. Bearing in mind that the currency position is fully hedged, this is the desirable result.
2. If the funds received are invested in other assets, such as investments in foreign subsidiaries that are carried at the historical exchange rate, then revaluing the forward commitment at spot rates will produce net foreign-exchange gains and losses on an apparently fully matched position.

   This would seem somewhat inappropriate. If such positions can be identified then the forward commitment to reexchange should not be revalued but held at the contracted rate, which is equivalent to the initial spot rate.

   Of course, this relates to the accounting treatment in the parent company only. On consolidation, the impact of exchange rate movements on investment in foreign subsidiaries should (in accordance with SSAP 20 and FAS 52) be dealt with as a movement in reserves and hence the unrealized gain or loss on the currency swap hedge should also be reflected directly in reserves.

   Identification of matching commitments is not always easy to

Table 4.5 General ledger

	DM			Sterling					Commitment Ledger	
	Investment in Subsidiary	Liquid Funds	Forward Suspense	Debtors	Investment in Subsidiary	Foreign Currency Liquid Funds	Bank	(Profit) and Loss	DM	£
July 1, 19X6 Exchange of currencies Commitment to reexchange		9,000,000				3,000,000	(3,000,000)		(9,000,000)	3,000,000
September 30, 19X6 Revaluation of DM at spot: DM9,000,000 – 2.80						214,285 3,214,285		(214,285)		
Revaluation of commitment at spot Accrual of periodic payment: £165,000 × 3/12			(214,285) 41,250					(214,285) (41,250)		
December 31, 19X6 Revaluation of DM at spot DM9,000,000 – 2.85						(56,391) 3,157,894				
Revaluation of commitment at spot Accrual of periodic payment: £165,000 × 3/12			56,391	41,250				(56,391) (41,250)		
19X6 financial year-end	—	9,000,000	(157,894)	82,500	—	3,157,894	(3,000,000)	(82,500)	(9,000,000)	3,000,000

Table 4.5 (continued)

	DM			Sterling					Commitment Ledger	
	Investment in Subsidiary	Liquid Funds	Forward Suspense	Debtors	Investment in Subsidiary	Foreign Currency Liquid Funds	Bank	(Profit and) Loss	DM	£
January 1, 19X7 Investment made in German subsidiary	9,000,000	(9,000,000)			3,157,894	(3,157,894)				
July 1, 19X7 Accrual of periodic payment: £165,000 × 6/12				82,500				(82,500)		
Receipt of interest differential				(165,000)			165,000			
December 31, 19X7 No revaluation of DM investment Revaluation of commitment at spot: DM9,000,000 – 3.10			254,668					(254,668)		
Accrual of periodic payment: £165,000 × 6/12				82,500				(82,500)		
19X7 financial year-end	9,000,000	—	96,774	82,500	3,157,894	—	(2,835,000)	(502,168)	9,000,000	3,000,000

June 30, 19X8							
No revaluation of DM investment							
Revaluation of commitment at spot: DM9,000,000 ÷ 3.15			46,083				(46,083)
Accrual of periodic payment: £165,000 × 6/12				82,500			(82,500)
July 1, 19X9							
Receipt of interest differential			(165,000)		165,000		
Liquidate investment	(9,000,000)	9,000,000		2,857,143	(2,857,143)		300,751
Reexchange of currencies		(9,000,000)	(142,857)	(3,157,894)	3,000,000	9,000,000	(3,000,000)
				(157,894)			
	—	—	—	—	—	—	—
	(9,000,000)	—	—	—	330,000	9,000,000	(330,000)

achieve. If this is not possible then the forward commitment should be revalued at spot rates ruling at the balance sheet date and any losses (or possibly gains) should be included in the profit and loss account.

3. The accruing of the periodic payments makes sense in view of the interest arbitrage theory. Taking the foregoing example, if the sterling funds passed to the German company on inception had been funded by an overdraft costing 10% per annum, and the Deutschmarks received had been invested in a Deutschmark deposit yielding 4 1/2%, then the U.K. company would have a loss equivalent to 5 1/2% on £3,000,000.

This equates to the periodic receipts by the U.K. company and represents a reduction in funding costs of the U.K. company. In the foregoing example, the £165,000 per annum receipts under the swap should therefore be credited to interest expense.

Cross-currency swaps. A cross-currency swap (also known as an exchange of borrowings) arises where two parties agree to service each other's external borrowings by making payments of both interest and capital on each other's behalf. Such an arrangement is usually established because one party has access to funding in a currency that is presumably expensive to the other party and vice versa.

One classic example of this was the swap between the World Bank and International Business Machines (IBM) in 1981. The World Bank had a demand for low-interest currencies, such as Swiss francs and Deutschmarks, and wished to diversify its source of funding. Simultaneously, IBM had a number of outstanding bond issues in Swiss francs and Deutschmarks which, because of the strength of the U.S. dollar, they wished to convert into dollar funding. The two parties therefore entered into an exchange of borrowings whereby the World Bank raised funds in dollars, sold the dollars spot for Swiss francs and Deutschmarks and hedged its dollar servicing commitment by buying forward dollars from IBM in exchange for Swiss francs and Deutschmarks. The transaction resulted in IBM having Swiss franc and Deutschmark assets and dollar liabilities, and the World Bank having Swiss franc and Deutschmark funding. Both parties had therefore achieved their economic objectives.

The exchange of borrowings could relate to a number of different interest-rate structures:

Swaps

1. Floating against floating (same basis—say LIBOR).
2. Fixed against fixed.
3. Fixed against floating.
4. Floating against floating (different basis—say LIBOR versus prime).

As has been mentioned several times, the objective of accounting for new treasury instruments is to properly reflect the economic substance of the transaction while complying with the various statutory and regulatory requirements. This is not so easy to achieve in respect of exchange of borrowings.

Although the economic risk of each party is the borrowings of the other party, both parties continue to have a legal obligation under their "external" borrowings. It is not possible simply to substitute the other party's borrowings in the balance sheet, because under company law an entity is required to show its legal obligation on its balance sheet, unless there is a legal right of offset. No such legal right exists in a cross-currency swap. Each U.K. counterparty to an exchange of borrowings must therefore show the "external" borrowings on its balance sheet and not that to which it is commercially exposed.

However, it is possible to achieve the economic objective without contravening company law. This can be done by revaluing at spot rates both the "external" borrowings and the "economic" borrowings under the swap, and reflecting any gains or losses in the profit and loss account as they arise, with an offsetting suspense account in the balance sheet. Movements in the suspense account will represent the amount to be taken to the profit and loss account each accounting period, and on maturity the suspense account will clear automatically as the currency funds are settled. As with currency swaps the periodic payments representing interest-rate differentials should be accrued evenly over the period to which the payments/receipts relate. The suspense account should be reflected on the balance sheet, separate from the external borrowings.

Example

In January 19X7, Clearco Limited—a U.K. company—has borrowings of $5,000,000 but requires Dutch guilders (DFLs). The dollar borrowings

Chapter 4

are fixed at 9% for five years. A German company has Dutch guilder borrowings but wishes to make an investment in the United States and hence requires dollars. The Dutch guilder borrowings are variable rate, fixing every January 1, and mature in five years. The variable rate is at LIBOR + 1/2%.

Clearco Limited and the German company enter into a cross-currency swap under which Clearco will meet the interest and principal obligations of the German company's guilder funding, and the German company will settle the dollar obligations of Clearco. The financial year-end of Clearco is December 31.

The balance sheet of Clearco immediately prior to the agreement to exchange borrowings is as follows:

Clearco—Balance Sheet at December 31, 19X6

	$	£
Assets		
Deposit with bank—dollars	5,000,000	3,125,000
Liabilities		
Bank borrowings—dollars	(5,000,000)	(3,125,000)

Note: £/$ exchange rate at December 31, 19X6 = 1.60.

On January 1, 19X7, Clearco exchanges the $5,000,000 for guilders at the then spot rate of 2.30, resulting in a receipt of DFL 11,500,000.

Inception
The initial exchange is illustrated in Figure 4.7.

Figure 4.7

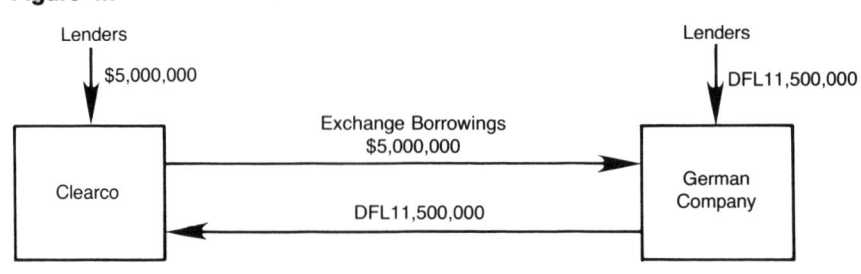

At each annual anniversary
During the life of the agreement each party agrees to service each other's borrowings as illustrated in Figure 4.8.

Swaps

Figure 4.8

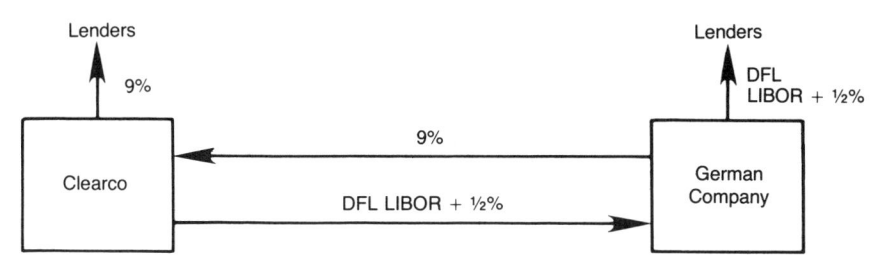

```
Lenders                                    Lenders
  ↑                                          ↑ DFL
  │ 9%                                       │ LIBOR + ½%
  │                                          │
┌─────────┐      ←─── 9% ───          ┌──────────┐
│ Clearco │                            │ German   │
│         │      ─ DFL LIBOR + ½% →    │ Company  │
└─────────┘                            └──────────┘
```

Maturity

On maturity, the parties reverse the initial exchange so that Clearco returns DFL 11,500,000 to the German subsidiary so that the loan can be paid off and the German subsidiary pays $5,000,000 to Clearco so that the dollar funding can be settled (Figure 4.9).

Figure 4.9

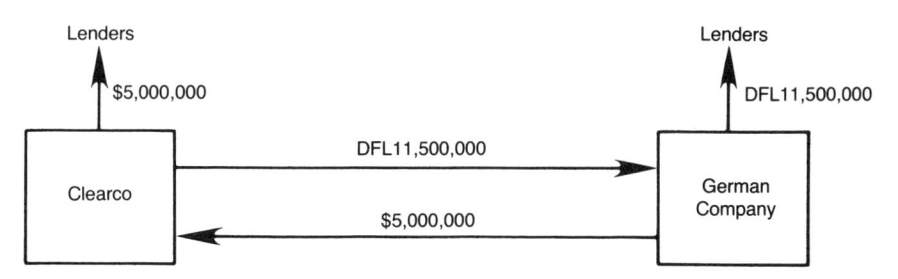

```
Lenders                                    Lenders
  ↑                                          ↑
  │ $5,000,000                               │ DFL11,500,000
  │                                          │
┌─────────┐    ─ DFL11,500,000 →      ┌──────────┐
│ Clearco │                            │ German   │
│         │    ← $5,000,000 ─          │ Company  │
└─────────┘                            └──────────┘
```

It can be seen that Clearco has acted as a surrogate borrower of dollars for the German subsidiary, which has acted as a surrogate borrower of Dutch guilders for Clearco.

One year's Dutch guilder interest rates during the period of the swap are as follows:

Year Ended	Average Interest Rates (%)	Sport Exchange Rates at December 31 $/£	DFL/£
December 31, 19X7	5 5/8	1.55	3.71
December 31, 19X8	5	1.45	3.55
December 31, 19X9	5 1/4	1.50	3.60
December 31, 19Y0	5 1/2	1.52	3.65
December 31, 19Y1	4 3/4	1.40	3.40

Accounting entries
The accounting entries for Clearco appear in Table 4.6.

This example shows the workings of the suspense account in order to achieve a proper reflection of Clearco's economic exposure of borrowings in Dutch guilders rather than in U.S. dollars.

The suspense account automatically clears on the reexchange of dollars for Dutch guilders, leaving a sterling equivalent of £883,640 (DFL 3,004,375), as the bank overdraft and a deficit on the profit-and-loss account of an equal amount. This profit and loss account deficit is as follows:

Sterling equivalent of interest cost of DFL borrowings under the swap (174,360 + 161,972 + 167,708 + 173,287 + 160,662)	837,989
Foreign-exchange loss arising on the difference between interest expense at historic rates and at closing rates	45,651
	£883,640

Hence Clearco has reflected in its books of account the cost of borrowing Dutch guilders, even though its legal obligations were in dollars. The foreign-exchange loss of £45,651 could have been avoided by hedging the £/DFL exposure in the forward market.

For balance-sheet presentation purposes, one key issue concerns the treatment of the suspense account. In the foregoing example, throughout the period of the swap, the balance on the suspense account is a debit. The borrowing is obviously a liability that reflects the sterling equivalent of the dollar borrowings. The question that arises is how should the suspense account be treated in the balance sheet. The company has a dollar liability to the lender and a receivable from the swap counterparty. There is no right offset between these two amounts. Accordingly, since the suspense account represents a receivable it should be included as an asset in the balance sheet and not as a deduction from the liability.

Table 4.6

	Bank	$ Borrowing	DFL Bank	$ Borrowing	Sterling $ Bank	DFL Bank	Suspense	Profit and Loss	Memorandum DFL	$
Balance sheet December 31, 19X6	5,000,000	(5,000,000)		(3,125,000)	3,125,000					
January 1, 19X7 Exchange borrowings	(5,000,000)		11,500,000	3,125,000	(3,125,000)				(11,500,000)	5,000,000
December 31, 19X7 Pay lenders 9% on dollar funding $5,000,000 × 9%	(450,000)				(290,323)			290,323		
Swap payments From German company $5,000,000 × 9%	450,000				290,323			(290,323)		
To German company DFL 11,500,000 × 5 5/8%			(646,875)			(174,360)		174,360		
	—	(5,000,000)	10,853,125							
FX gains/losses Revalue at spot: $5,000,000 at 1.55 = £3,225,806 DFL 10,853,125 at 3.71 = £2,925,371 DFL 11,500,000 at 3.71 = £3,099,731 $5,000,000 at 1.55 = £3,225,806 126,075				(100,806)		(25,269)	126,075	100,806 25,269 (126,075)		
Balance December 31, 19X7	—	(5,000,000)	10,853,125	(3,225,806)	—	2,925,371	126,075	174,360	(11,500,000)	5,000,000

Table 4.6 (continued)

	$ Bank	$ Borrowing	DFL Bank	$ Borrowing	Sterling $ Bank	DFL Bank	Suspense	Profit and Loss	Memorandum DFL $
December 31, 19X8* To German company DFL 11,500,000 × 5%	—	(5,000,000)	(575,000) 10,278,125			(161,972)		161,972	
FX gains/losses: Revalue at spot: $5,000,000 at 1.45 DFL 10,278,125 at 3.55 DFL 11,500,000 at 3.55 = 3,239,437 $5,000,000 at 1.45 = 3,448,275 208,838				(222,469)		131,847	82,763	222,469 (131,847) (82,763)	
				(3,448,275)	—	2,895,246	208,838	344,191	
December 31, 19X9 To German company DFL 11,500,000 × 5 1/4%	—	(5,000,000)	(603,750) 9,674,375			(167,708)		167,708	
FX gains/losses: Revalue at spot: $5,000,000 at 1.50 DFL 9,674,375 at 3.60 DFL 11,500,000 at 3.60 = 3,194,444 $5,000,000 at 1.50 = 3,333,334 138,890				114,941		(40,212)	(69,948)	(114,941) 40,212 69,948	
				(3,333,334)	—	2,687,326	138,890	507,118	

December 31, 19Y0					
To German company					
DFL 11,500,000 × 5 1/2%	—	(5,000,000)	(632,500)	(173,287)	173,287
			9,041,875		
FX gains/losses:					
Revalue at spot:					
$5,000,000 at 1.52					
DFL 9,041,875 at 3.65			43,860		(43,860)
DFL 11,500,000 at 3.65				(36,813)	36,813
= 3,150,685					
$5,000,000 at 1.52				(101)	101
= 3,289,474					
138,789			(3,289,474)	3,477,226	138,789	673,459
December 31, 19Y1					
To German company					
DFL 11,500,000 × 4 3/4%	—	(5,000,000)	(546,250)	(160,662)	160,662
			8,495,625		
FX gains/losses					
Revalue at spot:					
$5,000,000 at 1.40			(281,954)		281,954
DFL 8,495,625 at 3.40				182,149	(182,149)
DFL 11,500,000 at 4.50					
= 3,382,353					
$5,000,000 at 1.40				50,286	(50,286)
= 3,571,428					
189,075			(3,571,428)	2,498,713	189,075	883,640
Settlement on maturity					
of swap	5,000,000		3,571,428	(3,382,353)	(189,075)
	(5,000,000)		(3,571,428)		
Repayment of dollar loan		5,000,000			11,500,000
	—	—	—	883,640	883,640

*Ignores entries for the payment of interest to the lenders of the $5,000,000 and the equal and opposite receipts from the German company—no net cash flow or profit and loss effects.

Table 4.7 shows the balance sheet of Clearco at each year-end.

Table 4.7

	12/31/87	12/31/88	Time (Months) 12/31/89	12/31/90	12/31/91
Assets					
Bank balances	2,925,371	2,895,246	2,687,326	2,477,226	—
	3,051,446	3,104,084	2,826,216	2,616,015	—
Suspense accounts	126,075	208,838	138,890	138,789	—
Liabilities					
Bank overdraft	—	—	—	—	883,640
Borrowings	(3,225,806)	(3,448,275)	(3,333,334)	(3,289,474)	—
	(3,225,806)	(3,448,275)	(3,333,334)	(3,289,474)	(883,640)
Net liabilities	(174,360)	(344,191)	(507,118)	(673,459)	(883,640)
Profit and loss account	£174,360	£344,191	£507,118	£673,459	£883,640

Financial institutions

The accounting for swap transactions undertaken by financial institutions is not such a clearcut matter as that for corporates. The reasons for financial institutions using the swap market are typically fourfold:

1. To hedge interest-rate or currency exposures in the same way as corporates.
2. To obtain cheaper funds than otherwise available, usually through being a floating-rate payer under a swap and obtaining sub-LIBOR funds; the counterparty typically being a lesser-rated corporate borrower.
3. To provide customers with a swap facility, usually in relation to a new issue of debt.
4. As part of a financial arbitrage strategy.

Swaps

In practice, it is often very difficult to determine why a financial institution has entered into a swap transaction. There is also a need to identify separately short-term interbank swaps, carried out as part of the institution's short-term interest-rate management, from swaps entered into through the capital market, which tend to be longer term.

Traditionally the basis of accounting for interest-rate and currency-based products has been dependent on the reason for undertaking the transaction in the first place. The resulting concept of hedging and speculation has led to the accounting principles of amortization and revaluation respectively. For many institutions, this will continue to be the case. Those that deal in relatively small volumes and do not run large outright currency or interest-rate positions should be able to identify specific deals as either for hedging or for speculative purposes, and account for them accordingly. Also it should be possible to maintain adequate systems of control to ensure that once a hedge has been identified by dealers, it continues to be effective as a hedge and hence support the hedge accounting method.

Matched intermediaries

Some financial institutions enter into swap transactions solely as "matched intermediaries." In other words, the institution is acting as principal in two swap transactions that are equal and opposite in their terms (see Figure 4.10).

Typically, the intermediary will earn its income from taking a turn on the periodic payments made during the swap. This income is to remunerate the intermediary for the following:

1. Arranging the transaction.
2. Accepting the credit risk of both parties.
3. Administering the swaps.

Figure 4.10

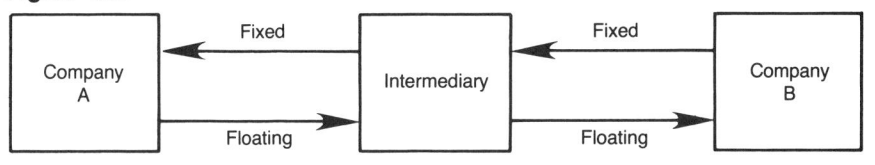

```
┌─────────┐  ←──── Fixed ────  ┌──────────────┐  ←──── Fixed ────  ┌─────────┐
│ Company │                    │ Intermediary │                    │ Company │
│    A    │                    │              │                    │    B    │
└─────────┘  ──── Floating ──→ └──────────────┘  ──── Floating ──→ └─────────┘
```

Chapter 4

Under the matching principle, it would appear correct to recognize the arrangement portion of the income at the start of the swap and to defer the amount relating to credit risk and administration. However, in practice these amounts are not separately identifiable, although an estimate of the income relating to the credit risk could be derived from the following formula:

$$NP \times V\% \times n = CS = \text{amount of intermediary's fee in respect of credit risk}$$

where
- NP = notional principal
- $V\%$ = expected annual change in interest rates (based on an assessment of volatility)
- n = number of years of swap agreement
- CS = commercial spread (difference between loan rate and funding rate) applicable to the counterparty risk, for a standard commercial loan transaction.

For example, a swap may have the following specification:

Notional principal—$1,000,000
Term—5 years

The swap intermediary takes a turn of 1/8% per annum, believes that interest rates could change by up to 3% in a year, and that it would expect a spread of 3/8% for a standard commercial loan to the swap counterparty.

The intermediary's total income is $1,250 × 5 = $6,250

The amount relating to credit risk could be assessed as

$1,000,000 × 3% × 5 = $150,000
$150,000 × 3/8% = $562.5

The $562.5 represents the annual assessment of credit risk by the swap intermediary.

In considering the various fee components, it is useful to review current thinking in the United States. The recently issued SFAS 91 (accounting for nonrefundable fees and costs associated with originating or acquiring loans and initial direct costs of leases) rejected the idea that arranging a loan is a separate service from the loan itself. Many people in the United States believe that swaps are analogous to loans for this purpose, and that accordingly no upfront income should be recognized on an interest-rate swap. Those that attest to this view maintain that if the bank incurs direct arrangement costs that they may be deferred and amortized over the life of the swap.

However, the practice of many banks both in and out of the United States continues to be to define the elements of the swap fee relating continuing services and spread these accordingly and to reflect the remainder as upfront income.

The most prudent method of accounting for the intermediary would be to accrue the period payment over the life of the swap and thereby recognize the income evenly during the swap. However, this may not properly reflect the economics of the intermediary's position.

This could be achieved by calculating the present value of the future turn on the periodic payments and to spread evenly over the life of the swap that proportion relating to credit risk assessed on the basis described above (although theoretically the credit risk reduces over time) and the administration. The balance would be considered an arrangement fee that should be recognized at the start of the swap. However, from a practical point of view this method may be difficult to implement.

Perhaps the most pragmatic method of accounting is to recognize at the start of the swap the present value of the future turn on the periodic payment and to assess the credit risk and make appropriate provisions as necessary during the term of the swap agreements. Because, legally, the intermediary has principal obligations to both parties to the swap, the periodic payment and receipts should continue to be accrued over the life of the swap, with an adjustment being made for the intermediary's turn, which has already been recognized.

Swap traders

For the more active participants in the market, there are additional considerations. The swaps market is now very substantial within the global capital markets and most of the major institutions around the world have an active swaps business. These major players typically handle their swap books in one of two ways:

1. For each individual swap taken onto the books without a matching counterparty swap, the position is hedged through an appropriate treasury instrument. The hedge will be unwound if a matching swap is undertaken in due course. This would be regarded in the market as "warehousing" a swap.
2. A swap portfolio is maintained, and hedging action is taken against the exposures arising from the portfolio. It is not the strategy to identify a perfect match for each individual swap taken onto the books.

Within the two methods of handling a swap book, it is possible that position limits will be delegated to the swap book enabling short-term interest rate or currency positions to be taken, or for longer-term mismatch positions to be established, in the event that a swap position is closed without matching the rollover dates on the floating side of an interest-rate swap.

In view of the liquidity now existing in the swaps market and the range of alternative liquid products that are available for hedging purposes, it is arguable whether hedge accounting is appropriate in any significant swaps operation, regardless of the strategy applied in running the book.

Imagine the scenario of a swap intermediary that takes a fixed against floating interest-rate swap onto its books as a floating-rate payer, but without any matching swap transaction. It is exposed to future increases in interest rates and decides to hedge by buying the relevant financial futures contracts. At a later date, it identifies an interest-rate swap in the same currency for a similar notional principal but with different rollover dates. At that time, it closes the futures contract, enters into the swap, and hedges the mismatch risk by selling the appropriate future-rate agreements (FRAs).

It then identifies a swap to match perfectly the original swap, through to maturity. It therefore assigns the mismatch swap in the secondary market and buys the appropriate FRAs to close the FRA position now created. Yes, the institution has ended up with a square position, but for practical purposes it is highly unlikely that the accounting system could properly handle the accounting treatment of the other hedge contracts.

A further problem is one of hedge identification, particularly where a swap book is run on the portfolio approach. It is highly improbable that a swap trader will either be able or willing to identify hedge contracts.

So what does all this mean? For institutions that run relatively active and sizable swap books, the only appropriate method of accounting is to mark all positions, including other transactions taken out for hedging purposes, to market.

This will give rise to unrealized gains and losses, which will usually be recognized in the profit and loss account as they arise. The major advantages of revaluation are as follows:

1. It is a simple method of computing profitability.
2. It avoids the distortions that can arise from hedge accounting.
3. It provides critical management information in certain areas:
   (a) measurement of position against maximum loss limits;
   (b) assessment of credit risk for intermediary institutions.
4. Where positions have been properly hedged a regular revaluation of all transactions involved will effectively serve to amortize any "locked-in" gain or loss on the position.

How are swaps revalued?

Although no formal market exists from which prices could be obtained to revalue an open position in interest-rate swaps, it should be possible to achieve an accurate measure of the exposure by either using rates quoted on the dealers' screens by banks or money brokers (probably applicable to short-term interest-rate swaps only) or, more likely, by calculating the cost/profit of closing the interest-rate swap position.

The process of revaluing an interest-rate swap involves the dis-

Chapter 4

counting of future cash flows resulting from the swap to the present day, by means of net present value calculations. A key variable in the net present value calculations is what discount rate to use. There are two options, as follows:

1. To use a constant par yield rate applicable to all future cash flows. An example of this would be the semi-annualized Treasury bond redemption yield of the relevant Treasury bond maturity.
2. To use zero coupon curve rates; a different rate for cash flows in each year. The coupon curve rate is widely available through financial information screen services and relevant market journals. The rate represents the market rate for the fixed side of a fixed against dollar floating interest-rate swap, where the floating side is LIBOR. Such rates are available by currency across a range of maturities.

The use of unique rates for each future year is more desirable as this method views the swap as a collection of distinct future flows and recognizes the fact that, say, a five-year swap is really equivalent to five separate swaps.

The zero coupon rates are derived from coupon curve rates. They represent the discount rates required to give the swap a net present value of nil, whereby the fixed side of the swap is the coupon curve rate. The following example demonstrates the way in which zero coupon rates are derived:

Example

Assume the following coupon curve for Swiss Franc swaps:

One-year swap	4.00%
Two-year swap	4.30%
Three-year swap	4.50%
Four-year swap	4.60%
Five-year swap	4.70%

Zero coupon rates are such that discounting all the cash flows of a five-year 4.7% swap at five different zero coupon rates for each year will produce a net present value of nil.

Swaps

The one-year zero coupon rate is equal to the coupon curve rate; 4%, since there is only one cash flow. To determine the two-year zero coupon rate, discount the cash flows of a 4.3% swap as follows (assuming a swap principal of 100 units):

Period	Cash Flow	Discount Rate	Net Present Value
0	(100)	—	(100.00)
1	4.3	4.0%	4.135
2	104.3	Y	95.865*
			Nil

*100 − 4.135

The two-year zero coupon rate Y is the rate which, when applied to the two-year flow of 104.3, gives a net present value of 95.865:

$$95.865 = 104.3 \times \frac{1}{(1 + Y/100)^2}$$

This makes Y = 4.3067

Having obtained the zero coupon rates for years 1 and 2, the rate for year 3 can then be obtained by discounting the flows of a three-year 4.5% swap:

Period	Cash Flow	Discount Rate	Net Present Value
0	(100)	—	(100)
1	4.5	4.00%	4.3269
2	4.5	4.3067%	4.1361
3	104.5	Z	91.5370[2]
			0.000

[2] 100 − 4.3269 − 4.1361

The zero coupon rate for year 3 therefore satisfies the following equation:

$$91.5370 = 104.5 \times \frac{1}{(1 + Z/100)^3}$$

This makes Z = 4.5137

Similar calculations will give the remaining Swiss Franc zero coupon rates for years 4 and 5 as 4.6177% and 4.7244% respectively.

Having obtained the zero coupon rates by currency, a swap can be revalued by discounting all future flows (using current LIBOR rates to arrive at floating flows) to the present day.

Example

Bank A has on its books a dollar fixed-against-dollar floating-interest-rate swap, with an outstanding maturity of three years and a notional principal of $1,000,000 in U.S. dollars. The details are shown in Figure 4.11.

Assume dollar zero coupon rates are 7%, 8% and 8.5% for years 1, 2 and 3 respectively and assume that the current 12-month LIBOR rate is 9%. Then the three future flows would be $1,000,000 \times (9 - 8)\% = 10,000$ each, being net payments. These would be discounted as follows:

$$\text{NPV Flow 1} = 10,000 \times \frac{1}{(1 + 0.07)^1} = 9,346$$

$$\text{NPV Flow 2} = 10,000 \times \frac{1}{(1 + 0.08)^2} = 8,573$$

$$\text{NPV Flow 3} = 10,000 \times \frac{1}{(1 + 0.085)^3} = \underline{7,829}$$

$$\$25,748$$

Bank A will therefore record a loss of $25,748 by processing the following entry:

| Debit | = Profit and loss account | $25,748 |
| Credit | = Sundry creditors | $25,748 |

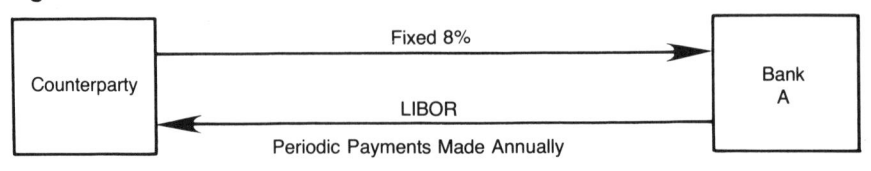

Figure 4.11

Counterparty → Fixed 8% → Bank A
Counterparty ← LIBOR ← Bank A
Periodic Payments Made Annually

Asset-based swaps

An asset-based swap transforms a fixed-rate asset into a floating-rate asset or vice versa. This kind of swap produces what is known as a "synthetic asset."

A typical asset-swap transaction might be where bank A purchases a fixed-rate bond from bank B, which also provides an interest-rate swap to transform the stream of fixed-rate income on the bond into a stream of floating- or variable-rate income. From an accounting point of view, the key issue is whether the substance of the transaction or the pure legal form should be reflected in the accounts of the entity that has engaged in the swap.

Clearly in such a case the correct legal position would be to reflect a fixed-rate bond, both in the balance sheet and in the profit and loss account and treat the swap as a separate transaction. While this does not reflect the economic substance of the asset acquired, there are likely to be problems in treating the bond as a floating-rate asset, owing to rules concerning set-off of assets and liabilities. Unless the swap is written by the same party that issued the bond, the transactions should be treated separately. However, it should be possible to ensure that the method of profit recognition properly accords with the economic substance of the transactions.

A security may be acquired for one of two purposes:

1. *Investment,* where the owner intends to hold the security until maturity. In this case, it is usual for the asset to be carried at cost as adjusted for any amortized premium or discount.
2. *Trading,* where the above criterion is not net then the asset would either be carried at the lower of cost and market value, or at market value.

If the fixed-rate bond is acquired for investment purposes, then the payments/receipts due under the swap should be accrued during each swap period. The accrual of the interest due on the bond will then be eliminated by the fixed amount payable under the swap, leaving the floating interest receivable under the swap as the net income. In practice, the swap payment/receipt will usually be settled net, which when accrued will form an adjustment to the fixed income on the bond. Therefore, the profit and loss account will reflect a floating-rate income profile.

If the fixed-rate bond is acquired for trading purposes and carried at market value, then it would also be appropriate to revalue the swap. Consider the scenario whereby a securities trader holds some fixed-rate bonds and has also entered into an asset swap to receive floating interest in exchange for fixed interest. Assume that interest rates then rise, causing a fall in the value of the bond, which results in a charge to the profit and loss account. This loss will be wholly or partially offset by the gain that would be expected on the interest-rate swap. Therefore, in such a case, it would be appropriate to revalue the swap so that the net position in the profit and loss account reflects the effect of an increase in interest rates on a floating-rate bond, not a fixed-rate bond.

CHAPTER 5
Currency and interest-rate options

The product

An option is a contract conveying the right (not the obligation) to buy or sell a specified financial instrument at a fixed price before or at a future specified date.

Before covering some of the features of options, it may be useful to consider some of the basic terminology that is associated with options in order to give a clearer understanding of their operation.

Basic terminology

The writer (sometimes referred to as the seller) of the option is the person who is required to carry out the terms of the option at the choice of the holder. The holder (sometimes referred to as the buyer) of the option is the person who has the right to exercise the option.

A *call option* confers on the holder the right to buy the underlying financial instrument. Conversely, a *put option* confers on the holder the right to sell the underlying financial instrument.

A *traded option* is freely transferable, whereas a *dealer's option* is typically not transferable.

A *European option* is exercisable only on the expiration date, whereas an *American option* is exercisable at any time up to the expiration date of the option.

Valuation

An option is typically valued according to a mathematical formula known as the *Black-Scholes model,* although several derivatives of this model have recently been developed. There are two basic variables that are relevant to the valuation of an option.

1. *Time value*. This is the value that is attributed to the benefit of being able to exercise the option during its period of currency. This value will be a function of both the volatility of the price of the underlying financial instrument (delta ratio), and the volatility of that volatility (gamma ratio).
2. *Intrinsic value*. This is the favorable difference between the price at which the option is exercisable (strike price) and the value of the underlying financial instrument.

The combination of these two elements produces a total value for the option, which is known as the option *premium.*

An option may be "in-the-money," "at-the-money," or "out-of-the-money," which, for a call option, means that the strike price is alternatively less than, equal to, or greater than the value of the underlying financial instrument. In other words, in-the-money options have intrinsic value, at-the-money options are where the strike price is equal to the underlying spot price, and out-of-the-money options have no intrinsic value.

Figure 5.1 provides a useful way of remembering the "money" concept.

Figure 5.1

	Strike Rate > Current Rate	Strike Rate < Current Rate
Call	Out	In
Put	In	Out

Uses

There are many ways in which options may be used, although, broadly, these uses may be summarized in four main categories:

1. Speculation.
2. Hedging.
3. Trading.
4. Income enhancement.

Speculators

A speculator will take an open options position that may have no connection to his or her main business. He or she is simply taking a view on how the market is going to move. The advantage of buying an option for the purposes of speculation is that the return is highly geared in relation to the cost of the underlying financial instrument, and the amount of loss that can be made is limited to the premium paid. This is in contrast to the speculator who writes an option, since the profit is limited to the premium received but the loss is potentially unlimited.

Hedgers

The main economic purpose underlying the use of options is to act as a device for transferring price, foreign-exchange, or interest-rate risk to the speculators, from those wishing to avoid that risk (hedgers).

Chapter 5

The advantage to hedgers of using this market is that for a comparatively low cost, exposures can be controlled while maintaining the ability to profit from favorable changes in price, foreign exchange, and interest rates.

One of the principal advantages of using options within a hedging strategy is that they can be used to eliminate downside risk without totally negating all the benefit of a potentially beneficial upturn. That is to say, the potential profit that may be derived from a beneficial upturn in the underlying financial instrument is only reduced by the amount of the premium, and not—as in the case of futures, for example—ceded to the counterparty in the hedging operation.

Furthermore, the amount of the risk that the company wishes to "insure" against may be tailored to that company's requirements. Thus if a company had a large U.S. dollar deposit, and wished to guard against only a large fall in interest rates, it could buy an out-of-the-money put option that carried the desired "trigger" rate of interest. Thus, if interest rates fell below this trigger level, the option could be exercised, but if they rose, the cash loss would be limited to the premium paid.

Traders

This classification is concerned with the trading activities of financial services organizations. Options may be bought and sold as part of an overall trading strategy that will encompass positions in different instruments on different exchanges and possibly in both dealer and traded options.

There are numerous trading strategies that may be invoked including those that are totally speculative in nature, such as taking an open position, and those for which the risk is minimal, such as straddles, spreads, and conversions.

A straddle is a strategy designed to take advantage of a perceived imperfection in the pricing of the option due to an incorrect assessment of the volatility of the underlying market. Thus, a dealer may buy both a put and a call ("buying a straddle") for the same option at the same exercise price and for the same expiration month and would thereby profit if the prices moved significantly up or down. Conversely, the reverse of the above operation ("selling a straddle") could be invoked to profit from insignificant movements in prices.

A spread is a strategy designed to take advantage of limited price movements. Thus, if a trader anticipated that the price was going to move upwards, he could buy a call option and then sell an identical call option but at a higher exercise price ("bull call spread"). The maximum profit will be the difference in the exercise price less the net premium paid, while the maximum loss is limited to the initial investment.

A conversion is a complex strategy designed to take advantage, with minimal risk, of a pricing anomaly between options and futures. Thus, if a trader were to buy a put and sell a call of an identical option relating to a particular futures contract, and thereby establish a synthetic short futures position, the value of this position on expiration should be equal to the value of an equivalent long futures contract. If it is not, a profit may be locked in with almost no risk attached.

Income enhancement

The term *income enhancement* relates to the generation of premium income from the sale of options.

For example, if a company is holding a foreign currency deposit, and anticipates that the foreign currency is going to weaken, but at the same time does not mind exchanging the deposit at a slightly lower rate, then the company could sell an out-of-the-money put option exercisable at that lower rate of exchange. Provided the exchange rate does not fall to this lower rate, the company will enhance any exchange gain or interest income arising on this deposit, by the premium income received on selling the put option.

It should, however, be emphasized that the writing of options generally carries a high degree of risk and is only likely to be profitable for the professional players in the market.

Trading strategies

Set out below are examples of some of the more sophisticated trading strategies. This may also clarify some of the trading strategies that have been outlined above.

Sell futures contract/buy call option

This strategy enables the investor potentially to generate profits on a highly leveraged basis, while limiting the size of his or her otherwise unlimited downside risk.

Thus, an investor who expected interest rates to rise could sell short a CD futures contract at a price equal to the strike price on the CD call option. If the interest rates rise as forecast, the investor will make a net profit as soon as the profit on the futures contract exceeds the premium that was paid for the option. On the other hand, if interest rates rise, the investor's loss will be limited to the cost of the option premium.

Sell futures contract/write put option

This strategy enables the investor to realize a high return on his or her investment during relatively "flat" markets (i.e., when no large price fluctuations are anticipated). This strategy is not appropriate where the underlying market is extremely volatile.

Thus, the investor may write a put option at a strike price below the price at which he or she has sold short the futures contract. If the value of the futures contract falls, the investor may earn a maximum profit of the difference in price between the strike price of the option and the price of the futures contract, plus the option premium that he or she will retain. Conversely, if the value of the futures contract rises, the investor will only make a net loss once the losses on the futures contract exceed the premium income from the option. However, above this point the losses are unlimited, and it is for this reason that this strategy is unlikely to be appropriate in volatile markets.

Write a put-call straddle

This strategy can generate good returns where the investor either expects the market to remain flat, or to be volatile within a narrow range. However, as with the previous strategy, it should be emphasized that this strategy is risky if the market is likely to extend out of the predicted range.

Thus, an investor could write March calls at a strike price of 70 and March puts at a strike price of 65. The investor will retain the full amount of the premiums if the price of the underlying instrument remains in the range of 65 to 70. He or she will however make a net loss if the price moves out of this range to such an extent that the gross loss exceeds the total premium received.

Traded stock options

Traded options are similar to interest-rate and currency options except that the underlying securities are the shares of large publicly quoted companies or a basket of their shares in the form of publicized indexes.

In the United Kingdom, there are currently traded options in respect of the shares of over 40 companies, the principal market for these options being on the floor of the Stock Exchange itself. Similar markets have been established in most of the world's leading stock markets.

In common with all other options, traded options are of two basic types—calls and puts—giving the right to buy or sell at a specific price, respectively.

Each market typically establishes a standard contract size of a fixed number of shares. This contract size may vary for those companies whose equity has an unusually high or low market price.

The Stock Exchange traded options have a maximum life of nine months and expiration dates are fixed at three-month intervals. This means that at any point in time, traded options will be quoted at three different expiration dates.

Margining

Margining procedures are broadly similar to those required for futures contracts.

Those who initially write the option are required to lodge an initial margin. This is calculated by reference to the price of the underlying equity and the exercise price of the option. In London, all clearing and margining is processed by the London Options Clearing House. Further margin calls are assessed on a daily basis by reference to daily movements in the price of the underlying equity.

Margin need not necessarily be lodged in the form of cash, but can also be the ordinary shares and American Depository Receipts (ADRs) of the underlying equity, or U.K. and U.S. government stock. In certain circumstances, concessions on the amount of margin lodged may be made where spread or straddle positions exist.

Acounting for foreign currency and interest-rate options

Background

The purchase of a currency or interest-rate option contract is an acquisition of an asset. In the case of a currency option, this is a right but not an obligation to acquire foreign currency at a particular designated strike price by or at a future date. Interest-rate options take two principal forms: They may either fix the maximum rate of interest on a predetermined credit, or be an option on a long-term financial asset.

After the future date specified, an option has no value and expires. Prior to that date, the value of the option will be determined by two factors: the intrinsic value—the difference between the strike price and the current exchange or interest rate (where the strike price is in favor of the holder, or in-the-money)—and time value, which is affected by a number of matters, typically time left until expiration of the contract, currency or interest-rate volatility, and supply-and-demand considerations.

Options on foreign currency and interest rates have been written in the over-the-counter (OTC) market for many years but on a relatively limited basis. Significant growth has been experienced recently and has coincided with the introduction of exchange-traded options in the late 1970s and early 1980s. The growth of exchange-traded options has been complemented by growth in the OTC markets.

This growth has been primarily user-driven, and reflects the desire of large companies and financial institutions to manage interest-rate and foreign currency risk. The recent volatility of interest and foreign-exchange rates, over which firms have no direct control, has been a significant factor in creating this demand.

Foreign-exchange options on the OTC market are traded in several of the world's financial centers. Most activity is concentrated in the London and U.S. markets. Organized exchanges exist in Amsterdam, Chicago, Philadelphia, Montreal, Sydney, and London. Interest-rate options are less well developed and market activity on both the OTC and exchange-traded markets is concentrated in the United States.

Professional standards

To date, there have been no rules or guidelines laid down by U.K. or U.S. accounting bodies on accounting for currency or interest-rate option contracts. A number of U.S. and U.K. accounting standards are however relevant. In the United States, Statement of Financial Accounting Standards (SFAS) 52 "Foreign Currency Translation," SFAS 80 "Accounting for Futures Contracts," and SFAS 12 "Accounting for Certain Marketable Securities" AICPA Issues Paper 86-2 "Accounting for Options" and, in the United Kingdom, Statement of Standard Accounting Practice (SSAP) 20 "Foreign Currency Translation" are all relevant sources of guidance in determining the accounting policy that should be applied in respect of option contracts.

None of the standards noted above makes specific reference to the treatment of options, although SFAS 52 deals in detail with the treatment to be given to forward-exchange contracts and introduces the concepts of hedging and speculation. These issues are developed further in SFAS 80, which deals exclusively with futures transactions, other than foreign currency futures contracts.

SFAS 52 and SFAS 80 are the primary authoritative accounting pronouncements that address financial instruments that are often used for hedging, as are options. The two statements are, however, not consistent in all respects and it is necessary to select from alternatives the most appropriate treatment of an option. In these situations, account must be taken of the "one-sided" nature of options, which make the risk and reward characteristics of options different from those of futures and forward contracts.

Accounting entries

In arriving at an appropriate accounting treatment, three separate phases require consideration:

Chapter 5

1. The initial entries to record the purchase or sale of an options contract.
2. Calculation of profit or loss arising in respect of an options contract—that is, valuation.
3. Recognition of profit and loss.

Initial entries. The basic accounting entries in respect of a sale or purchase of an option are straightforward.

PURCHASE. When a put or call option is purchased, cash will be paid away to the writer or seller of the option in the form of a premium, representing the time value and—for in-the-money options—the intrinsic value of the option. The premium may be regarded as an asset acquired, and a balance sheet premium suspense account should be established to account for the transaction. The other side of the entry is to cash or a broker account.

SALE. The treatment of a sold option transaction should mirror that described above. Thus, the premium received should be credited to a premium suspense liability account. In addition to premium received, certain entries will be required to record any margins paid to cover losses that may arise on a short position when revalued to market prices.

Margins consist of two elements: the initial margin, and the variation margin that may be required to reflect deterioration in the value of a short position over the life of the option. Any initial margin paid should be debited to a separate margin account held in the balance sheet. Variation margins should be recorded separately to facilitate management control of positions held. Margins should never be debited to the premium suspense liability account as this will hinder the calculation of profits and losses.

The subsequent treatment of the premium paid or received will vary and will depend not only on whether a long or short position is held, but also on the purpose for which the option was purchased or sold.

In the United States, there is a view that in certain circumstances the intrinsic value and time value of an option should be separated. Subsequently, the time value should be amortized over the life of the option and the intrinsic value accounted for as a hedge (see below). The rationale for this approach is that the time value of an option is in some circumstances equivalent to an insurance premium. Accordingly, the "premium" should be written off over the period to which it relates.

There are, however, certain drawbacks to this approach. First, it is necessary to identify the method by which the "premium" should be written off. A straight-line approach may not be appropriate. Second, other things remaining equal, the effect of marking to market an options position (see Valuation, below) is to write off the time value as it erodes during the life of the option.

Valuation. The valuation of open option positions is straightforward in respect of traded options. These are quoted on an exchange and therefore a ready market value exists for all such options. In respect of OTC options, no market exists and alternative procedures must be adopted. There are essentially two possibilities:

1. Option pricing is generally performed using pricing formulae. The most well-known formula is the Black-Scholes, which is based on the concept that the options should be priced in such a way that opportunity for risk-free arbitrage between the option and the underlying commodity should not exist. Various derivatives of the Black-Scholes have been developed that vary or change the assumptions made; however, the basic rationale remains the same. Providing that the holder or writer of an option is aware of the model used and assumptions made, it is possible to recalculate the value of an option at any time taking into account any changes in the initial variables used in calculating the option price.
2. For a trader who is holding an option, the pricing formula is probably unknown. To obtain a valuation, it should be possible to go back to the writer of the option and request a current valuation, which would be derived by the writer as in (1) above.

Once the current profit or loss on an option has been determined, it is necessary to consider how to deal with it.

Recognition of profit and loss. There are four main groups of options use:

1. Speculators.
2. Hedgers.
3. Traders.
4. Income enhancers.

The motives of each user group are different and will affect the accounting policy to be adopted.

There are essentially two ways of accounting for options positions:

1. *Mark to market.* This approach requires that all options are marked to market and that both realized and unrealized gains and losses resulting from a change in the market value of options held are recognized currently in the profit and loss account income statement. The American Institute of Certified Public Accountants (AICPA) has produced an accounting issues paper entitled "Accounting for Options" which although not authoritative identifies the issues and provides a source of views regarding accounting for options. In this, they recommend that all options that do not qualify for hedge accounting be marked to market.
2. *Lower of cost or market.* The application of this accounting basis results in the recognition of unrealized losses but not of unrealized gains. In the case of written options, valuation on this basis would be at the higher of the premium received or market value.

The latter alternative will only be appropriate where it is consistent with accounting policies adopted in respect of related items. For example, a commodity dealer that carries its inventory at the lower of cost or market may account for options that do not qualify for hedge accounting at the lower of cost or market.

The recommended policy for each user group is as follows.

SPECULATORS. A speculator is an entity that takes positions that have no connection with its main business. Such positions will be taken on the basis of future expectations of price movements or of volatility.

Because a speculator holds options that are not connected with other activities of the entity, the mark-to-market basis described above is recommended. This approach is consistent with SFAS 52 and SFAS 80 and is in line with current trends in accounting for financial instruments. However, speculators that are not financial institutions will frequently only recognize gains when realized and carry open long positions at the lower of cost and market value.

HEDGERS. The basic economic purpose of an option is to provide a mechanism for transferring foreign-exchange or interest-rate risk from those wishing to avoid risk to those willing to assume it in anticipation of profit. Basically, hedging involves taking opposing positions in the cash and options markets to protect against unfavorable price movements.

There are many different strategies that may be adopted to hedge positions using options; however, all strategies fall broadly into two basic types:

1. Hedges of *existing* assets, liabilities, or firm fixed-price commitments.
2. Hedges of *probable* or anticipated futures transactions but to which an entity may not yet be legally committed.

The accounting treatment in each of these two cases will be different and is discussed below.

First, however, it is necessary to determine whether an option qualifies for hedge accounting. In establishing this fact, a number of criteria should be met:

1. The price behavior of the hedge and the item being hedged should show a high degree of positive correlation.
2. The options position should reduce the foreign-exchange or interest-rate exposure.
3. The options position should be designated as a hedge.
4. If the hedge has been established in anticipation of a commitment, that commitment should reasonably be expected to be fulfilled.
5. In respect of written options, they should not only meet the criteria in (1) to (4) above but also must be so deep in-the-money that it is reasonably assured that they will remain so throughout their term. In

this case, the written option will effectively take on the characteristics of a futures contact.

Where these conditions are met, hedge accounting is appropriate. Hedge accounting is based on the concept of symmetry of accounting between the option and the related asset, liability, or transaction being hedged. The recommended treatment is as follows:

1. *Hedge of existing asset, liability, or transaction.* If an option is bought against an existing asset or liability, then where the hedged asset or liability is being revalued to market, unrealized profits or losses on the option position should be credited or debited to the profit and loss account. If the hedged asset is being carried at the lower of cost and market, the reverse treatment should be accorded to the option position (i.e., value at the higher of cost or market). This latter approach would normally result in profits on option positions being recognized only when they are realized. If the hedged asset or liability is an interest-bearing financial instrument carried at amortized cost, gains and losses on the option should be amortized over the life of the instrument.
2. *Trade commitment.* Unrealized gains and losses on hedging a firm trade commitment should be deferred until the commitment matures.

    It is necessary to monitor the position of the underlying commitment throughout the life of the option contract. If the commitment is cancelled before the option is exercised, the previously deferred gains or losses should be taken to profit and loss, together with any subsequent differences.
3. *Potential commitment.* The position regarding potential commitments requires further examination. An example might be a manufacturer who believes he may order goods for delivery in three months' time but is unsure whether or not he will place a firm order. Another example is a company entering into a tender for a large overseas fixed-price contract that wishes to protect the foreign-exchange exposure that could arise.

    Factors that should be considered in determining whether to defer unrealized differences on potential commitments include the following:

(a) whether the significant characteristics and expected terms of the anticipated transaction are known;
(b) the likelihood that the transaction will occur.

In assessing (b), consideration should be given to the frequency of similar transactions in the past, the ability of the entity to carry out the transaction, the length of time to the transaction date, and the extent of losses or disruption of operations that could occur if the transaction did not take place.

Generally speaking, if a transaction is possible but not probable, any option obtained to reduce the possible exposure will not qualify for hedge accounting. It should be noted that in the United States, trades undertaken to protect adverse movements in respect of potential commitments do not qualify as hedges.

Let us now consider two examples, first where a trade commitment exists and second where a potential commitment is due to crystallize.

Example—Foreign currency option transaction hedging a trade commitment

On July 1, a U.K. company is committed to the sale, in the United States, of a large quantity of its product. Delivery and invoicing are due to take place in two months, and payment one month thereafter.

The sale price is £1,500,000 and is due for settlement in dollars. The current exchange rate is $1.50: £1. The U.K. company is exposed to strengthening of sterling against the dollar.

The treasurer of the U.K. company decides to hedge this exposure in the options market by acquiring options to purchase £1,000,000 at the current exchange rate (the option will therefore be purchased at-the-money). The premium paid for the purchase of the option is £20,000. The option expires on September 30, the day that payment is due from the company's customer.

During the life of the option, the following movements in the exchange rate and the market value of the option take place:

	\multicolumn{5}{c}{Time (Months)}
	July 1	July 31	August 31	September 30	September 30
Exchange rate	1.50	1.45	1.4	1.48	1.55
Market value of option (£)	20,000	15,000	10,000	Nil	50,000

Chapter 5

The alternative exchange rates at September 30 are used to demonstrate the impact on the company of the option expiring both in- and out-of-the-money.

Accounting entries

July 1
The premium paid is an asset and should be recognized as such:

    Dr Premium suspense (balance sheet account)   £20,000
    Cr Cash   £20,000

July 31
The option held by the company has fallen in value by £5,000. As yet, however, there is no matching asset in the balance sheet (receivable being hedged) and thus the loss should be deferred:

    Dr Deferred loss (balance sheet account)   £5,000
    Cr Premium suspense   £5,000

August 31
Delivery has been made and an invoice raised. The loss on the option should now be taken to profit and loss.

(i) Recognition of sale ($1,500,000 × $\frac{1}{1.45}$ = £1,034,483)

    Dr Receivable   £1,034,483
    Cr Sales   £1,034,483

(ii) Recognition of loss on option

    Dr Profit and loss account   £10,000
    Cr Deferred loss   £ 5,000
    Cr Premium suspense   £ 5,000

September 30

Assumption 1
The option has expired out-of-the-money and must be written off in full. The receivable is settled and converted at the prevailing spot rate of 1.48.

Currency and Interest-Rate Options

Dr Profit and loss		
— premium		£ 10,000
— foreign-exchange movement		
(£1,034,483 − £1,013,513)		£ 20,970
Dr Cash ($1,500,000 × 1/1.48)		£1,013,513
Cr Receivable		£1,034,483
Cr Premium suspense		£ 10,000

Assumption 2
The option has expired in-the-money as the exchange rate has moved unfavorably against the dollar receivable balance. The company may either exercise the option, or sell it back to the writer for its intrinsic value on expiration. Let us assume that the company does the latter. The necessary accounting entries will be as follows:

(i) To recognize the profit on the option
Dr Cash	£50,000
Cr Profit and loss	£50,000

(ii) To write off the balance on premium suspense
Dr Profit and loss	£10,000
Cr Premium suspense	£10,000

(iii) To record the cash receipt and write off the foreign-exchange loss
Dr Cash ($1,500,000 @ 1.55)	£ 967,742
Dr Profit and loss—foreign exchange	£ 66,741
Cr Receivable ($1,500,000 @ 1.45)	£1,034,483

Company balance sheets. The table below summarizes the company balance sheet at each stage of the transaction described.

Debits (Credits)			Time (Months)		
Account	July 1	July 31	August 31	September 30	September 30
Premium suspense	20,000	15,000	10,000	—	—
Deferred loss	—	5,000	—	—	—
Receivable	—	—	1,034,483	—	—
Cash	(20,000)	(20,000)	(20,000)	993,513	997,742
Profit and loss	—	—	(1,024,483)	(993,513)	(997,742)

Chapter 5

In order to assess properly the impact of the option on these results, let us consider the position had the receivable not been hedged:

	Time (Months)	
	September 30	September 30
Cash	1,013,513	967,742
Profit and loss	1,013,513	967,742

As can be seen, the company has limited its losses to £2,258 under assumption (2) (1,000,000 − 997,742). Furthermore, while the opportunity for windfall profits has been reduced the company will benefit from any favorable movement in the exchange rate, the impact of which is greater than £20,000. Any other favorable movements, such as that under assumption (1), will reduce the cost of the hedge.

The position may be shown diagrammatically as in Figure 5.2.

Figure 5.2

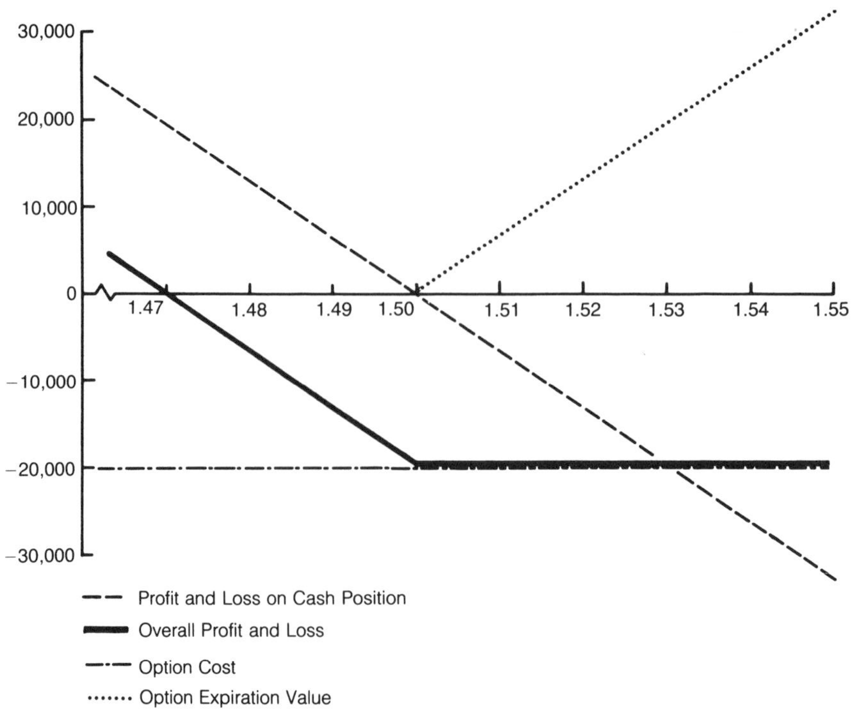

– – Profit and Loss on Cash Position
▬ Overall Profit and Loss
–·– Option Cost
······ Option Expiration Value

Had the exchange rate fallen to $1.47 on expiration, the option would break even:

$$\begin{aligned}1{,}500{,}000 \,@\, 1.47 &= £1{,}020{,}000 \\ \text{Less cost of option} &= \underline{20{,}000} \\ &\,\underline{\underline{£1{,}000{,}000}}\end{aligned}$$

Example—Interest-rate option transaction hedging a contingent asset

On June 1, a U.K. insurance company is expecting to receive £1,000,000 inflow of premiums in three months' time. The treasury manager intends to invest the money in long-term gilts but is concerned that there may be a decrease in interest rates before the money is received. This would increase the cost of the gilts to be purchased and consequently reduce the yield that he expects. As a result, he decides to purchase an appropriate call option on the London International Financial Futures Exchange (LIFFE).

The option purchased to hedge the cash market position will be an option on a long-gilt future. This is appropriate, since the purchase of a future fixes the price at which a cash bond can be purchased, and the purchase of a call option will fix the futures price and thus the cash market price.

The current futures price of LIFFE long gilt futures in 91-21/32. The company intends to purchase September 20 call options with an exercise price of 92-00 for a premium of 3-24/64. Note: Each option represents £50,000 nominal value long-term gilt with a 12% coupon. The premium payable totals £33,750 (3-24/64 × £500 × 20).

Accounting

First, it must be established whether the option qualifies for hedge accounting. The £1,000,000 receivable is not yet in the books of the company and will be established as a receivable in month 3. However, historically the premiums have always been received as they relate to the renewal of existing policies.

The significant terms and characteristics of the anticipated transaction are known, it is probable that it will occur, and therefore hedge accounting should be applied.

During the life of the option, the following price movements take place:

Chapter 5

	Time (Months)			
	June 30	July 31	August 31	August 31
Futures price	92-00	93-00	90-00	96-00
Option price	3-00	4-00	—	4-00

The accounting entries are straightforward:

June 1
The company has purchased an asset with a value of £33,750. This will be accounted for in the same way as any other option premium:

Dr Premium suspense (balance sheet account)	£33,750
Cr Cash	£33,750

June 30
After one month, interest rates have fallen and the futures price has risen. The option purchased is now at-the-money, has no intrinsic value, and has lost a small part of its time value. The position being hedged does not exist in the accounts of the company and thus the loss on the option position should be deferred (24/64 × £500 × 20 = £3,750).

Dr Deferred loss (balance sheet account)	£3,750
Cr Premium suspense	£3,750

July 31
The option is now in-the-money, and has remaining time value. The position being hedged is still not in the books of the company and the profit should be deferred ((4-00) − (3-00) × £500 × 20 = £10,000).

Dr Premium suspense	£10,000
Cr Deferred income (balance sheet account)	£ 6,250
Cr Deferred loss	£ 3,750

August 31

Assumption 1
Interest rates have risen and the option has expired out-of-the-money. The remaining premium suspense must be written off, and the

£1,000,000 will be invested in the cash market after clearing the cash shortfall. Thus:

Dr	Cash	£ 33,750
Dr	Profit and loss—write off option premium (net)	£ 33,750
Dr	Investments	£ 966,250
Dr	Deferred income	£ 6,250
Cr	Profit and loss—premium income	£1,000,000
Cr	Premium suspense	£ 40,000

Assumption 2
As anticipated by the treasurer, interest rates have fallen and the gilt price has gone up. The option expires in-the-money and will be sold back to the writer by the company. The company is then able to go into the market to purchase the long-dated gilts required for its investment portfolio.

The resulting accounting entries will be as follows:

(i) Write off the option value
Dr	Deferred income	£ 6,250
Dr	Profit and loss	£33,750
Cr	Premium suspense	£40,000

(ii) Record the insurance premium income
Dr	Cash	£1,000,000
Cr	Insurance income	£1,000,000

(iii) Record the sale of the option
Dr	Cash	£40,000
Cr	Profit and loss	£40,000

(iv) Record the purchase of the gilt
Dr	Investments	£1,006,250
Cr	Cash	£1,006,250

Company balance sheets. The table on the next page summarizes the company balance sheet at each stage of the transaction described:

Chapter 5

Account	June 1	June 30	Time (Months) July 31	August 31	August 31
Premium suspense	33,750	30,000	40,000	—	—
Cash	(33,750)	(33,750)	(33,750)	—	—
Deferred loss	—	3,750			
Deferred income	—	—	(6,250)	—	—
Profit and loss	—	—	—	(966,250)	(1,006,250)
Investments	—	—	—	966,250	1,006,250

Had the company done nothing, its balance sheet at August 31 would have been as follows:

Investments	£1,000,000
Insurance income	£1,000,000

At first glance, it would appear that the decision to purchase the option has been very costly in one instance and resulted in only a small gain where the option finished in-the-money. However, let us consider the relative yield of each position by looking at the nominal value of the gilts purchased.

	Nominal Value Purchased
Assumption (1) with option	
(966,250 @ 90)	1,073,611
without option	
(1,000,000 @ 90)	1,111,111
Assumption (2) with option	
(1,006,250 @ 96)	1,048,177
without option	
(1,000,000 @ 96)	1,041,666

Where the option finished out-of-the-money as under assumption (1) the company will always be able to buy £33,750 less than if no option had been purchased. In this particular instance the difference in nominal value is £37,500:

$$33,750 \times \frac{1}{0.9} = 37,500$$

In the second instance, the company has benefited and the maximum extent of loss will always be limited. It should be noted that although the company appears to have profited more where its option expired in-the-money, its holding of stock is greater under assumption (1) and the company has derived greater benefit from the fall in gilt prices, as is to be expected.

TRADERS. Organizations coming under this heading would normally include banks and other financial concerns.

Options may be both bought and sold as part of an overall dealing strategy involving positions in different instruments, on different exchanges and, possibly, positions in OTC as well as traded options.

All open positions should be marked to market and the result compared with the balance on the premium suspense account. Unrealized losses should in all events be recognized and unrealized profits will usually be taken to the profit and loss account as they arise.

Caution should be exercised in relation to the recognition of unrealized profits arising on OTC options. In such cases, a view should be taken on the extent to which the underlying market in the options is liquid for the relevant maturity dates and strike prices. It may well be that the illiquidity of some OTC options may encourage the deferral of premium income.

The following example outlines the treatment of a typical trading strategy.

Example—Trading spread transaction

A U.K. company trades in options and futures in the currency markets. Over a period of three days it performs the following transactions:

Day Transaction
1 Purchases a three-month futures contract to buy $1,000,000 in sterling at a rate of $1.50 to the pound.
   Cost on delivery: £666,667
2 Purchases a put option with an expiration date co-terminous with that of the futures contract. The put option gives the trader the right to sell $1,000,000 at $1.55.
   The option is out-of-the-money.
   Cost: £5,000

Chapter 5

3	Sells a call option with an expiration date co-terminous with that of the futures contract. The call option gives the purchaser the right to buy $1,000,000 at $1.55.
The option is in-the-money.
Premium income: £30,506
(intrinsic value £21,506, time value £9,000)

By buying a put and selling the call, the trader has established a synthetic short futures position at an exchange rate of $1.55.

Whatever the rate prevailing at the expiration date, this position will be liquidated at $1.55. If the rate is above $1.55, the trader will exercise his put option. If it is below $1.55, the holder of the call will exercise his option.

The trader has thus apparently sustained a loss if his two positions are matched.

Long
$1,000,000 @ 1.50   666,667
Short
$1,000,000 @ 1.55   (645,161)
Loss   £21,506

However, the trader has also paid and received premiums on the options bought and sold.

Premium received   30,506
Premium paid   (5,000)
Net income   £25,506

The overall position may be summarized thus:

Loss on "futures" positions   (21,506)
Profit on options   25,506
Net profit   £4,000

At whatever price is prevailing at expiration, the trader will always make a profit of £4,000. This may be shown diagrammatically as in Figure 5.3.

Figure 5.3

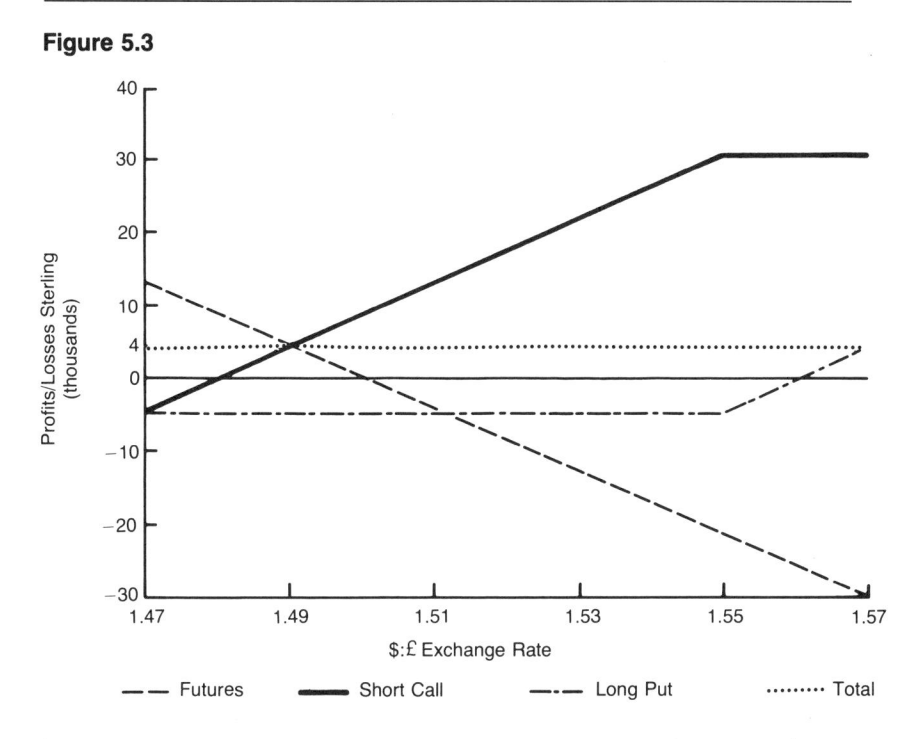

[Chart showing Profits/Losses Sterling (thousands) vs $:£ Exchange Rate, with lines for Futures, Short Call, Long Put, and Total]

Let us assume that the exchange rate remained constant at $1.50 throughout the three-day period. How was the transaction possible?

Many things affect options pricing, including the expected volatility of the market over the life of the option. If on day 3 something happened that changed the market's expectation of future volatility, the time value of an option could rise significantly, as is the case in this example. Of course, in the real world such an event would be likely to affect the futures and the spot price as well as the options price. The example has been simplified in order to identify more clearly the accounting treatment applicable.

The appropriate accounting treatment is as follows:

Day 1.
The trader has purchased a future and will account for any margin payable. In addition the trader will establish a memorandum account. The future would normally be marked to market over its life and any profits or losses would be credited or charged to profit and loss as they arose.

Day 2.
The trader has paid a premium of £5,000 to purchase the put option. As in the previous examples, the premium should be posted to a suspense account. If the option is designated as a hedge, the option would be marked to market over its life to mirror the treatment of the futures position. If not designated as a hedge, the treatment should be consistent with that applied to the other trading instruments held by the trader.

Day 3.
The trader has received £30,506 as a premium arising from sale of the call option. The spread of £4,000 has been locked in. If the trader marked this position to market, to match the treatment of the other legs of the strategy, charges or credits to profit and loss might arise that would distort the commercial reality of the position (i.e., a £4,000 profit).

Providing the trader designates the position as a locked-in strategy and intends to hold the position to expiration, an alternative treatment is recommended. The profit of £4,000 should be credited as deferred income and amortized over the life of the strategy. It should be noted that this treatment will match income with any funding cost associated with the strategy.

If at any time the trader decides not to hold the position to expiration, but is considering unwinding the position, the three legs of the strategy should be marked to market and any profit or loss arising should be credited or charged to profit and loss.

INCOME ENHANCER. In addition to their use as hedges or speculative instruments, options may be used individually or in combinations to perform additional functions. One of the most common uses is for income enhancement.

Options may be used to enhance the income from existing liquid assets. Let us assume that a U.K. company holds U.S. dollars on deposit with its bank and the U.S. dollars were acquired at a price equal to today's spot price. The treasurer may decide that he expects a weaker dollar, but is happy to convert his U.S. dollar holding at an exchange rate slightly lower than the current rate. He will therefore sell the appropriate number of put options at a strike price below the current rate (out-of-the-money). If it is assumed that the current sterling exchange rate is $1.45, the U.K. trader may sell put options at, say, $1.40. These options will give the buyer the right but not the obligation to sell sterling to the company at the strike price. The company will then receive premium income for selling the put options with an expiration date in, say, three months' time.

Common sense may indicate that this premium should be amortized to the profit and loss account equally over the remaining period of the option. However, it should be noted that there is an underlying risk associated with the options that the company has sold. Assuming, as in this example, that the company has an underlying currency deposit of U.S. dollars, this will be revalued to market in line with exchange rate movements. In the same way there should be a revaluation of the option contract to market. In both cases the difference will be taken to the profit and loss account.

The way in which the premium will be amortized to the profit and loss account in this case is worthy of note. Since the options sold only have time value (they have no intrinsic value because the options have been sold out-of-the-money), it is interesting to observe the decay of the option price up to the expiration date. Research has indicated that time value will not reduce on a straight-line basis but will decay more rapidly in the latter part of the option period. Assuming that the strike price of the option is never matched by the exchange rate, a major portion of the premium income will probably be credited to the profit and loss account during the final month of the option.

CHAPTER 6

Interest-rate caps, collars, and floors

The product

Caps, collars, and floors may be seen as yet another tool for transferring interest-rate risk away from the corporate sector into the financial sector. These instruments are essentially a form of interest-rate volatility protection that enable the corporate manager to fund his or her medium-term projects with short-term money in the confidence that substantial increases in interest rates will have no ill effects on the company's profit and loss account.

Interest-rate cap

An interest-rate cap is an agreement between a bank and a corporate borrower with floating-rate debt whereby the bank, in return for a premium, undertakes to cap the cost of this debt over an agreed rate for an agreed period of time. That is to say, the bank will pay any interest costs arising as a result of the increase in the cost of the debt above the agreed cap rate.

Suppose that a company is considering investing in a project that is forecasted to be profitable until the cost of funds relating to the project exceeds 14%. If the borrower is able to borrow at LIBOR + 1/2%, and

LIBOR currently stands at 11%, there is clearly a risk that the borrowing costs may exceed 14%. However, in return for the payment of a lump-sum premium, the borrower may "cap" the interest rate on this loan at 14% and thereby ensure that, all other things being equal, the project will remain profitable during the life of the cap (ignoring the cost of the premium). Also, the company will continue to take the extra benefit from the interest rate remaining below this level.

The pure cap is inextricably linked with the underlying borrowings and results in a high concentration of risk on one party. The stripped cap on the other hand is detached from the underlying borrowings and enables a market in caps to develop, thereby distributing the risk and reducing the premium that the borrower is required to pay.

Interest-rate floor

A floor is an agreement between a bank and a corporate lender with floating-rate loans whereby the bank, in return for a premium, agrees to set a floor on the interest income that the corporate lender will derive from its loans. That is to say, the bank will pay any lost interest income arising as a result of a fall in the interest rates below the agreed floor rate.

Suppose that a company is funding its floating-rate assets with a fixed-rate loan at 12%. If the return on these assets falls below 12%, they will no longer be profitable to the company. Again, by the payment of a lump-sum premium, the company can set a "floor" on the interest that it will receive from these assets at 12% and thereby ensure that, all other things being equal, the assets will generate a net return during the life of the floor (ignoring the cost of the premium). Also, the company will continue to take the extra benefit of any rise in interest rates.

Interest-rate collar

A collar is a combination of both a cap and a floor that enables a party with a floating-rate stream of funds to lock into a predetermined interest-rate band.

Suppose that in the situation described above for the cap, the corporate manager had taken the view that interest rates were not going to fall below 8%, or alternatively he wanted to maintain the downside

Interest-Rate Caps, Collars, and Floors

protection afforded by the cap but wanted to reduce the cost of the premium. In return for the payment of a premium, likely to be 30% less than that for the cap, depending on where the floor was set, the company could set a "collar" of between 8 and 14% on the interest payments that they would have to pay. The premium that is paid here is most simply viewed as a net premium, whereby the company pays a premium for the collar, and receives a premium in return for the floor.

This collar ensures that the project will remain profitable, although now no benefit will be derived by the company in the event that interest rates fall below 8%.

These points are illustrated in Figure 6.1, which shows the comparative position of a borrower who chooses alternatively fixed, unhedged floating, capped floating, and collared floating loans.

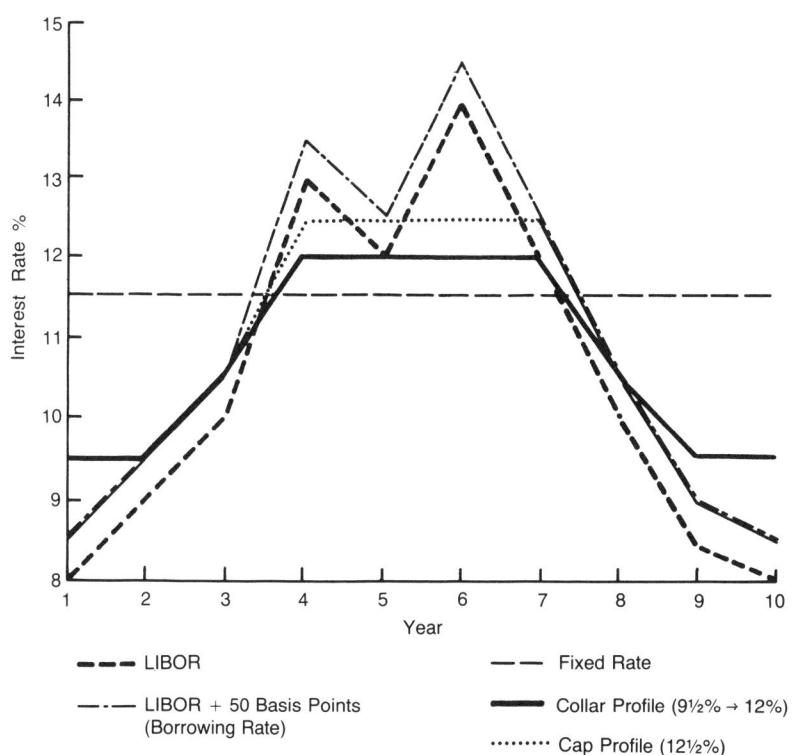

Figure 6.1 Comparative borrowing costs

- - - LIBOR
— · — LIBOR + 50 Basis Points (Borrowing Rate)
— — Fixed Rate
——— Collar Profile (9½% → 12%)
········· Cap Profile (12½%)

Uses

The most prolific cap users are risk-averse corporations seeking protection against large adverse movements in their floating-rate loans. Alternatively, these instruments are extremely useful to the company involved in medium-return projects, such as construction and leasing, and companies funding themselves for leveraged buyouts.

Caps will generally be preferable to floating-rate index options where the loan structure is not compatible with the floating-rate index options available on the market. This is typically the case with loans maturing in more than three years. Also, the swap markets are only available to the bigger players, and are not suitable where the borrower wishes to maintain his current low level of borrowing while ensuring against any large increases in future rates.

There are, however, a number of factors that have had a restraining effect on the use of these instruments.

1. The payment of a substantial upfront premium, which, typically, may range between 1 and 5% of the principal loan, depending on the strike level of the cap and its maturity period, is at best incompatible with the company's cash, and at worst may put a severe strain on the company's liquidity.
2. There may be adverse fiscal consequences from the payment of an upfront premium.
3. Any hedging policy is always viewed in hindsight as being suboptimal. That is to say, if retrospectively the cap was found not to be needed, the company frequently sees itself as having paid a premium for nothing, or as having selected the wrong strike level. It may be little consolation to a company that an alternative hedging strategy, such as a swap, would have resulted in a greater effective loss.
4. There is a credit risk associated with a cap in so far as, if the interest rate exceeds the strike level of the cap, the writer of the cap is liable to make a compensating payment to the company. There is no margining system as with the futures markets. Also, where the caps are "stripped" from a floating-rate note (FRN) for example, the credit risk changes between traders in the market.

Markets

The major writers of these instruments are the large international investment banks. The advent of the stripped interest-rate cap has enabled a market in caps to develop and, as mentioned earlier, this ability to diversify the risk has reduced the premium payable for the caps.

Stripped caps are traded in London and New York and the market for three- to five-year caps is now becoming quite liquid, with about twenty major players.

Accounting for interest-rate caps, collars, and floors

An interest-rate cap (otherwise known as an interest-rate guarantee) is a relatively new financial instrument designed to protect borrowers of floating-rate funds against excessive upward movements in interest rates. Such an instrument has the features of an interest-rate option, but since caps tend to be longer term they would be regarded as long dated option contracts. As with many new financial products, caps were initially written by banks in response to customer demand to protect the cost of funds against volatile adverse movements in interest rates. As banks were prepared to take the interest-rate risk onto their books they needed a mechanism for hedging the risk and hence an interbank market in caps has evolved.

An interest-rate floor is really the converse of a cap. It protects investors in floating-rate instruments against excessive downward movements in interest rates, while being able to take credit for upward movements in rates. It is an instrument mainly designed to protect or enhance the yield on portfolios of floating-rate instruments, such as FRNs.

An interest-rate collar is really a combination of a cap and a floor, whereby the buyer of the collar purchases a cap and sells a floor to the writer of the collar.

This means that the buyer has capped the cost of floating-rate borrowings but limited the potential gain from reductions in interest rates to the floor rate. The driving force in developing the product was the lower premium rates available compared with the pure cap that was seen as being expensive.

For example, an interest-rate cap may provide protection against rises in interest rates above 11% and allow the buyer to take full credit for any favorable movements. Hence, if rates were to rise to say 15%, the writer of the cap would have to pay the buyer an amount equivalent to 4% on the agreed principal amount, whereas if rates had fallen to 6%, the buyer would simply pay 6% to the lenders. A collar written in similar circumstances may have the specification of providing protection in excess of 11% but with a lower limit of, say, 8%. Therefore, if interest rates fell to 6% the buyer would have to pay 2% to the writer of the collar.

The specifications of an interest-rate cap or floor are set in the same way as an over-the-counter option. For a cap, the strike price is the rate above which the writer (or seller) of the cap will compensate the buyer (i.e., when the cap is in-the-money). The expiration date is the date at which actual interest rates are compared with the strike rate and if the cap is in-the-money the appropriate amounts are paid by the writer to the buyer. If the cap is out-of-the-money (current interest rates are less than the strike rate), the cap simply lapses. The expiration date will usually coincide with the rollover date on the buyer's underlying borrowings. Clearly, the converse of these specifications applies to interest-rate floors.

In return for providing the buyer with interest-rate protection, the writer receives a premium. As for currency or interest-rate options, the premium will usually be based on two factors:

1. *Intrinsic value*—the difference between the strike rate and the actual interest rate, where the actual rate is higher (i.e., the cap is written in-the-money).
2. *Time value*—mainly comprising volatility. The longer the period to expiration and the greater the historical volatility of the relevant interest rates, the higher the premium.

There is no traded market in caps, collars, or floors. All quotes are made by dealers to meet the particular requirements of the customer. There are currently no standard terms and conditions for such instruments, as exists in the interbank market for future-rate agreements and interest-rate swaps (laid down by the British Bankers Association).

As already mentioned, interest-rate caps tend to be longer dated options designed to protect the interest risk on medium- to long-term floating-rate debt. Full protection can only be achieved by buying a series of caps with expiration dates coinciding with the rollover dates on the floating-rate debt. For example, to fully protect a five-year FRN issue, on which the interest rate is set every six months, it will be necessary to acquire ten caps with expiration dates coinciding with the six-month interest fringe. This is termed a "strip" of caps, the premium for which would be paid at inception, although the strike prices applicable to each cap would not necessarily be the same, and this would be reflected in setting the premium. It is possible that stripped caps may be unbundled from the related cash market issue and traded separately.

Accounting

As for ordinary option contracts, caps and floors present an asymmetrical risk profile between the writer and the buyer. The potential profit of the writer is restricted to the amount of the premium received while he or she is exposed, in theory, to an unlimited loss. Consequently, the buyer has a maximum cost equal to the premium paid but, in theory, has unlimited profit potential. This is an important consideration in establishing the appropriate accounting treatment for the writer and for the buyer.

Interest-rate caps

A key factor in establishing the accounting principles for interest-rate caps is the reason for entering into the transaction. A buyer will typically use the market for one of two reasons:

1. To hedge against increases in interest rates on variable-rate borrowings.
2. To hedge against written caps.

Variable-rate borrowings. When a cap has been purchased to protect against the effect of an increase in interest rates on variable-rate debt, it could be regarded as an integral cost of funding and accordingly

Chapter 6

the cost of the premium should be spread evenly over the life of the cap. The buyer of a cap is in effect ensuring against future events that would have a detrimental effect on the profitability of its company and the premium paid is analogous to an insurance premium.

Economically, the buyer has made the decision to accept a cost of funding slightly above prevailing actual rates, in order to ensure against significant future adverse movement in rates. It would therefore seem appropriate to reflect the "total" cost of funding in the accounts, regardless of when they are prepared.

Example

On January 1, 19X7, company A issued $10,000,000 of floating-rate notes (FRNs) maturing in five years' time, on December 31, 19Y1. The interest rate on the FRNs is set at London Interbank Offered Rate (LIBOR) plus 20 basis points, which is fixed semi-annually on June 30 and December 31.

Company A is concerned at the recent volatility in U.S. interest rates and decides to hedge against excessive upward movements by purchasing a strip of interest-rate caps covering each rollover period. The cost of the cap is set at 1/2% for each six-month rollover (i.e., 1% per annum). The total cost of the cap is therefore $500,000, which is paid on January 1, 19X7 (for illustrative purposes, the pricing ignores the time value impact on the premium).

At the inception of the contract, U.S. dollar six-month LIBOR is standing at 7%. The strike rate on each of the caps is 8%.

Average LIBOR and actual funding costs over the first two periods are as follows:

	LIBOR	Funding Costs
June 30, 1987	9%	9.20%
December 31, 1987	6.5%	6.70%

The accounting entries are therefore as follows:

6 months to June 30, 1987

(i)   Dr   Premium suspense $500,000
       Cr   Cash $500,000
       Being payment of cap premium

(ii) Dr Profit and loss—interest expense $460,000
    Cr Cash $460,000
    Being interest on $10,000,000
    at 9.2% for six months
    (provided on a straight-
    line basis over the
    six-month period)

(iii) Dr Sundry debtors $60,000
     Cr Profit and loss $60,000
     Being the anticipated
     receipt under
     the interest-rate cap—
     $(9.2\% - 8\%) \times \$1{,}000{,}000 \times \dfrac{180}{360}$

(iv) Dr Cash $60,000
    Cr Sundry debtors $60,000
    Being receipt of the intrinsic
    value under the cap

(v) Dr Profit and loss $50,000
    Cr Premium suspense $50,000
    Being amortization of
    one-tenth of the cap
    premium

6 months to December 31, 1987

(vi) Dr Profit and loss—interest expense $335,000
    Cr Cash $335,000
    Being interest on $10,000,000
    at 6.7% for six months

(vii) Dr Profit and loss $50,000
     Cr Premium suspense $50,000
     Being amortization of
     one-tenth of the cap
     premium

Chapter 6

In summary:

	FRNs Issued	Premium Suspense	Cash	Profit and Loss
Issue of FRNs	(10,000,000)		10,000,000	
Purchase of cap		500,000	(500,000)	
6 months to June 30, 1987 (cumulative)				
Interest expense			(460,000)	460,000
Recovery under cap			60,000	(60,000)
Amortization of cap premium		(50,000)		50,000
	(10,000,000)	450,000	9,100,000	450,000
6 months to December 31, 1987 (cumulative)				
Interest expense			(335,000)	335,000
Amortization of cap premium		(50,000)		50,000
		(50,000)	(335,000)	385,000
	(10,000,000)	400,000	8,765,000	835,000

The accrual method of accounting results in the following effective funding costs being shown in the accounts of the company:

	Average Borrowing	Total "Interest" Cost	Funding Rate
6 months to June 30, 1987	$5,000,000	450,000	9%*
6 months to December 31, 1987	$5,000,000	385,000	7.7%**

*Since the cap rate is set at 8% and the annualized cost of the cap is 1%, the maximum total cost of borrowing is 9%. When the cap is in-the-money the accrual method of accounting produces the correct result.

**When the cap is out-of-the-money, as in this case, the effective funding cost is the actual rate (6.7%) plus the cost of the premium (1%); again, as reflected by the accrual method of accounting. As the cap was acquired out-of-the-money, the premium represented wholly time value, which is also the position at December 31. Although time value does not decay evenly over the life of the cap, straight-line amortization is usually a good enough approximation for accounting purposes.

In terms of financial statement disclosure, the purchase of a cap has limited impact. If material, it would be appropriate to show the premium suspense account in the notes to the accounts analyzing debtors, and also splitting it down between the amount to be amortized over the next year at the amount to be amortized thereafter.

The underlying borrowings would be shown as usual in the balance sheet with the relevant footnote disclosures, which might include a note to indicate the maximum cost of the borrowings (having taken into account the cost of the premium).

The writer of a cap. The writer of a cap is usually a commercial bank or an investment bank responding to customer demand and attempting to generate income without using balance sheet assets.

Accounting for an interest-rate cap in the books of the writer can be an extremely complex—and often theoretical—process. For a start, there is no traded market in caps and hence determining a market value is difficult. Second, an in-the-money cap position may be hedged in a variety of ways, none of which will be perfect (only buying a cap with the same specifications would be) and some of which may be balance sheet items and some of which may be off-balance instruments. The problem can be demonstrated by considering the following scenario.

A bank writes a five-year cap with a strike rate of 8%. Current interest rates are 7% and hence the cap is written out-of-the-money; the premium paid has no intrinsic value. At this point the bank has no need to hedge since with this interest-rate relationship it is not exposed. Suppose interest rates start to move up and when they are at 7 1/2% the bank decides to hedge 75% of the principal amount by going short of Treasury bonds. Interest rates continue to climb and at 8 1/2% the bank decides to fully hedge and covers the remaining 25% by allocating a short maturity gap position in its money book to the cap desk. Assume that prior to the cap expiration date interest rates rise a further 50 basis points to 9%, but then in response to a significant economic event fall quickly to 7%. As soon as the interest rate falls below 8% the hedges become speculative positions that if not closed will, by definition, be loss making.

Consider the three possible methods of accounting for the cap:

1. *Amortize the premium received on a straight-line basis over the life of the cap* (i.e., mirror the treatment of the buyer). This makes no rational economic sense. The method of income recognition would be wholly unaffected by economic events (although provisions would be made for possible future losses) that determine the hedging actions of the dealers and the value and effectiveness of such actions.
2. *Amortize the time value of the cap such that it decays in accordance with the theoretical profile, and revalue the intrinsic value.* This is perhaps technically the most correct method of accounting but from a practical point of view is extremely difficult to implement.
3. *Revalue the cap and recognize gains and losses as they arise.* This is probably the preferred approach, since it is pragmatic while economically realistic. However, there are drawbacks.

In the above scenario, assume the bank's accounting policy for securities is to carry them at the lower of cost and market value (for long positions) and the greater of cost of market (for short positions) and not to revalue money market maturity gaps. As the rates move through 8% and the cap goes into-the-money, a revaluation of the premium will show a loss.

If the hedge is effective the Treasury bond will be showing a profit because the price will have fallen below cost. However, in accordance with the accounting policy the loss on the cap would be recognized, whereas the unrealized gain on the bond would not. The results would therefore not show the correct position. Similarly, this would also be the effect of the money market mismatch position.

If the accounting policy for securities is to carry them at market value then clearly 75% of the hedge would be properly reflected, whereas the remainder would continue to be distorted. Additionally, when the interest rate comes back down to 7% the loss on the Treasury bond will be properly recognized but no profit and loss account impact will result from the money market positions.

The above should show the difficulties in arriving at a workable but economically sensible method of accounting for caps. In the final analysis, the best accounting method will be the one that most closely approximates the economic reality. Whatever the conclusion, symmetry of accounting between the underlying position and the hedging transactions is the most essential element in arriving at the most appropriate solutions. It seems appropriate that the revaluation approach be adopted and that efforts be made to ensure that as far as possible the hedging instruments are also revalued to market, regardless of whether they are cash or off-balance-sheet hedges.

This does raise the final issue, which is how to revalue a cap if there is no traded market? As with over-the-counter options the dealer could either try to obtain a quote in the interbank market or revalue the cap using the same pricing formula as that originally used. The only problem with the latter approach is ensuring that the volatility factor used in the revaluation is appropriate.

From the above, it follows that caps purchased to hedge caps sold should be revalued at gains or losses recognized as they arise.

Interest-rate floor

The accounting considerations in respect of interest-rate floors are identical to those reviewed for caps. It will be appropriate to differentiate between the various users of the market. Those who are buying floors to hedge their asset portfolio, but are not actively engaged in trading new instruments, will have different considerations from the institutions that are writing floors for their customers.

The accounting treatment for the hedging buyer will depend on the strategy behind the underlying asset to which the floor relates. If the asset has been acquired for investment purposes and is carried in the balance sheet at cost, then the floor premium could be regarded as an integral part of the yield and therefore, like caps, should be spread evenly over the period to which the floor relates. When the floor is in-the-money, accrued receipts on the floor should be taken to income. This is the most likely scenario for most buyers of floors.

If the underlying asset has been acquired for trading purposes and is carried at the lower of cost and market value or at market value, then it is recommended, assuming the asset is quoted "ex-interest," that the coupon on the security be accrued, and the value of the floor assessed at the fixing dates to determine whether there is any income receivable under the floor contract.

Example

An investor buys $10,000,000 of floating-rate notes (FRNs) that he intends to hold for a certain period, but not until maturity. The investor's policy is to mark such investments to market. The investment is funded by a fixed-rate deposit. In order to protect the yield on the FRN, the investor decides to buy an interest-rate floor with a strike rate of 7%. The FRN fixes at LIBOR, which at the time the floor is purchased is 8%. Assume that the following rates prevail during the period when the investor holds the FRNs.

Time (Reporting Period)	LIBOR (%)	Floor
0	8	Out-of-the-money
1	5	In-the-money
2	7	At-the-money
3	9	Out-of-the-money

On the date the floor is acquired, the premium paid represents an asset and should be debited to a premium suspense account and held on the balance sheet. At time 1, the floor has an intrinsic value equivalent to 2% (7% − 5%). If time 1 coincides with a fixing date on the FRN then 2% would be receivable from the writer of the floor and should be recognized as income in the profit and loss account. At time 1, the floor will have lost some time value and this should be written off in the profit and loss account. Although time value does not decay evenly over the life of the floor, it would appear reasonable in most cases to write off this element of the premium on a straight-line basis.

If time 1 had not coincided with the fixing date on the FRN, the market value of the security would, to some degree, reflect this by an increase in the price. It would not be appropriate to recognize the potential 2% receivable under the floor until the date of the fixing is reached.

At times 2 and 3, the floor only has time value and hence the premium will continue to be amortized, with no receivable being established in respect of the floor contract.

If the FRN is sold with the floor, then the sale proceeds would be compared with the carrying value of the FRN and the balance on the premium suspense, and the difference (profit or loss) reflected in the profit and loss account.

Interest-rate floors are often used together with an interest-rate swap to lock in a profit on the swap while retaining the opportunity to maximize

Interest-Rate Caps, Collars, and Floors

Figure 6.2

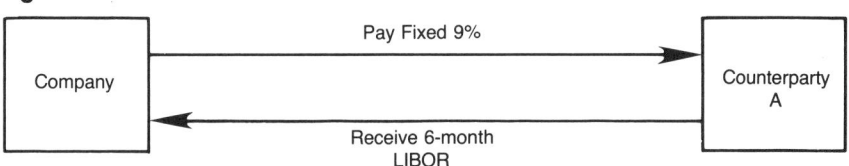

```
                    Pay Fixed 9%
   ┌─────────┐  ──────────────────▶  ┌──────────────┐
   │ Company │                        │ Counterparty │
   │         │  ◀──────────────────   │      A       │
   └─────────┘   Receive 6-month      └──────────────┘
                      LIBOR
```

the profit potential of the deal. For example, say a company has entered into the five-year interest-rate swap transactions illustrated in Figure 6.2. Following inception of the swap, interest rates have risen and the company wishes to take its profits in the transaction. It therefore finds another counterparty that will pay 11% fixed against a six-month LIBOR, which is currently at 10% (Figure 6.3). The company then enters into an interest-rate floor agreement with another counterparty, which agrees to pay the company the difference between LIBOR and the floor rate of 10% (in the event that LIBOR is less than 10%). The premium paid for the floor is 1%. Clearly, the company has entered into the floor agreement because it believes interest rates will fall to less than 9% (10% − 1%).

Accounting treatment. The accounting treatment of the floor should be consistent with the method of accounting for the other transactions in the deal. If the policy of the company is to revalue its swaps, then on closing out the swap position it will recognize the present value of the 2% spread that is locked in for the duration of the swap. In this case it would make sense to also revalue the floor premium to market and recognize currently any unrealized gains and losses on the floor contract.

If the policy of the company is to amortize all swap payments and receipts over the relevant period, the premium paid for the floor should

Figure 6.3

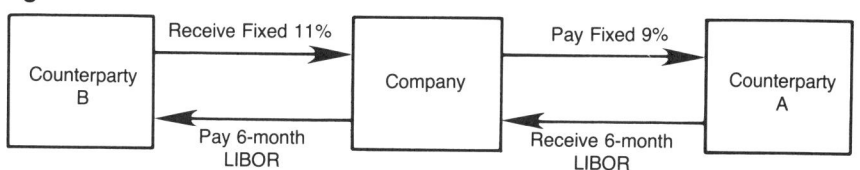

```
                Receive Fixed 11%              Pay Fixed 9%
  ┌──────────────┐ ──────────▶ ┌─────────┐ ──────────▶ ┌──────────────┐
  │ Counterparty │              │ Company │              │ Counterparty │
  │      B       │              │         │              │      A       │
  └──────────────┘ ◀──────────  └─────────┘ ◀──────────  └──────────────┘
                  Pay 6-month                Receive 6-month
                     LIBOR                        LIBOR
```

be amortized evenly over its life and any receipts from the floor counter-party be spread evenly over the relevant six-month period.

Interest-rate collar

The purchase of an interest-rate collar should be accounted for in a similar way to that previously described for an interest-rate cap. The only difference will be that the purchase of a collar may result in amounts having to be paid away to the writer, in the event that interest rates fall below the floor rate of the collar. When the collar is purchased to hedge variable-rate borrowings, any payment to the writer should be treated for accounting purposes in a similar way to any receipt in the event that interest rates rise above the cap rate. That is at the fixing date, although it may be necessary to make provision for losses if the entity's financial year-end is between fixing dates.

The accounting considerations for the writer of interest-rate floors and interest-rate collars are the same as those described previously for interest-rate caps.

CHAPTER 7

Risk control

This chapter deals with the risk aspects of the new financial instruments. The following sections have been applied to the area of risk control:

1. Discussion of general risks.
2. Risks by financial instrument.
3. Internal controls—the new environment.

The discussion in this chapter must be considered as an indication of the types of risk and their control, associated with the new financial instruments discussed. The new instruments and markets in those new instruments are changing rapidly. The markets are extremely volatile and therefore the procedures for the assessment of risks and their control must be variable to meet the markets' changing requirements.

Discussion of general risks

Financial transactions reallocate various categories of risk among lenders, borrowers, and financial intermediaries. These risks can be analyzed into key control areas that will require different emphasis on controls within each financial institution.

Before discussing the risks from the perspective of the individual firm or bank, it is important to assess the impact of the new instruments on the financial system as a whole, the financial system risk.

Financial system risk

A main conclusion of many observers with respect to new financial instruments is that market participants, at least those with access to all markets, are able to adjust their profits in most categories of risk more precisely with the new instruments than previously. Overall, this enables credit to be extended by lenders to borrowers, while the various categories of risk historically associated with credit extension can be separated and spread more widely and, in particular, can be transferred to those who can match it with an offsetting exposure or to those who specialize in management of risk for a fee.

The above argument is often extended to reach the conclusion that banking innovation is an unambiguous social good. That is, the effects in the aggregate are the simple sum of effects for individual economic agents, without any significant negative side effects (externalities).

However, the question of whether new financial instruments contribute to an increase in systemic risk depends in part on whether the various risks inherent in them are appropriately priced. That is, whether they produce sufficient profit margins *on average* to cover potential losses from market, credit, or other risks, both in the short and the long run.

It seems reasonable that there must be some cost of acquiring the knowledge and experience required for efficient pricing. These "learning costs" may appear in the form of underpriced transactions, which could generate either near-term or future losses. Such problems would seem most likely to crop up in rapidly growing new markets, and be of significance if new instrument activity were particularly concentrated among a small group of market participants.

Further, there appears to be a general tendency for new instrument markets systematically to underprice specific risks of a new market during a phase of development. New financial instruments in general are not subject to protection by the patent laws, as are many manufactured products, and this may help to explain the tendency new instrument markets have of quickly becoming extremely competitive.

Initially profitable margins earned by the innovator are narrowed to razor-thin amounts by new entrants seeking to establish a presence in a new market begun by others, normally other firms that have been traditional competitors. This pattern may in part be explained by the tendency of major financial institutions to seek to maximize profits in the long term, and thus to compete aggressively in the short run to maintain market share. It is frequently argued that the fine margin characteristics of some of the most competitive new instrument markets are insufficient to justify the range of risks involved, and that margins will widen as markets mature.

Market pricing of financial risks in the long run

Traditional risk-pricing approaches were used over the last decade by banks to price credit transactions. During this time, financial institutions generally, and international banks in particular, accumulated sizable amounts of assets that subsequent events indicated were underpriced.

This occurred mainly because of the deceleration of inflation and the associated rise in real interest rates in the 1980s that affected a very broad range of the assets on the books of banks, not just a few isolated loans. Throughout the period during which those assets were being accumulated, lending margins over the cost of funds were under continuous downward pressure from intense competition in banking markets. The rise in real interest rates in the 1980s made it clear that risks associated with these assets were far greater than anticipated, leading to a very substantial augmentation of credit spreads in many of these classes of loans.

It is probable that this will always happen, at least to some degree, given the highly competitive nature of national and international financial markets and the great difficulty in long-term economic forecasting.

At present, real interest rates appear to be well above historical levels, and again it seems both unreasonable to think that they will remain so indefinitely, and impossible to predict when and under what circumstances they will return to more normal levels. It is even possible that some unanticipated event might push interest rates even higher for a time before they come back down to historical levels.

To put the question in more practical terms, a financial institution may well see perfectly clearly, with hindsight, what mistakes were made in lending during the late 1970s and seek to apply those lessons to the future. That suggests that banks should seek wider profit margins in all activities in order to accumulate greater loss reserves appropriate to the newly perceived risk levels. However, it has proved difficult to maintain wider spreads, partly because of the repayment problems of borrowers in difficult straits and also—more importantly—in the face of competitive pressures.

Further, the greater use of off-balance-sheet transactions and securitization of assets together makes it far more difficult to determine the risk exposures of various sectors of the economic structure. The implication of these notions is that, if possible, all transactions, and especially innovative ones, should be priced to contain margins for loss above that implied by short-term expectations. However, an institution that does so, contrary to market trends, cannot hope to remain active and competitive in the short term, mainly because the going price in financial markets at any given moment is set by the individual participant willing to accept the thinnest risk spread.

To the degree that short-run competitive pressures progressively squeeze the cushion against solvency risk (make more "efficient" use of capital resources), the capacity of the financial structure to temper the effects of macro-economic stress may be reduced and central banks may be forced to change the liquidity and solvency rules.

Risk concentration

Quite aside from the issue of risk pricing, the financial system can be vulnerable if there are large concentrations of the normal market and credit risks that arise in credit transactions. For these purposes, it is important to distinguish between market risk, which in the aggregate must sum to zero, and credit risk, which by its nature cumulates in direct proportion to the volume of financial contracts outstanding. That is, all financial contracts are two-sided with respect to market risk: The holder of a fixed-rate bond has at least a paper gain if interest rates fall, while the issuer of that bond has an equal and offsetting loss. From a systemic perspective, there is no net change. In that same contract, the credit risk is one-sided once the asset has been issued. Thus, events that affect the ability of the debtor to pay have an implied impact on the creditor, while there is no reverse exposure.

New instruments allow price risk to be separated from credit risk to a large degree and the market risk to be transferred to another institution that has an offsetting exposure on its balance sheet. To this extent, systemic risk is reduced, since the creation of new instruments cannot create net new price risk, but instead is used to match offsetting real exposures. But creation of new transactions to accomplish this purpose does create a new credit risk, since the two institutions are now linked, probably through at least one intermediary, and thus the financial health of one becomes partly dependent on that of the other and on that of the intermediary. This risk is increased where there is only a limited number of institutions in the new markets.

Risk assessment and risk taking by individual firms

With traditional banking or securities market instruments, the risk characteristics were well understood and were generally consistent from one transaction to the next, even though their numerous risks were bundled together. Pricing of such instruments never did and still does not include separate charges for the various risks. Rather, experience determined prices that were thought likely to protect the lender on an overall basis. Since this approach was well accepted, both management and outside observers felt comfortable that balance sheet analysis could produce a reasonably clear picture of overall risk.

In contrast, new instruments require new, specially designed analytic techniques to price the risks involved. Banks and investment banks have worked out approaches to the accounting for these transactions, generally by trying to adapt approaches used for conventional instruments. There remains considerable variety in approaches, and as yet few institutions fully disclose these transactions in published financial statements.

Therefore, one has to ask whether the difficulties of risk assessment of new instruments, and the fact that these are less visible to outside observers, lead an institution to take greater overall risk.

The proliferation of new instruments and their complexity implies that risk assessment on an instrument-by-instrument basis should be augmented by the development of a comprehensive risk assessment that specifically examines how the individual risks fit together from the perspective of the institution as a whole.

Growth of multinational portfolios

The global integration of financial markets has been closely associated with a parallel trend for financial portfolio managers to increase the share of foreign currency denominated assets. Such actions can be taken for a variety of purposes, including that of hedging. As the practice has grown, it is useful to ask whether some cases might involve lessened or heightened exposures to market risk. Greater diversification of portfolio might well reduce risk exposures. At the same time, there may be reasons to believe that assets managers deliberately increase the risk exposure of the portfolios they run in order to improve performance.

Portfolio managers can of course hedge currency risk when acquiring assets abroad, but to do so would necessarily sacrifice all or most of any potential gain arising from interest-rate differentials. Quite to the contrary, it is widely known that both cross-currency investments and borrowings are frequently unhedged. Decision makers instead are content to monitor markets to determine the appropriate time to cover.

Further, given that previously much of this liquidity presumably would have been invoked locally, the growth of multinational portfolios seems clearly to increase aggregate exposure to market risk.

An assumption underlying the increased trading resulting from global integration is that asset prices vary and markets function as they have in the past; that is, that both asset and currency markets maintain depth and liquidity in the face of attempts to hedge or reverse these exposures. However, information on economic and other events is available virtually instantly around the globe, and common interpretation of specific events may produce common reactions, which in turn can overload markets and destroy liquidity. Thus, it would seem that the trend toward greater international management of portfolios in the aggregate can increase the risk of currency and interest-rate volatility, increasing sharply at times when it is most damaging.

The increasing international trading of all financial instruments also complicates the problem of ascertaining risk and could potentially add to the risk of the financial system. First, the laws of other countries may govern contracts, and may or may not be well known to all involved. This is especially important in the context of unbundled, off-balance-sheet transactions, where in many cases the legal standing of the contract has yet to be tested in any country. Also, the new instrument markets have grown up very much on an international basis, and an element of country risk may indeed enter a transaction that is otherwise purely domestic if one counterparty in a large set of transactions is located offshore.

The volatility of markets

It is likely that volatility causes innovation as much as innovation causes volatility. The precise effect of new financial instruments on the volatility of markets is difficult to assess. First, the rise in volatility has coincided with a shift to floating exchange rates and major changes in the thrust and implementation of monetary policy.

Second, price deregulation in the form of lifting of interest-rate ceilings or of exchange controls has meant that, independent of innovations in financial instruments, interest rates on existing instruments have had more scope to vary than would have been possible under similar circumstances in the past.

Third, a number of new instruments have arisen from a need to hedge against this volatility. Futures markets for interest rates, for example, did not exist before interest rates became more volatile.

Finally, financial innovation and the separation of different risks may have contributed to a redistribution of the impact of volatility within the economy. Although volatility may have increased, the effect reduced owing to the redistribution. However, such redistribution may have led to a more fragile financial structure, which itself may have contributed to volatility.

Volatility of markets is also dependent on the trades in that market and the technology associated with it; in particular, the effect of the actions of speculators in the market, whether stabilizing or destabilizing.

If speculators are to be a stablizing agent then certain conditions must prevail: first, the speculators' forecasts should be reasonably correct and reflect fundamental factors, such as the demand and supply for the cash instrument by nonspeculators; second, speculators must generally refrain from joining "bandwagons"; and third, speculators should refrain or be unsuccessful in attempts to rig the markets (that is, they should be unable to benefit at the cost of other market participants by exaggerating swings from new information or producing capricious price movements).

The effect of technology on the volatility of markets has been the significant increase in the efficiency with which information is disseminated and interpreted in world financial markets, both cash and futures.

The effect of this efficient distribution on the volatility of the markets depends on the correct interpretation on average of that information. On the other hand, the effect of the information may be destabilizing. While traders and investors may get the direction of change right in many cases, rarely do they get the amount right. Thus, it is difficult to know when a market move starts, when it will stop or, more precisely, when it should stop (when a new "equilibrium" has been reached). The market's response to new information also depends on how it compares with market expectations.

A further effect that technology may have on the volatility of the markets is where traders use automatic dealing. Thus, market movements may be exaggerated or fluctuate excessively as a result of technological advancements without reassessment of the market information by the traders.

Now we will turn to the individual risks and their effect on the new financial instruments.

Market or price risk

Market risk is the risk that the market value of a financial instrument (adjusted to exclude accrued interest) will decline over time as a result of changes in exchange or interest rates.

Market risk arises whenever variability in exchange and interest rates changes an asset's market price and thus affects the value of that asset or a portfolio of assets. Unlike credit risk, market risk deals only with price variability, which exists regardless of an individual debtor's financial status or the nature of a particular contractual arrangement.

Credit risk

Credit risk is the risk that a counterparty to a financial transaction will fail to perform according to the terms and conditions of the contract (default), either because of bankruptcy or for any other reason, thus causing the asset holder to suffer a financial loss.

The measurement and evaluation of credit risk has become a major factor in the effective management of risk, for both domestic and international participants.

The major credit risks are as follows:

1. Failure to recognize the ultimate credit risk associated with a transaction.
2. Failure to identify the risks involved in establishing custody and ownership of securities.
3. Danger through being exposed at different centers simultaneously and on the same security or instrument.
4. Technical shortcomings that delay contractual fulfillment or render it impossible.

The new market environment will cover a broader range of participants whose credit position is less well known and will therefore necessitate more extensive searches and client data bases. The sovereignty of counterparties is crucial to the proper assessment of credit risk (see below).

The wide variety of globally tradeable products by different arms of the same organization exposes each participant to a concentration problem. Concentrations of exposure are difficult to monitor because of the problems in setting up systems and measuring exposures that are comparable. The credit risk resulting from concentration of assets is more important than the exposure to a particular instrument although both will need to be monitored. Most organizations currently do not have systems to measure, monitor, and control worldwide exposures to any particular credit risk.

New instruments may be split into two groups with respect to credit risk: those that involve an extension of credit and those that do not. Of the new instruments discussed in this section, only repurchase agreements and note issuance facilities (NIFs)/revolving underwriting facilities (RUFs) perform the economic function of extending credit, and with NIFs/RUFs, only in the minority of cases in which the facilities are actually drawn.

Credit extension involves bearing credit risk, equal to the full principal amount, and extending to the maturity of the credit obligation. Market acceptance of new credit instruments, therefore, has generally depended on their perceived low credit risk, which derives either from the high credit standing of the borrower or, in the case of securitized credits, from the past low default rates on the large number of underlying assets of comparatively small denomination. With some securitized credits, there are explicit insurance schemes protecting some portion of the principal credit risk.

For those instruments whose prime function is not the extension of credit (i.e., options, swaps, FRAs, and undrawn NIFs), the credit risks are significantly less than for conventional credit-extension instruments, either because the credit risk is limited to a fraction of the full face value or because most are used primarily as backup lines. This means that their economic function is to improve the liquidity of the borrower. Where NIFs are drawn, the credit risk to the provider of funds is less than in a conventional syndicated bank loan because of frequent rollover. The banks that issue the standby commitments associated with these facilities take longer-term risk, but in principle it is as much liquidity as it is credit risk, since the agreements generally require the banks to provide access to low-cost borrowing only on the condition that the financial standing of the borrower does not deteriorate materially. Of course, whether these covenants will function as designed in times of serious financial market stress remains to be seen.

Therefore, the key risk feature of instruments that do not extend credit (i.e., swaps, options, and FRAs) is that they all serve the economic function of permitting a market participant to hedge a market risk or to convert a market risk from one form to another, and they do so with an associated credit risk that is generally a rather small fraction of the principal amount.

Technology risk

A number of risks arise owing to the increasing dependence placed on information systems and the related technological support. These include the following:

1. High volumes of market-making business require state-of-the-art technology that will need to be evaluated and developed as appropriate to meet the demands of a changing marketplace.
2. Inadequate hardware, software, and support systems.
3. Insufficient training of relevant staff and management.
4. Failure to satisfactorily isolate computer installations and terminals from sabotage and/or fire.

The importance of technology to the success of participants in the global environment cannot be overemphasized. The failure of a computer system for a participant holding positions could lead to a significant loss following a change in price. It is therefore essential that participants have adequate backup and support systems.

Settlement or delivery risk

Settlement risk is the risk that arises at the time of liquidation when a bank pays out funds before it can be certain it will receive the proceeds from the counterparty and comprises the following possible elements:

1. Nonfulfillment of a contract by the bank, the client, or the counterparty.
2. Failure to deliver the correct stock on the settlement day.
3. Failure to deliver the correct stock to the correct location.

It is likely that errors arising from the above will be caused by the following:

1. Increases in transaction volumes causing administrative backlogs and uncontrolled settlement procedures.

2. Inadequate knowledge of local procedures.
3. Inadequate awareness of the different regulatory environments operating in the different settlement areas.

Although the risks are of an operational nature, the extent of any loss will usually be a factor of adverse price movements in closing out a position not properly settled.

The process of global integration and deregulation of financial markets has dramatically increased the volume of transactions in financial markets, especially in relation to the liquidity base of collected funds against which transactions are cleared. Communications, payments, and transactions processing systems have been revolutionized, a process of change that is both in response to the increased flows and probably also a cause of further growth in transactions volumes. These trends obviously depend heavily on improved technology, which is the main vehicle through which transactions costs have been steadily and dramatically lowered.

Much attention has been paid to protecting these expanded transactions processing systems against error and breakdown of all kinds. Nevertheless, some believe that overall error rates in transactions processing worldwide have increased somewhat. The key question is whether there are scale effects; namely, whether overall transactions volumes have become so huge that, even with low error rates, the inevitable breakdown at a major concentration point in the funds transfer system can involve very large amounts.

As the total volume of transactions has grown explosively, both customers and the banks processing these transactions have moved to economize on the cash balances maintained to settle accounts. This has been achieved by the development of automated transactions processing systems by most financial institutions. Much attention has been devoted to developing mechanisms to control risks, including means to resolve disputes as a result of processing errors. Nevertheless, major disruptions of the transactions process have occurred, as yet without systematic damage, and central bankers remain concerned that competitive pressures to cut transactions cost may make it difficult for financial institutions to retain even the present degree of control and protection.

Market liquidity risk

Market liquidity risk is the risk that a (negotiable or assignable) financial instrument cannot be sold quickly close to full market value. Market liquidity can change gradually over time, or rapidly in times of crisis.

The new instruments by definition are trading in new markets, where the liquidity of the market has yet to stand the test of time and, in particular, to function effectively through periods in which associated markets experience major stress. In addition, all instruments trade either partially or entirely in over-the-counter markets, where liquidity can rapidly disappear.

Even without a major disruption of the main credit markets, the COMEX gold options markets experienced a major problem in the spring of 1985 involving the bankruptcy of three exchange customers and serious repercussions for other customers not directly involved in the problem. This example demonstrates that both liquidity and credit risk remain even in the context of an exchange. Less forcefully, it also demonstrates that markets in new instruments can suddenly lose liquidity, adversely affecting liquidity and price movements in associated markets.

Country and transfer risk

The risk here is that all or most economic agents will become unable to fulfill international financial obligations (country risk). More specifically, the risk is that a given country will find itself unable or unwilling to service all international financial obligations because of an overall shortage of foreign exchange, even though all or most economic agents within that country remain solvent (transfer risk). Country or transfer risk generally applies to all types of financial instruments in the same manner.

Transaction-type risk

The nature of the risks relating to the type of transactions will be affected by the volume of transactions and the development of new products. The main transaction-related risks are as follows:

1. Failure to execute the bargain correctly (e.g., buy instead of sell).
2. Failure to deal at the correct price and/or for the correct amount.
3. Failure to deal in the right instrument.
4. Failure to comply with the overriding settlement rules for each transaction type.
5. Failure to recognize a risk inherent in the transaction through lack of experience or misunderstanding.
6. Failure to ensure that margin calls are made on more volatile instruments such as options or futures.

Errors in these areas will normally arise for one of the following reasons:

1. Inexperienced traders (i.e., lack of understanding).
2. Inadequate internal controls over the dealing function.
3. Inadequate dealer support and back office systems.
4. Human error.

The risk measurement system will need to monitor each exposure by evaluating each transaction from execution date to value date and from value date through to actual payment/settlement of the transaction.

Other risks

Inevitably there are many other risks associated with a rapidly changing business environment.

Some of the generic risks applicable to the dealing of financial instruments are as follows:

1. Inadequate capital to support the size of operation.
2. Failure to hedge open positions adequately and general lack of understanding of hedging techniques.
3. Failure to carry out proper management review functions in critical areas.
4. Failure to monitor activities or performance of personnel.

5. Danger of overstretching on a global basis, for profitability and market share.
6. Inadequate control of brokers'/traders' limits on positions and authority to transact business.
7. Failure to comply with the rules and regulations of the Securities and Investments Board, the self-regulatory organizations, and the Bank of England.
8. Misappropriation of assets by theft or instructions to counterparties.
9. Failure to compute correctly the taxation liabilities arising from transactions in the global market.

The current market environment will require a greater awareness by management of the restrictions on activity, the requirements of the regulators, and the need to balance profitability and risk exposure. It is the management of risk that will determine profitability.

Risks by financial instrument

In this section the effect of the risks detailed in the first part of this chapter will be discussed with respect to specific financial instruments. A summary is given in Appendix I.

Currency and interest-rate options

Options, both currency and interest rate, differ from all other financial instruments in the patterns of risk that they produce. Both market and credit risk patterns are asymmetrical between writers and buyers of options. With respect to price risk, the holder of an option has the possibility of unlimited profit should the option move increasingly into-the-money, while the loss is limited to the amount of premium paid should the option expire at- or out-of-the-money. Conversely, the option writer's income is limited to the amount of premium earned, while in principle the loss is unlimited should the option move increasingly into the money.

Therefore writing an option involves the seller in a contingent liability; the bank must perform at the choice of the buyer. In one sense, the contingencies are fairly straightforward, since buyers will only exercise in-the-money options, although this depends on the price movement of the option.

Banks may wish to limit their exposure to counterparties. In writing options, bank writers assume market risk while the buyer assumes credit risk, with the possibility that the writer will be unable to perform. Between the transaction date and the payment of premium, the writer of the option is exposed to the buyer for the amount of the premium.

Thereafter, and through the life of the contract, the buyer must take the risk that the writer will fail to meet his obligations, while the writer incurs no credit risk since the buyer has no obligations to perform.

After exercise, there are also several possible settlement risks, but all involve obligations to perform by both parties. With foreign currency options, both parties are obligated to deliver one of the two currencies involved, whether the option is a put or a call. With interest-rate options, exercise obliges the writer to purchase or deliver securities, while the buyer must deliver securities or cash.

The option writer can seek to hedge against the effect on the value of the option of an adverse movement in the price of the underlying item. Given the asymmetrical pattern of risks, the only certain way to hedge an option completely is through purchase of an equivalent option, identical with respect to all attributes of the exercise price, face value, and expiration date. The premium cost of an option purchased as a hedge will probably roughly equal that received for an option written. Therefore, if options written are hedged with identical options purchased, the trading profit opportunity will in principle be limited on average to a bid/offer spread between the two.

One of the attractions of trading options on exchanges is that contracts are standardized, and thus it is possible to hedge or close out an options position completely. In contrast, banks may wish to limit their exposure to counterparties in respect of over-the-counter options. In writing options, bank writers assume market risk while the buyer assumes credit risk, with the possibility that the writer will be unable to perform. The over-the-counter market may lack sufficient depth and liquidity to hedge the customized options written for customers by precisely matched purchased options. The option writer may be able to purchase a "similar" option whose contract specifications may differ in one or more of several features, such as underlying instrument, face value, exercise price, and maturity.

However, as with all new financial instruments, they are by definition trading in new markets where the liquidity of the market has yet to stand the test of time and, in particular, to function effectively through periods in which associated markets experience major stress. The liquidity of exchanges is superior to over-the-counter markets, where liquidity can rapidly disappear, but is partially dependent on the liquidity of the market for the underlying instrument.

The liquidity risk is also affected by the problem that an individual market participant may dominate the market and so limit its scope to adjust position without exaggerated price movement. Consequently, banks may wish to limit their overall position in certain markets.

Interest-rate and currency swaps

In a conventional currency swap, specific amounts of two different currencies are exchanged at the outset, and are repaid over time according to a predetermined rule that reflects both interest payments and amortization of principal. Normally, fixed-interest rates are used in each currency.

Both price and credit risk are inherent in swap transactions. Price risk arises because interest or exchange rates can change from the date on which the swap is entered. Credit risk arises because a counterparty may fail to perform and that event may expose a swap participant to an unexpected and unintended mismatch.

Currency swaps allow participants to hedge certain narrow types of interest-rate risk. Swaps create the opportunity to fix interest differentials between rates in two currencies relative to market fluctuations. Currency swaps can thus be used for fine-tuning interest-rate risk without at the same time changing other risks (such as currency risks). However, hedging of interest-rate risk is usually done in single-currency interest-rate swaps rather than in currency swaps.

In an interest-rate swap, no actual principal is exchanged either initially or at maturity, but interest payment streams of differing character are exchanged according to predetermined rules and based on an underlying notional principal amount. As in currency swaps, price and credit risks are also inherent in interest-rate swaps. In addition to the price risk described above, basis risk arises with interest-rate swaps when the floating-rate indexes on two matched swaps differ.

These swap exposures can be analyzed on two levels: short-term exposure and long-term exposure. Short-term exposure is the delivery risk to each party on a payment-by-payment basis (i.e., the risk to a party making a payment that the other party will not make the corresponding payment). A party's delivery risk is increased if it is obligated to make a payment prior to the other party's corresponding payment. An extreme example would be a LIBOR against zero-coupon swap where one party pays six-month LIBOR to the second party semi-annually over a term of say five years and the second party pays the full amount of accrued interest at a fixed rate on maturity.

A more common example is one in which one party pays six-month LIBOR to another party that is paying an annual fixed amount. In each case, the first party may, for internal accounting purposes, treat each LIBOR payment made prior to the other party's payment as if it were an advance (i.e., direct, rather than contingent, credit exposure to the other party). Most intermediaries attempt to minimize settlement risk by matching the timing of each set of payments as closely as possible. Whenever possible, only net amounts are actually transferred.

In a currency swap, delivery risk receives greater attention because of the risk inherent in payments being made in different currencies and hence in different financial centers in different time zones such that one party may actually be required to deliver its currency to the other prior to its receipt of the payment due. In a currency swap in which there is an exchange of notional principal amounts at maturity, this risk is further increased because the final amounts are of course substantially greater than the individual periodic payments. Thus, as a currency swap approaches the maturity date, when the notional principal amounts must be exchanged, many institutions will gradually increase their exposure internally ascribed to the swap because of this currency delivery risk.

Swaps also have a short-term market risk where traders do not match each swap as it is taken on. Therefore, a position is taken based on the assumption that the offsetting side of the transaction can be completed without adverse change in the market during the interim period.

The long-term exposure is the value to a party, at any given time, of the swap over its remaining term—that is, the loss that a party would incur if the swap were to terminate. Termination of the swap will result in each party having lost the benefit of its bargain and be in a mismatched position, exposed to market risk, because interest rates or exchange rates may have changed from the date on which the swap was arranged.

Intermediaries must also be able to manage other types of market risk. They face basis risk, which represents the risk of matching the floating-rate side of a swap with a different floating-rate profile (for example, paying six-month LIBOR and receiving a margin over the Treasury bill rate). This risk should be monitored during the swap and the potential costs/benefits evaluated for budgeting and profit and loss purposes. Another type of risk arises when the reset date on swap flows differs from that on its hedge. The intermediary will hence be exposed to short-term interest-rate fluctuations that it may or may not hedge. This mismatch may be a factor in pricing the swap.

Matching or hedging swap positions does not reduce an intermediary's exposure to credit risk. An intermediary's credit exposure depends on the joint probability of an adverse move in interest rates and a performance failure by the swap counterparty.

This credit risk is limited to the replacement cost of the swap in the event of default, either with another swap or with a series of borrowings and investments, in either case to regain its bargain and to hedge its position. If the swap is replaced through a new swap, the gain or loss to each party is the amount it would receive from or the amount it would have to pay to a new entity to undertake obligations similar to those of the other party under the terminated swap.

If a series of borrowings and investments is selected as the means of replacement, the gain or loss to a fixed-rate recipient would be the profit or loss in acquiring a fixed-rate investment to match the fixed-rate income it was to receive under the swap. The gain or loss to a fixed-rate payer is its profit or loss in acquiring a fixed-rate liability to match that which it had under the swap, which gain or loss will be determined by the change in prevailing fixed rates since the date of the agreement.

Chapter 7

Most institutions will ascribe some long-term exposure to each swap they write. Some institutions use simple percentage rules of thumb, while others utilize sophisticated computer analyses. In any event, the exposure will clearly always be less than the notional principal amount involved and it may range, for example, from 10% in an interest swap to 25% or more in a currency swap. Thus, those responsible for the credit decisions would equate exposure under a swap with a $25 million notional principal amount to exposure under a $2.5 million term loan. Some maintain that while the term risk is greater at the beginning of a swap since it stretches out into the future, both credit and interest risk are less at that time because of the greater certainty that the counterparty will not default (assuming there has been an adequate initial credit investigation) and the lesser risk of dramatic fluctuations in rates having occurred. A contrary view is that the period of least risk occurs as the swap approaches termination since, then, the redeployment for the balance of the term effectively covers a shorter period, and even though rates may have moved dramatically or the creditworthiness of the counterparty declined, actual exposure is less (subject to delivery risk not being increased in a currency swap).

A company's exposure on an interest-rate swap could be summarized as in Table 7.1. Depending on the type of transaction, the risk on currency swaps will usually be both an interest-rate risk and a currency risk. A summary of the risk environment is given in Table 7.2. Arithmetically, the exposure represents the difference between the currency equivalents (in base currency) of the present values of the two payment streams discounted to the default or close-out date.

The currency risk represents an exposure to changes in the spot rates between the two currencies concerned. The degree of risk increases the longer the period to maturity.

Table 7.1

	Current Rate Lower Than Fixed Rate	*Current Rate Higher Than Fixed Rate*
Fixed-rate payer	Loss	Gain
Fixed-rate receiver	Gain	Loss

Table 7.2

		Fixed to Fixed	Fixed to Floating	Floating to Floating
Interest rate Currency	Currency 1	Yes	Yes	No
	Currency 2	Yes	No	No
	Spot foreign exchange	Yes	Yes	Yes

Yes = Risk position

The above discussion must be considered in the light of the market for interest-rate swaps. It should be noted that swaps are over-the-counter contracts and as such have limited market liquidity. This reflects the inverse relationship between maturity and liquidity: the longer the maturity, the more difficult it is to lay off the risk owing to the thinner liquidity of the longer-term market. Also, the longer the period the greater the risk of adverse interest-rate and/or currency movements. Such limited liquidity may increase the replacement cost and thus the credit risk of the swap.

Interest-rate caps, collars, and floors

The transaction can be likened to an interest-rate swap wherein the purchaser is the fixed-rate servicer and the seller is the floating-rate servicer.

The cap level is the equivalent of the fixed rate in the swap. On each payment date succeeding a reset date wherein the floating index exceeds the cap level, the seller, or floating-rate servicer, makes a net payment of the difference between the fixed rate (or cap level) and the floating index just as it would in an interest-rate swap with net settlements and matching payment periods.

The cap transaction differs from an interest-rate swap in that for periods in which the floating-rate index is reset at levels below the cap level, the purchaser does not make payments to the seller. The purchaser therefore retains the advantages of low short-term borrowing costs with the added benefit of a fixed maximum cost. These savings are minimally offset by the upfront cost of the cap, which generally adds approximately 50 to 70 basis points per year to the purchaser's all-inclusive financing costs.

The product also enables an institution that favors long-term market conditions but has no immediate long-term financing requirements to lock in a long-term rate at current levels without incurring additional debt. The cap seller benefits relative to an interest-rate swap in that credit exposure to the purchaser can be entirely eliminated.

Therefore, like swaps, caps, collars and floors are subject to the same risks as interest rate swaps, settlement, credit and market risk. Settlement risk is limited to the net payment with respect to the purchaser only. The seller (writer) of the cap's settlement risk is limited to the receipt of the upfront arrangement fee.

Similarly, credit risk is limited to the replacement cost of the contract, in the event of default by the seller.

However, the market liquidity risk is greater than that for interest rate swaps, as a result of the relative size and age of the market. On the other hand, market risk is limited to the variability of the market rate to the contracted level.

Interest-rate futures

By entering into a hedge, the financial manager is attempting to eliminate the market risk of adverse changes in interest rates. However, by entering into a hedge the manager is assuming the risk of a change in the relationship or spread between the market price of the cash instrument that is being hedged and the market price of the futures contract. This relationship is referred to as the basis. Although this must be recognized as a business risk of establishing a hedge, the basis movement has traditionally been less risky and more manageable than the interest-rate movements themselves. The change on the basis relationship must be monitored to determine whether an economic profit or loss will result from the hedge as a unit.

It can be seen that interest-rate futures are subject to market risk. They are also subject to market liquidity risk, although this is limited because futures are exchange-traded instruments.

Because futures contracts are exchange traded, there is no settlement risk; that is, the counterparty to a contract fails and the contract does not go through.

Credit risk is limited to the creditworthiness of the clearinghouse, the organization through which all trades are processed. The clearinghouse guarantees the commitments of the exchange traders. It is able to do this as each trader places deposits with the clearinghouse, which vary, on a daily basis, proportionally with the magnitude of the position taken by the individual trader.

Forward-rate agreements

A forward-rate agreement (FRA) is in effect an over-the-counter financial future. Like financial futures, FRAs enable banks to adjust their interest-rate exposure without altering their liquidity profile and with less impact on the size of the bank's balance sheet and credit exposures than by use of the interbank market. By comparison with futures, FRAs offer the features of simplicity, flexibility, absence of margins, and the possibility of an instrument tailored exactly to a bank's or a customer's interest-rate mismatch.

However, unlike futures, FRAs cannot be sold, but only reversed with another FRA. Credit risk on futures is uniform and considered to be very small, whereas on FRAs it will vary with the counterparty. Also, futures are traded at thinner spreads than FRAs.

The main risk involved in an FRA is the replacement risk: that if the counterparty fails, the other party is at risk to the extent that interest rates have moved so that it would otherwise have expected to receive a payment from the counterparty. The risk of loss, therefore, depends on both the movement of interest rates and the default of the counterparty, and is limited since there is no exchange of principal amounts.

FRAs also create interest-rate positions in the future. They are generally used to hedge existing positions, but could be used to open a position if a bank wanted to take a view on interest rates.

As described above, the size of the credit exposure on an FRA depends on the extent and direction of interest movements in the period up to the settlement date. Consequently, the eventual exposure cannot be known at the outset, although it will only be a small fraction of the agreed principal amount. FRAs raise the same issues for measuring exposure as do interest-rate swaps, such as estimating the volatility of interest rates. In practice, a more rough-and-ready approach is generally adopted because the periods covered by FRAs are much shorter than for swaps.

In most cases the credit exposure on FRAs is measured by setting a flat-rate amount against the counterparty's credit limit, usually 5% (sometimes 10%) of the principal amount. The 5% credit exposure is a rule-of-thumb adopted for convenience, and represents the potential loss from counterparty default if the reference interest rate for a three-month future period moves against the bank by 20 percentage points before the settlement date. For an agreement covering a six-month future interval, the 5% charge to a counterparty's credit limit represents exposure against a 10% move in the reference interest rate.

On the settlement date, the difference calculated between the agreed forward rate and the rate at that time is discounted (using the current rate) to take into account the fact that payment of the difference is made at the start of the agreed period rather than at maturity.

It should be noted that an FRA has more replacement risk than an interest rate future as the market for FRAs is less liquid since the instrument is often tailored to one user's needs. As mentioned previously, since FRAs iare not exchange traded there is liquidity risk as a result of the size of the FRA market.

Therefore, it can be seen that in normal circumstances, where FRAs are settled for cash, the credit and settlement risks are equal and limited to the market risk.

NIFs/RUFs

The risk incurred with note issuance facilities (NIFs), including revolving underwriting facilities (RUFs), differs among various aspects of the facility. NIF participants that provide an underwriting commitment incur a credit risk closely analogous to that inherent in a loan commitment, since they are obliged to acquire an asset at the discretion of the borrower. Most facilities entitle the borrower to draw on the bank line in case the paper cannot be placed within a specified margin of a reference rate. Where that difficulty is most likely to arise is when the credit rating of the borrower has deteriorated.

The risks incurred by banks participating in NIFs depend on the role they pay and the technique used. Most exposed are those banks that provide an underwriting commitment, whereas banks that take part in a tender panel have the choice whether or not to bid for notes. The banks are obliged to acquire an asset whenever the borrower chooses to call for funds, and do so as a maximum spread over LIBOR. For banks underwriting a facility using the single placement agency, dealership, or tender panel techniques, their obligation is closer to a contingent liability, since they will only be called upon to acquire Euronotes if these cannot be placed elsewhere. Moreover, this is likely to occur in circumstances when there are doubts about the creditworthiness of the borrower.

NIFs also involve liquidity risk. This is the risk that banks will be called upon to provide funds at a time when they cannot easily do so, either because the individual bank is unable to fund itself at market rates or because of the general conditions in the interbank market. While this risk has generally attracted less attention, banks now appear to be becoming increasingly concerned about funding risk and the extent to which they may be protected by documentation.

Banks holding notes issued under NIFs face straightforward credit risk on the issuer for the life of the notes. If the bank holding the note is not also an underwriter of the facility, then over the banking system as a whole there will be an element of double-counting of exposure since both the bank holding the note and the bank underwriting the facility will be recording exposures to the same borrower. Clearly, any sudden large movements in interest or exchange rates will affect the value of outstanding notes; but in this they do not differ from other short-term instruments.

Some protection against being required to buy the notes of a borrower in difficulties may be provided by "material adverse change" clauses or financial covenants in the underwriting agreement. However, such clauses are untested in law.

Repurchase agreements

Repurchase agreements are hybrids, having elements of buy-sell transactions and collateralized loans. The risks involved with such agreements will encompass those elements of the agreement.

The most important risk to be addressed is the business risk: the risk that a party entering into such agreements will misunderstand their terms and therefore misunderstand the economics of the transactions and incorrectly assess the risk it is in fact assuming, the return it hopes to earn, and the financing costs it is incurring. This in turn can result in incorrectly pricing the agreements or in incorrectly treating accrued interest in pricing the underlying securities. Repurchase agreements in particular are not always labeled as such, and parties to them may not always be aware of the risks and returns being contracted for and accordingly may not account for them properly.

All securities are subject to market risk in that their prices can change. The prices of government securities vary inversely with changes in interest rates; while price changes may be small, they can result in significant gains or losses because of the large amounts involved in many government securities transactions. Price changes may affect the ability of one party to a repo agreement to continue to finance it and the ability of the other party to replace the securities when the transaction is supposed to be reversed. Changes in prices also affect the margin in a transaction (the haircut) and may create a need for the seller-borrower to transfer additional securities or return cash. Accordingly, both parties should monitor the market value of securities subject to repo agreements, including accrued interest, on a daily basis.

As mentioned above, a repo agreement can be viewed as a loan of cash by one party and a loan of securities by another. When the agreement is completed, both loans are repaid. There is a risk that a buyer-lender who has sold or otherwise transferred the securities to third parties will not have sufficient resources at the maturity of the agreement to regain possession of the securities required for resale to the seller-borrower. There is also a risk that the seller-borrower will not have sufficient funds to repay the loan (repurchase the securities). Thus, credit risk is faced by both parties to the transaction. Government securities dealers are often organized as separate affiliates of securities broker-dealers, and parties to repo transactions should be careful to identify the specific entity with which they are doing business.

The risk that the issuer of the underlying securities may default is also present, except in the case of securities issued or guaranteed by the U.S. government or its agencies. This risk pertains to repo agreements involving bankers' acceptances, negotiable certificates of deposit, mortgage-backed obligations of nongovernmental enterprises, and similar instruments. If the issuer of the underlying securities defaults, both participants to the repo agreements are still obliged to perform and complete the transaction.

The credit risk to which a particular entity may be exposed can be affected by the extent to which the entity's repo position is concentrated in any one underlying security or with any one party. Credit risk is related to market risk in that changes in market prices in general and resulting economic losses may affect a seller-borrower's ability to repay the loan (repurchase the securities) or a buyer-lender's ability to return the securities. The extent of credit risk, therefore, may not be evident if the parties to the transaction do not continually review and evaluate their securities position based on market values, including accrued interest.

The extent of credit risk faced by a party that enters into a repo transaction with a government securities dealer is also related to the dealer's business policies and practices regarding control and use of collateral, the extent of the haircut on securities serving as collateral, the extent to which the dealer maintains a matched book, and the dealer's capitalization. In addition, uncertainties surround the legal status of the securities that the parties to repo transactions view as collateral.

In this respect, when a seller-borrower transfers securities to a securities dealer under a repo agreement, there is a risk that the dealer may not be able to reverse the transaction by selling the securities back at the agreed price. If the seller-borrower has the legal right to offset the securities against the borrower funds, the potential economic loss is limited to the excess of the market value of the securities plus accrued interest at the date of the sale over the amount borrowed, plus or minus any change in that market value and accrued interest. In that case, the risk of losing the collateral is essentially the same as market and credit risk. If the seller-borrower does not have the legal right to set-off, the potential economic loss extends to the full value of the securities, including accrued interest.

If a buyer-lender under a repo agreement with a securities dealer does not perfect a security interest in securities purchased, for example, by having a signed agreement and by taking possession, either directly or through a custodian acting as its agent, the potential economic loss also extends to the full value of the securities and the risk assumed becomes that of an unsecured lender; namely, credit risk. Collateral risk for the buyer-lender is reduced if definitive collateral is held by the dealer's custodian as the dealer's agent through specific identification of the assignee or if book entry collateral is transferred directly or by a notation entry.

When the definitive collateral is locked up by the dealer in safekeeping and segregated and identified by the customer, collateral risk will be reduced only if the dealer's system of internal control over securities held in safekeeping is adequate. Collateral risk is reduced further if the buyer-lender or its agent—which could be the dealer's bank acting as the lender's agent—takes possession of the collateral.

Synopsis of general internal controls applicable to trading operations

Set out below is a synopsis of general internal controls applicable to trading operations, which addresses some of the risks identified previously.

The overall objectives of any system of internal control would normally include the following:

1. Establishing the creditworthiness of each counterparty.
2. Ensuring that all trading activity meets with management's objectives (i.e., proper approval and within preestablished limits).
3. Identifying all open commitments and recording trades on a timely basis.
4. Monitoring realized and unrealized profits and losses and associated commission charges and fees.
5. Controlling cash movements and safeguarding funds.
6. Establishing effective management reporting.
7. Identifying and responding to external reporting requirements.

It should be noted that in developing any system of internal control, the company must give due consideration not only to the risks involved in not establishing the controls, but also to the cost of maintaining the control. Accordingly, a system of internal controls for trading will vary depending on the volume of transactions involved, the number of individuals involved in the trading and monitoring of these activities, the reasons for entering into the transaction, and the degree of sophistication of the control and of the electronic data-processing systems.

However, specific techniques should not serve to overcontrol the activity and thereby unnecessarily restrict the trader's flexibility.

While it is impossible to generalize for each situation, the sections that follow provide a brief description of certain basic internal control procedures that should be considered.

Procedure and policy manuals

As with any system of internal control, the trading policies, including the instruments to be dealt and the currencies in which dealings may be made, the procedures and the accounting guidelines relating to the trading activities should be documented in a formalized procedures manual. The manual should be approved not only by senior trading management, but also by top management in the accounting area.

The overall purpose for the company's trading activity, an approved list of counterparties, the sources for monitoring interest- and currency-rate movements where applicable, and the matters discussed in the following sections should all be included in the procedures manual. Proper authorization and approval policies should also be detailed in the manual.

Additionally, the procedures manual should outline the company's policies with respect to the training and supervision of personnel to ensure that all personnel involved are familiar with the concepts, terminology, and trading practices of the relevant market.

Credit limits

Trades should only be made with approved counterparties whose creditworthiness has been established. Similarly, the number of trades with any particular counterparty should be limited according to predetermined credit limits, approved centrally by management, and should include limits on contingent exposures.

The company should establish approved credit authorization procedures, which may include delegated limits to individual personnel and involvement of a credit committee or risk control function. Detailed procedures should include standard credit analysis procedures and consideration of specific swap-related risks such as volatility of interest rate and currency, term of swap, and liquidity of currencies concerned.

In exceptional circumstances, the management may request some form of credit enhancement (for example, a letter of credit) or collateral from counterparties. Where necessary, a letter of credit is usually written for the amount of the initial exposure. Collateral may be requested in the form of an initial margin that is reduced over the life of the contract, or the company may retain the right to make a call on collateral over the life of the contract if exposure increases. The contracts of some intermediaries include a two-way call for collateral—both the intermediary and his counterparty have the right to call for collateral from the other.

Actual exposures should then be monitored against limits on a regular basis with exceptions reported to senior management. Additionally, the total exposure in all markets to one credit risk should be monitored by a consolidation of the credit risks in all markets, including those risks of connected parties, both of the company and the counterparty.

With respect to some financial instruments, the credit risk is affected by the market risk—for example, interest-rate swaps. In these cases the company should perform the appropriate volatility analysis to determine anticipated fluctuations in interest rates that will form the basis for measuring exposure against limits at the inception and during the term of a swap. This process should be updated on a regular basis.

In addition, there should be a regular revaluation of the swap book assuming counterparty default, to determine potential exposure. The quality of credits should be reassessed where the swap is heavily out-of-the-money to determine whether any preventative action is required, such as requesting that collateral be placed. Similar considerations exist for FRAs, interest-rate caps, collars and floors, and dealer options.

Trading limits

Dealing with approved counterparties is recommended and only traders who have proven knowledge of the market and the related company policies and procedures should be authorized to trade.

Senior management should establish limits as to the maximum number of open positions, as well as the degree of fluctuation of "profit" and/or "loss" limits acceptable within the company's overall policy. In particular, stop loss limits should be imposed. These limits should be established for the company in total and for each individual currency and, if applicable, each individual trader. Limits on the overall net open position should be set and further consideration should be given to setting "gap" limits for each contract maturity date. Naturally, compliance with these limits should be monitored periodically by senior management.

Additionally, procedures should be established to ensure that the trading activity is integrated fully with the company's other positions and commitments.

Trade tickets

At the time a trade is made, the trader should prepare a trade ticket that originates the accounting and control information required. Trade tickets should contain all the information needed to record and settle the transaction properly (i.e., trade date, value date, purchase and sale, contract description, counterparty, quantity price, trader, etc.). When each ticket is prepared, a copy should be sent directly to the back office to ensure a timely recording of the transaction. Tickets should be prenumbered and controlled.

Accounting records

The accounting records required to control trading activities should be maintained by individuals who are independent of the actual trading function. The records should contain all the information necessary to verify open commitments, cash movements, support entries to the general ledger, and to generate the necessary internal reports needed by management to monitor trading activity. The form of the records will vary according to the trading activity, and the branch should use memoranda or contingent ledgers to capture the information where potential exposure arises on the transaction. These should be updated daily, as should the general ledger system, to record the trades. All trading activity should be recorded from the trade tickets (i.e., the trade date, trader, reason for the trade, etc.) and each trade should be verified subsequently by the accounting function by reference to the confirmation received by the counterparty.

Such confirmations should not be received directly by the traders. Additionally, it is likely that the day's trading activity will be confirmed verbally with the counterparties to avoid waiting for written confirmation of open commitments.

If it is the branch's intention to use an instrument as a hedge, it is important that the accounting records identify the specific existing asset or liability or commitment with which the instrument is associated. These records will be necessary to support the symmetry concept required to satisfy this specific criterion for hedge accounting.

Reporting

The primary objectives of a system of internal control over reporting are to ensure that the trading personnel are receiving accurate information in a manner required to undertake trading decisions and that senior management are being provided with adequate information to evaluate the trading performance or the results of a trading strategy.

Although the types of reports provided to trading personnel will vary according to the types of trading, the size and frequency of the positions, and trading volumes, traders should receive information at least daily. These reports should reflect all open contracts by maturity, the unrealized profit and loss on the open contracts, and the change in the unrealized profit and loss from the previous day. Additionally, the trader responsible for the trading activity should be receiving adequate information with respect to any movement in the value of a hedged asset, liability, or commitment as this will prove essential in determining the economic worth of maintaining the hedge.

With respect to reporting to senior management, the type and frequency of these reports will similarly vary depending on the size and nature of the branch's activity in the markets. However, reports will be necessary to reflect all open contracts on a maturity basis, along with the current trading activity and related economic income effects. These reports should display both realized gains or losses and changes in unrealized gains or losses resulting from market appreciation/depreciation on open positions.

From a review of open positions and current trading activity, management can determine if the preestablished limits with respect to individual trades, total open positions, and limits are being adhered to. These reports should be sufficiently detailed that management can make an overall effective performance evaluation of the trading activity.

EDP support

In most trading organizations, accounting and management information is wholly reliant on computer systems. Apart from the basic elements of EDP control that should exist in any computerized system, particular care should be given to ensure that systems are integrated to show consolidated interest rate and currency positions, are flexible enough to handle the increasing complexity of new financial instruments and have the capacity to process increases in trading volumes. Where large mainframe-based software packages are used by an entity, it will often be necessary to have a series of micro-based systems to support the trading in new financial instruments.

Finally, it is essential that appropriate back-up facilities are available, both in respect of front office trading systems and back office processing and support systems.

CHAPTER 8

United Kingdom taxation

Introduction

While bankers and treasurers may have seen the first obstacle in the market development of treasury instruments as understanding how they work and are priced, it soon became clear that a number of other issues also had to be addressed in order to facilitate the growth in volume and depth of the market. It was probably inevitable that among these was taxation. Tax advisers may on occasion be guilty of overestimating their level of importance to commercial transactions. In the area of treasury instruments, however, it has become clear that failure by users to consider the tax implications could potentially prove very costly. A transaction that was fully offset and hedged for treasury and accounting purposes when entered into can, as a result of tax considerations, quickly turn what was a nicely priced profit into an uneconomic posttax result.

One of the unfortunate results of the very rapid development of treasury instruments has been to demonstrate that, first, such instruments do not very often fit easily into existing U.K. tax legislation and tax case law. Second, in a number of instances the result of applying the Inland Revenue's interpretation of existing tax law was potentially to obstruct the development and marketing of such instruments. While in certain cases the Inland Revenue has subsequently either introduced appropriate legislation or agreed concessions, this does not cover all circumstances. The continued growth of the variety and types of instruments seen in the market will no doubt maintain this inevitable trend of the marketplace continually moving in front of the tax legislation.

Against such a background, this chapter will attempt to outline the framework of U.K. tax law within which the different users of treasury instruments must work and then to review the U.K. tax treatment of the various financial instruments that have been covered in previous chapters.

While reference will be made to the position of individual taxpayers, this chapter mainly considers the tax status of corporates since currently and in the foreseeable future they are likely to comprise the main users of such instruments.

Types of users

The U.K. tax system differentiates in its treatment of the users of treasury instruments based on the type of taxable activities which they perform. These can be very broadly categorized as follows, though inevitably there will be variations and exceptions in the tax treatment within each category.

Banks and financial institutions

Such taxpayers, by virtue of carrying on a finance trade, should face trading treatment on most of their activities. As a result, the issue of taxability or deductibility of most treasury instruments should typically not cause concern, although problems on the timing of taxability or deductibility can arise.

Trading activities

In this category, the taxpayer will be carrying on a taxable trading activity under Schedule D, case I. Since this is not a financial trade, they will need to carefully review the tax treatment of any treasury instrument used, ensuring this is on an acceptable basis. Also, with certain instruments such as currency swaps, these taxpayers face a distinction in tax treatment between trading income and capital gains. Income and capital gains are subject, in most cases, to tax at 35% in the case of companies, and a maximum rate of 40% in the case of individuals. For disposals prior to March 17, 1987, the effective tax rate for companies on such gains was 30%. In the case of individuals, the 1988 Budget proposes that capital gains will be taxable on increases in the value of assets after March 31, 1982 at the taxpayer's marginal rate of income tax (25% or 40%) with the benefit of an inflation indexation allowance in computing the gain. Individuals will also have an annual exemption allowance which for the tax year 1988/89 will be £5,000.

Investment activities

The characteristic of taxpayers carrying on investment activities is that they hold capital investments upon which they would face capital gains tax on disposal, their taxable income being the revenue from such investments. In the case of companies, the majority of such entities are classified as "investment management" companies and are subject to specific tax rules as to deductibility of management expenses (Section 75*). Such companies are, broadly speaking, at a disadvantage with trading companies in respect of the tax treatment of certain treasury instruments.

Exempt organizations

Such taxpayers with a status of being exempt from tax (for example, charities and pension funds) would typically not be concerned about the tax treatment of expenses or receipts. The main issue is that their use of treasury instruments does not prejudice their tax-exempt status by constituting a trading activity.

General U.K. tax principles

Any attempt to provide an outline of the U.K. tax system must inevitably leave itself open to the criticism that it did not provide full

*Statutory references are to the Income and Corporation Taxes Act 1988, unless specified otherwise.

coverage of all aspects. The main objective behind the comments below is to cover the salient aspects of the U.K. income and corporation tax system relevant to treasury instruments at the time of writing and also to highlight certain problem areas. It is hoped that these will in turn assist in the subsequent comments on the individual instruments.

Income versus capital

U.K. tax law has for a long time drawn a distinction as to whether an item of income or expense should be accorded "revenue'" or "capital" treatment. The distinction is critical because, in the case of expenses, it will determine in what form the taxpayer will obtain relief and offset for amounts disbursed in computing his tax liability. There is no statutory definition of what is "capital" or "revenue." The result has been a number of tax cases where the Courts have tried to establish guidelines, although these are by no means an ideal solution for all cases. The following appear to be the major tests which the Courts will apply based on these cases:

1. *Fixed versus circulating capital.* Using the economist's distinction to differentiate between items that represent the long-term capital or infrastructure of the business and those which, by their short-term use or character, are being "turned over" or circulated. As will be seen later, this test is most pertinent in the area of currency gains and losses.
2. *Enduring benefit.* To examine whether, in cases of expenditure, it creates a benefit to the trade that will last for several years.
3. *Characterization of asset.* To try to isolate the type of asset on which the expense was made or receipt received, and to then determine, if characterizable as capital, whether the item arose from acquiring or disposing of the asset or whether it represents amounts spent maintaining or generated from exploiting the asset.
4. *Incidence.* The distinction as to levels of recurrence of an expenditure or receipt will, in certain cases, assist in considering an item for revenue-type treatment.

These tests are far from satisfactory when applied to a variety of specific facts and, in certain cases, will not deny revenue treatment. They do, however, provide a loose framework in which to attempt an analysis where the position is not clear.

It should be noted that U.K. tax law does not support the approach that symmetry in fiscal treatment should exist between taxpayers. The fact that an amount is taxable as revenue in one person's hands does not automatically bestow revenue treatment on the U.K. payer. How payments and receipts are characterized for any U.K. taxpayer will always be based on his or her particular facts and circumstances, unless there are specific tax provisions overriding this.

Income tax schedules

Where an item is characterized as revenue, it is then necessary to determine under which schedule of the U.K. income tax code it is taxable or deductible. The trading activities of financial and nonfinancial taxpayers will fall under Schedule D, Case I (or, in the case of professions, Case II). The other schedules relevant to treasury instruments are Schedule D, Case III, covering receipts of U.K. source interest, discounts, and annual payments (where the item is in respect of a foreign security or debt instrument, it will fall to be taxed under Schedule D, Case IV) and Schedule D, Case VI, which represents a "sweeping up" Schedule to assess any income-type payments or receipts not brought into charge to tax under other Schedules. Again, there is no requirement that, because one taxpayer is accorded Case I trading treatment on an expense or receipt, symmetry of tax treatment should be granted to the payer.

Each of the Schedules is exclusive to itself and has its own provisions regarding methods of computation. The major area of potential difficulty for users of treasury instruments is that losses incurred under Schedule D, Case I, may generally be offset against all other income and gains in the year incurred (and if appropriate the prior year) but, when carried forward, can only be offset against future trading profits under Case I. Receipts in a subsequent period under Cases III, IV, or VI cannot therefore be offset by Case I losses brought forward. Of greater potential restriction is that revenue expenses and losses that are not accorded Case I treatment will normally fall under Case VI. Expenses and losses incurred in any period under Case VI can only be carried forward and relieved against future Case VI profits. On certain treasury instruments, this potential pitfall, with the effective quarantining of losses, is a potential cause of difficulty. Losses arising under capital gains transaction can only be offset against other capital gains of the taxpayer in that or subsequent periods.

Deductibility of expenses

The initial critical distinction, as covered above, is whether an expense incurred is revenue or capital. In order for revenue costs to be deductible under a particular Schedule, they have to satisfy the requirements of the specific provisions. For trading entities, these are contained principally under Section 74(a). This stipulates that expenses should be incurred "wholly and exclusively" for the purposes of the taxpayer's trade. While this would seem, initially, to provide an adequate basis for the claiming of a deduction by all taxpayers carrying on a trade, under the argument that their use of treasury instruments is trade related, it will be seen that this provision is more limited in its application.

For investment management companies the tax legislation only grants relief in respect of "expenses of management." This is not defined by the tax legislation, tax Cases being the only indicator. In general terms, it is limited to the majority of revenue-type expenses that such activities incur in running their business of managing investments. While in practice this is likely to be more limited than the expenses incurred by trading companies, such entities do enjoy one benefit, which is that all surplus management expenses of any year are carried forward against *all* future taxable income and gains, and not just income under a specific tax Schedule.

As covered above, expenses falling under Case VI are only deductible against other income taxable under that Schedule. The same position applies for expenses in respect of capital assets under the capital gains tax provisions.

Deductibility of interest

General concepts

In the Case of companies liable to U.K. corporation tax, specific tax rules exist governing the deductibility of interest. These rules, which have developed over time, may seem unnecessarily complicated to the nontax specialist. It is, however, necessary to attempt a general understanding, given their interplay with the tax treatment of treasury instruments, especially those used to protect against interest movements.

United Kingdom tax law does not define interest, and the fiscal definition has been established through tax Case law. The critical tests are that it represents "a payment by time for the use of money" (*Bennett v. Ogston* (1930) 15 TC 374) and that there exists an underlying loan between the payer of the interest and the lender (*Re: Euro Hotel (Belgravia) Ltd* (1975) STC 682).

A distinction in tax treatment also exists on whether interest is "short" or "annual." "Short" interest relates to loans that will last for less than one year from inception to repayment. "Annual" interest arises in respect of loans that will last longer than one year. The major impact of this difference is that U.K. withholding tax (currently 25%) only arises in respect of annual interest. This withholding will not arise in any of the following circumstances:

1. The interest is paid to or by a recognized U.K. banking business approved by the Board of Inland Revenue under Section 349. A recognized U.K. banking business could include the U.K. branch of an overseas bank.

2. The recipient of the interest is resident in a country which has concluded an appropriate double tax treaty with the United Kingdom and an appropriate withholding tax treaty exemption claim has been approved by the U.K. Inland Revenue.

3. The loan is a qualifying quoted Eurobond (Section 124).

Banking activities

The ability to pay and receive interest gross, without withholding by a recognized U.K. banking business, reflects the ability to have such payments treated as part of their Schedule D, Case I, results. Such taxpayers will claim relief on an accounts accruals basis, the only requirement being that such interest is paid in the ordinary course of their banking business. Such a requirement should be satisfied in the Case of the majority of transactions but under current Inland Revenue practice, payments of interest on loans of over five to seven years duration (the exact period will depend on the individual bank's circumstances) potentially fall outside the exemption.

Other loans that could fall outside the exemption (even though of a shorter duration) arise where the funds have one of the following characteristics:

1. The loan was subordinated.
2. The funds were used for specific fixed-capital purposes.
3. The funds were regarded by the appropriate Central Bank as expanding the entity's capital base.

Trading company

The starting position under U.K. tax legislation on deductibility of interest is that it is not deductible in computing trading profits under Schedule D, Case I, unless it is "short" interest. Such short interest must be trade related and not for the purpose of capital investment. The trading purpose test is overridden where the interest is paid to a recognized U.K. banking business, stockbroker, or discount house.

Where it is "annual" interest, such amounts are not deductible in computing trading profits under Schedule D, Case I, but are deductible as "charges on income" against the total profits (including income taxable under other Schedules and capital gains) of the company (Section 338). At the risk of making these rules seem to turn full circle, this provision is overridden (under Section 337 (3)) in the case of annual trade-related interest paid to a recognized U.K. banking business where the deduction is reinstated as allowable under Schedule D, Case I! The main benefit of this treatment is that such interest is deductible on an accounts accruals basis, whereas charges on income are only deductible on a payments basis. All other annual interest payments will constitute charges on income with the need to review the withholding tax considerations covered above.

Investment management companies

Companies not carrying on a trade will need to ensure that payment is to a recognized U.K. banking business, stockbroker, or discount house in order to obtain a deduction for short-interest costs. In respect of annual interest, including payments to a recognized U.K. banking business, relief will be given as a charge on income.

U.K. branches of nonresident companies

It should be noted that, in all the above cases, in order to qualify for relief as a charge on income, the payment is required to be made by a U.K. resident company. This cannot be satisfied where the taxpayer is the U.K. branch of an overseas resident company, even though such branch profits are subject to U.K. corporation tax. In such situations, the only method of obtaining U.K. tax relief is where the head office of the company is in another country that has concluded a tax treaty with the United Kingdom that includes an appropriate nondiscrimination article. The benefit of such articles is that they put the U.K. branch of the overseas company on the same fiscal footing as a U.K. resident company, and this extends to deduction of charges on income.

Discount versus interest

United Kingdom tax law has created a distinction between interest and discounts in respect of payments and tax relief. The above rules relating to interest do not apply to discounts, even though such amounts may be computed by reference to interest rates and time periods. For trade-related discounts—for example, discounting of short-term bills of exchange and promissory notes—the amount should be deductible under the Section 74 tests of "wholly and exclusively." The problem arose in the United Kingdom with development of zero coupon bonds and the subsequent commercial paper, where the underlying debt does not qualify as trade related or is of a long-term capital nature.

Appropriate legislation was introduced in 1984 and 1985 so that, structured correctly, discounts should, like interest, be deductible to most taxpayers. Relief is given by computing the discount on a compound yield basis so that the appropriate element of accrued discount is deductible as a charge on income on the earlier date of redemption (the anniversary of the bond's issue or the date of interest payments, if any, on the security).

Costs of finance

Until the Finance Act of 1980, U.K. tax law did not grant relief for the various costs of arranging loan finance—for example, arrangement commissions, guarantee fees, underwriting, and sundry issue costs. These costs, normally referred to as "nothings," did not qualify for tax relief, except in the case of financial institutions, since they related to raising loans of a medium- to long-term nature and so were regarded as "fixed" and not "circulating" capital items. While interest paid on such loans would qualify under the relevant provisions outlined above, the arrangement expenses were not revenue and fell outside the scope of Section 74.

Owing to representations, legislation was introduced in 1980 that granted a tax deduction to trading and nontrading companies for such costs where they relate to a "qualifying loan." Briefly stated, these are loans raised to provide finance to that company or its trading subsidiary, and such amounts are not convertible into equity in the three years after the making of the loans. These provisions were subsequently extended to apply to the 1984 legislation on discounted securities.

Critical issues for treasury instruments

The main impact of the above tax provisions for users of treasury instruments is that two potential problems surface, as follows:

1. The great majority of instruments are transacted in such a way that the user has the benefit of separating the funding decision (who does

he raise the loan finance with?) from the cost of funding (the interest cost and using treasury instruments to monitor his interest exposure). This results very often in the treasury instrument being transacted with a person who is not the original loan creditor. The relevant payments made do not therefore constitute *interest on money* or *discounts* for U.K. tax purposes under the criteria outlined. As a result, they are not deductible under those specific tax provisions, even though the interest incurred on the original loan is.

2. For the same reasons, the arrangement costs incurred (if any) in setting up the treasury instrument will not be in respect of raising a "qualifying loan," because they reflect the taxpayer's decisions on interest exposure and not the obtaining of loan finance. Again, they therefore fall outside the strict definition of the tax legislation and specific provisions for relief.

These problems will be reviewed more fully in the sections on specific instruments.

Capital gains tax

The taxing provisions relating to capital gains only arise in respect of capital assets and then only in respect of items that do not fall to be included as income under one of the income tax schedules. Expenses and losses under the capital gains rules can only be offset against other capital gains of that period or carried forward for future offset against other capital gains of the taxpayer.

The principal benefit of capital gains in the United Kingdom is that such treatment qualifies for an indexation allowance in computing any gain. The computation of any indexation allowance is based upon the increase under an Inland Revenue published price index and is applied to the original acquisition cost (or market value at March 1982, if the asset was owned at that date) over the lesser of the whole period of ownership or from March 1982 onwards.

The principal benefit of capital gains in the United Kingdom for individuals of being taxed at a lower rate of tax (30%) than the top rate of income tax (60%) will cease under the Budget proposals. These will provide that for all gains after April 5, 1988, only the element of gain accruing after April 1982 (if the asset was owned at that date) or if later the date of acquisition, will be subject to tax. The computation of such gains will include an indexation allowance based upon the increase over the period of ownership under an Inland Revenue published price index that commenced in April 1982. The resulting gains will for a company by taxed at 35% and for individuals at their marginal rate of income tax (25% or 40%).

The list of chargeable assets under the capital gains legislation is comprehensive and includes foreign currency, whether held directly, in a bank account or to be acquired under a forward currency contract. There are a limited number of exemptions, most notably in respect of debts that are not "debts on security" and, in the case of individuals, foreign currency held and used for their own personal needs.

The time of disposal for capital gains tax purposes is when the contract (or other form of agreement) is exchanged between the parties and not when the contract is concluded by delivery if this is at a later stage. The only exception to this rule is when the contract is conditional, in which case the date of disposal is when that condition is fulfilled (Section 27, Capital Gains Tax Act (CGTA) 1979).

One particular issue in respect of option instruments is that the capital gains legislation treats them as "wasting" over their life. This results in the original acquisition cost or option premium paid being depreciated for capital gains purpose, such that, at the end of the option life, they have no base cost.

This problem is illustrated by the following example:

Three-month option premium at a cost of 300.

Depreciating cost over life

End of month 1	200
End of month 2	100
End of month 3	Nil

Option sold at end of month 2 for 250

Economic loss: 300 − 250 = (50)
Taxable gain: 250 − 100 = 150

Although certain amendments have been introduced to the tax law in this area, this unsatisfactory tax treatment can still arise in certain cases.

Currency gains and losses

The impact of the U.K. tax treatment of currency gains and losses is only likely to arise on a limited number of treasury instruments, notably currency swaps and currency options. This is because, first, a number of treasury investments are sterling denominated and therefore do not produce any currency gains or losses. Second, in the case of most interest treasury instruments, it should be possible to demonstrate that the item is of a revenue nature (since it relates to interest which, by characterization, is a revenue not a capital item) and therefore fails to be taxed under one of the relevant income tax schedules.

The present U.K. tax law in relation to currency gains and losses is in many aspects unsatisfactory. The disparity in treatment of currency gains and losses can be particularly critical on transactions such as currency swaps where the treasury and accounting objective is to create a hedged transaction that is not affected by subsequent adverse currency exchange rate movements. However, the corresponding U.K. tax treatment of such transactions seeks to break up or "fragment" such transactions, so that, reviewed in post-tax terms, the hedge may, without appropriate planning, trigger a tax cost that renders the transaction uneconomic.

Revenue versus capital

The starting point for understanding the tax issues arising from currency gains and losses is as under general income tax law, whether an item arises on the capital or revenue account. Currency gains and losses arise for consideration in filing U.K. tax returns because sterling is the base currency for U.K. tax purposes. The translation of any set of financial statements into sterling for such tax returns (as well as any other statutory reporting) will produce currency gains and losses of two types. These will be, first, gains and losses "realized" on transactions completed and consumated in the year and, second, "revalued" gains and losses, being the year-end balance sheet revaluation of transactions that are still open—for example, trade account receivables and payables and open contractual commitments, such as foreign exchange.

Such accumulated gains and losses, with certain limited U.K. accounting exceptions, will require inclusion in the profit and loss account for the relevant period of the taxpayer. In submitting a tax return, it is then necessary to analyze this total in its component parts to determine whether an item is accorded revenue or capital treatment. Also, for reasons covered below in the case of capital items, it needs to be decided whether it is related to a chargeable capital asset (capital gains) or a capital liability (nontaxable/deductible).

A currency gain or loss of itself has no specific characteristics as it is the result of an accounting convention and fiscal requirement to produce financial results in one base currency denomination—U.K. sterling. The required approach is therefore to look to the "underlying" transaction that generated the currency gain or loss. Where this does not immediately link it to a specific asset or liability, it is necessary to look at the wider ancillary evidence, such as management's intentions and documented decisions in entering into the transaction.

While it may seem a very simplistic approach, it is often possible to identify the true character of many currency gains and losses by adopting a balance sheet approach to review the underlying rationale and motive behind the currency gain or loss. This approach is valid even where the transaction had been completed and is not reflected in the balance sheet at the year-end. For a company engaged in Schedule D, Case I, trading activities, the following would be a typical tax analysis of its balance sheet:

	£		£
Share capital	NT	Fixed assets	C/R
Loan capital	NT	Investments	C
Current liabilities	R	Current assets	R

R: The economist's distinction of circulating versus fixed capital is followed, such that trading related items that arise through the Case I trade will be accorded revenue treatment and taxed accordingly.

C: Where assets are not part of circulating capital and so not taxed under the income tax schedules, they will (with limited exceptions) fall to be taxed under the capital gains provisions. The computation of such capital gains, as well as taxing the economic profit or loss of the transaction, will also include the currency gain and loss over the period of ownership. This is computed by comparing the original exchange rate with sterling at the date of acquisition with the proceeds translated into sterling at the exchange rate ruling when disposal occurs (based on the case of *Bentley v. Pike* (1981) STC 360, 53 TC 590).

The one exception to this rule is a capital asset that has qualified for U.K. tax depreciation allowances by remains designated in a foreign currency—for example, plant and machinery assets used in an overseas branch of a U.K. company. The drawback of tax depreciation allowances up to the maximum of sterling amounts previously claimed will comprise part of revenue profits, buy any excess in sale proceeds over original sterling cost will be accorded capital gains treatment (Section 31, CGTA 1979).

NT: Where a *liability* is not part of "circulating" capital, any currency gain or loss on revaluation or repayment does not form part of trading results under Case I. Also, because capital gains is a tax on chargeable *assets*, it does not fall under the capital gains tax provisions. Under current U.K. tax law, any currency gain or loss on such items falls outside the scope of the U.K. tax system and is neither taxable where a gain, nor deductible where a loss. While share capital (where nonsterling designated) forms part of this category, the more problematic issue is on loans that are in nonsterling currency and, by their terms, outside trading treatment.

It should be noted that it is the character of the underlying liability that determines this tax status and not the use to which the loan proceeds are put. The demonstration of a nonsterling loan as being used to purchase trading stock or paying trade liabilities, or as an offsetting match for the purchase of a capital investment—for example, shares in an overseas subsidiary in the same currency—does not impact the nontaxable treatment.

Chapter 8

Marine Midland and the Inland Revenue Statement of Practice

The fiscal "Catch-22" under the above analysis especially of nontaxable liabilities was first highlighted in the case of *Davies v. Shell Co. of China* (1951) 32 TC 133, where it was in the taxpayer's favor to argue such a gain was nontaxable, since the loan liability was designated in Chinese dollars that had depreciated against sterling and thus showed a profit. The subsequent liberalizing in the 1970s onward of financial markets with a move from fixed parity exchange rates has seen a greater volatility of sterling against other major trading currencies. This has often produced the invidious situation that a foreign currency loan taken out to obtain a lower tax deductible interest funding cost has often, by the time of repayment, appreciated against sterling and triggered a currency loss that is nondeductible for U.K. tax purposes.

This dichotomy was highlighted in a recent case that was seen by some tax advisers as being of potentially major significance—*Marine Midland Ltd. v. Pattison* ((1984) STC 10 [1984] AC 362, House of Lords). The main facts of the case are very simple. Marine Midland Ltd. was a U.K. subsidiary of a U.S. parent company, which carried on a banking trade in the United Kingdom. To finance this trade, two U.S. resident subsidiaries of its U.S. parent subscribed for US$15 million of subordinated unsecured loan stock in 1971. The U.K. company lent these dollar funds as part of its normal banking business in making loans to customers. In 1976, the U.K. company redeemed the loan stock by using sufficient of its total pool of dollar funds. Throughout the existence of the loan stock, the bank had revalued the dollar asset and liability as part of its normal trading position, such that the gain on the dollar assets (sterling depreciated against dollars over the period of this transaction) was netted off against the loss on the dollar liability in reporting its sterling taxable profits. On repayment in 1976, based on comparing the spot rates in 1971 at drawdown with those at repayment, a loss in sterling terms of £2.5 million had arisen on the *loan liability,* even though, in dollar terms, there was no loss.

The Inland Revenue took the position that this loss arose on the capital account and was nonallowable for tax purposes, whereas the corresponding gain, since it related to trading assets of a bank (loans receivable), was taxable under Schedule D, Case I. The Inland Revenue approach was overruled by the Court of Appeals and the House of Lords and, in doing so, introduced a new concept to currency gains and losses of "matching." This held that, on the above facts, there had not been any economic or taxable gain or loss, since the original currency received had been retained throughout and finally repaid as such.

The perceived extension of U.K. tax laws by professional advisers from the decision of Marine Midland in the area of currency gains and losses led to a subsequent Inland Revenue Statement of Practice on exchange rate fluctuations (see Appendix II). It should be appreciated that a Statement of Practice does not have the force of law and represents no more than a suggested Inland Revenue approach to a particular issue.

In its present form, the statement seems an unsatisfactory answer to the tax treatment of this major treasury issue. This is because of the following:

1. The statement concerns itself only with the computation of trading profits and the tax adjustment required for trading profits as reflected in the profit-and-loss account of the taxpayer. The tax treatment of capital gains and capital transactions is not affected under the statement.

2. To the extent foreign currency assets and liabilities are translated into sterling in producing sterling accounts, the bringing into account of unrealized gains and losses for tax purposes, regardless of prior case law on the point of realization versus revaluation, was not finally an issue considered in the courts in the Marine Midland decision. Indeed, the Inland Revenue's concept of taxing revaluations, on the basis they are realized profits under the U.K. Companies Act 1985, is open to argument.

3. The currency transactions envisaged by the Inland Revenue are necessarily simplistic in providing examples. In practice it is likely to still leave open questions, since the statement does not address multicurrency transactions where no realization into sterling occurs. Also, banks and multinational corporations increasingly finance and hedge their operations through a variety of currencies and not through a simple flow through, as occurred in the case of Marine Midland.

4. The position of exchange gains or losses arising on capital *assets* is that they will be either taxed or relieved twice. This is by virtue of first being included in the currency adjustment to the profit and loss account and, second (and quite separately), in the computation of any capital gain arising on the sale of the asset, since, as indicated under point (1), the computation of capital gains remains unaffected by the statement.

5. The major question of what distinguishes "capital" and "trading" remains undefined. The statement commences with the Inland Revenue stating that this principle remains as far as they are concerned, although the U.K. courts that found in favor of the taxpayer did not have to address this point in reaching their decision.

The overall conclusion is that, far from being a major case in advancing U.K. tax law on currency gains and losses, the Marine Midland decision is likely to be ultimately seen as a case of limited application based on its very specific facts and circumstances. The U.K. distinction of capital versus revenue and the Inland Revenue's limiting of the decision to trading and not capital gains transactions (and so ensuring that any realization of nontrading currency into any other form of capital asset is outside the "matching" principle) leads to the inevitable conclusion that, in looking to the tax treatment of currency gains and losses, the existing U.K. tax law pre-Marine Midland will continue to be applied in the majority of cases.

A case which was recently decided by the Court of Appeal could potentially alter this situation. The case of *Beauchamp (Inspector of Taxes)v. F. W. Woolworth Plc* was won by the taxpayer before the Special Commissioners, reversed in the Inland Revenue's favor on appeal to the High Court (1987, STC 279), and has been recently reversed back in the taxpayer's favor before the Court of Appeal. The main facts were that the company had raised two loans in Swiss francs, in 1971 and 1972 respectively, totalling 100 million Swiss francs. The Exchange Control regulations then in force required a minimum borrowing period of five years. Due to the decline of sterling between the establishing of the loan and repayment, losses of £11.4 million were incurred on repayment of the two loans.

The taxpayer claimed a trading deduction for these losses which was denied by the Inland Revenue on the basis that the terms of the two loans characterized them as capital liabilities. The company was successful on its appeal before the Commissioners. It contended that the purpose of the loans was solely to fund its trade over a short-term cash flow problem and so represented temporary facilities rather than additions to the capital employed in the business. The High Court ruled that the Commissioners had erred in law and the substantial period covered by the terms of the loans rather than what the company used the funds for was the test to apply.

The most interesting aspects, however, arose before the Court of Appeal which reversed the decision back in the taxpayer's favor on two points:

1. The relevant legislation upon which the Inland Revenue relied in applying the 'capital' argument was Section 74(f) which denies losses 'deducted in respect of any capital withdrawn from, or any sum employed or intended to be employed as capital in, the trade'. By tracing this wording back to the original legislation of the Income Tax Act 1842, it was decided Parliament had only sought to deny a deduction for the withdrawal of capital. As a result, the provision only applied to the repayment of the loans themselves and not to the currency exchange losses incurred in connection with such repayments.

2. It was considered that the Commissioners in considering the taxpayer's purpose in raising the loans (being to obtain cash for general trading purposes over a five year period which in turn had been forced on them by the Exchange Controls then applying) and giving this more weight than the fixed amount of the loans over a long-term period, had not been unreasonable in their finding based on the facts. It was therefore not open to the Courts to alter this as a question of law.

It is likely that the case will proceed to the House of Lords for a final ruling. That decision, especially if it upholds the Court of Appeal's finding on Section 74(f), could alter quite dramatically the existing U.K. tax law in this area.

In concluding this particular topic, it is worth noting that the

United Kingdom together with the limited number of countries that follow the U.K. tax principles under their own domestic systems (principally Ireland and certain Commonwealth countries), are in an increasing minority in such a treatment of currency gains and losses. The majority of Western European and other major developed countries do not follow the capital versus revenue distinction and do not differentiate between assets and liabilities in taxing or allowing relief. Where such a distinction did exist, there has been a trend in recent years to remove this disparity—for example, in Australia and the United States. It remains to be seen whether any legislation will be introduced to bring the United Kingdom into line with the tax treatment in other countries or bring capital liabilities into the scope of U.K. tax in some form.

Taxation of specific treasury instruments

In looking at the specific instruments, it is intended to break these down by categories in recognizing that, for each grouping, it is possible to identify certain common tax issues. The categories that will be covered are as follows:

1. Interest-rate treasury instruments (financial futures, future-rate agreements, interest-rate options, caps, collars, and floors)
   (a) Exchange-traded
   (b) Over-the-counter.
2. Swaps (interest and currency swaps)
   (a) General aspects of swaps
   (b) Specific issues under currency swaps.
3. Currency options.

Interest-rate treasury instruments

There is a need to break down this group into exchange-traded and over-the-counter. This is due to U.K. tax law amendments since exchanges such as LIFFE opened, creating this fiscal distinction. As will be seen, the current rate of U.K. tax law has created a differential which, for certain taxpayers, could impact their decision as to which market to use.

Exchange-traded instruments

Background. The development of financial exchanges around the world that have standardized contracts and settlement terms allow two main benefits. The first is a credit risk benefit in that any user is dealing with a trader behind whom stands a recognized financial exchange structure in the event of default. Second, by representing a market of "open outcry" it is comparatively easy for any user to gain quick access to current pricing under any traded contract; to lay off risk by entering that market and concluding a contract; or to crystallize a profit or loss by closing off an existing contract.

The United Kingdom followed the U.S. lead when it established LIFFE, which has since been duplicated in other financial centers around the world in developing 24-hour trading. When the exchange was preparing for opening in 1982, it entered into discussions with the Inland Revenue to try to agree on guidelines as to likely tax treatment of the contracts to be initially traded. These initial guidelines are reproduced in Appendix III and reflect the situation that there was no specific tax legislation on the issue of how futures contracts should be treated at that time.

Initial U.K. Inland Revenue Approach. Relying on old cases such as *Cooper v. Stubbs* (1925) 10 TC 29, and *Townsend v. Grundy* (1933) 18 TC 140, both of which concerned transactions in cotton futures and predated the introduction of capital gains tax in 1965, the Inland Revenue considered that, in most nonfinance trades, the basis of assessment for LIFFE interest contracts would be Schedule D, Case VI. This approach was to be relaxed in the case of banks and other financial institutions, where it was felt there was a sufficient nexus with their normal trading activity to satisfy the "wholly and exclusively" tests of Section 74.

The issue of Schedule D, Case VI, treatment was an initial indication of how, without change, the tax treatment could differ with the commercial objectives. Financial futures were intended to provide a hedge on underlying interest rates which, for liabilities, would be a deductible trading expense (either in computing trading profits in U.K. bank interest or as a charge on income against total profits) or, for assets, taxable investment income. The problem of Schedule D, Case VI, treatment was that, for tax purposes, it would fall outside this approach. A company with brought forward Case I losses could not offset those losses against Case VI profits and, of more concern, losses incurred under Case VI could only be offset against future Case VI profits. This would potentially apply to both trading and investment management companies.

Allied with an Inland Revenue approach to apply Schedule D, Case VI, and so treat LIFFE transactions as sundry taxable income, was a concern that other market users would also face a tax disincentive. The two major categories were first speculators who, because they were not carrying out sufficient levels of transactions, could not claim trading treatment, but also could not obtain the more beneficial tax regime of capital gains. Second, U.K. tax-exempt organizations, especially pension funds, were concerned that continual use of LIFFE would expose them to an Inland Revenue argument that this was outside the scope of their tax exemption, and so a tax charge could be incurred. This unsatisfactory tax situation led to extensive lobbying by interested parties for a better tax regime in attracting more users to the market.

Amendments to U.K. tax treatment

Tax-exempt organizations. The first amendment to the U.K. position was for tax-exempt organizations in Section 45, Finance Act 1984 (now Section 659), but only in respect of pension funds and related annuity businesses, and not charities. The provision stated that, where such organizations entered into contracts dealing in financial futures or traded options, it would be regarded as an investment. As a result, they should not face trading treatment on such transactions from July 1984. It should be noted that, while "traded options" are defined as options dealt with on an Inland Revenue recognized stock exchange (under Section 841) or LIFFE, "financial futures" are not limited to only those dealt in on "recognized futures exchanges" (Section 114)). This seems to represent an oversight under the legislation and creates potentially a wider market, without any geographical limitations, to that available for other U.K. users (refer below).

Other U.K. users. In Section 72, Finance Act 1985 (now Section 128), the situation for other taxpayers was amended in that transactions in traded futures and options contracts that are *not* part of a trade were to be taxed under capital gains rules, so removing the Schedule D, Case VI, rule. This amendment, which applied to both commodity and financial futures as well as traded options, however created the distinction that only contracts traded on a recognized stock exchange or recognized futures exchange would be accorded this treatment. Failure to transact on such approved exchanges would result in the old rules still applying. Initially, the Inland Revenue only recognized one futures exchange—LIFFE in London. Also, by virtue of its being an SEC-approved stock exchange, and therefore a U.K. Inland Revenue approved exchange, the Philadelphia Stock Exchange was also included. A current listing of non-U.K. futures exchanges is included in Appendix VI.

An additional benefit of this legislation was that it also granted such exchange-traded contracts nonwasting treatment. In respect of interest-rate options, the fact that no option rights were exercised or sold by the expiration of the option term does not prevent a capital loss from being claimed equivalent to the *full* option premium paid at the outset.

While the legislative changes were welcomed in clarifying the situation for nonfinancial trade taxpayers, subsequent discussions with the Inland Revenue by interested parties led to an Inland Revenue press release on November 29, 1985 (reproduced in Appendix IV). This indicated that the mere fact the taxpayer was not carrying on a finance trade did not automatically result in capital gains treatment applying. Instead, relying heavily on the old case of *Emanuel (Lewis) & Son Ltd. v. White* (1965) 42 TC 369, the Inland Revenue reserved the right to review each case on its facts.

The Emanuel case concerned a fruit and vegetable merchanting company which, by carrying out numerous transactions involving surplus cash for the buying and selling of shares through the stock exchange, was able to establish that it was carrying on a trade of dealing in securities. The Inland Revenue using this precedent could therefore seek, in appropriate circumstances, to deny capital gains treatment where the taxpayer involved is speculating on a sufficient scale. As with so many issues in tax law, the starting point as to whether trading is taking place is dependent on the specific facts. Over time, a number of general "badges of trade" for tax purposes have been developed. These include the following:

1. Number of transactions.
2. Motive of taxpayer for entering into the transactions.
3. Amount of time devoted to this activity and experience of the markets.
4. Undertaking of trading decisions.
5. Method of financing.

However, in the context of futures or options transactions, such tests cannot be so easily applied. Instead, they would need to be tailored to this activity by particular reference to the following:

1. The level of income or profits generated by such transactions.
2. An underlying intention test, say, by showing a connection with a capital asset that the deal is not pure speculation.
3. The level of activity, based on number of transactions, frequency of turnover and length of ownership, and amounts involved.

It would, however, seem correct to state that under both this Inland Revenue approach and the current tax law for exchange-traded options and futures contracts, the taxpayer either faces trading treatment under Schedule D, Case I (either as a trade-related transaction or by sufficient levels of speculation), or taxation as capital gains. This in total represents a more satisfactory position than originally existed, with the spectre of Schedule D, Case VI and its inherent problems.

Over-the-counter (OTC) instruments

Background. While the above covers the tax treatment of exchange-traded interest treasury instruments, the marketplace has also developed outside the recognized exchanges. In part, this reflects certain major financial institutions being of sufficient size to write and trade their own futures and options book and so cut out the intermediation of an exchange. Also exchanges by establishing set contracts and settlement dates do not quote directly for every user's specific exposures or treasury needs. This scenario has produced a number of situations where financial institutions, in dealing with other financial institutions and corporate customers, have developed a secondary "over-the-counter" (OTC) market. This is characterized by counterparties matching each other's requirements so that the instrument is tailored by the writer to the user's specific needs.

Examples of such instruments are FRAs, collars, caps, and floors. The growth of transactions being written in the OTC market has, in turn, led to sufficient depth in volumes handled that there is now a growing ability for the original user to sell on such instruments where, because of interest-rate movements, they have acquired inherent value.

Tax issues. Since such instruments are not currently quoted or traded on Inland Revenue recognized stock or futures exchanges, the above legislative amendments granting capital gains or Schedule D, Case I, treatment were of little benefit.

The Inland Revenue approach on such instruments was to follow broadly the original LIFFE guidelines, such that financial institutions could, in most cases, contend Case I treatment on payments and receipts but, that for other taxpayers, Case VI (and *not* capital gains) was the correct basis of assessment. Also, pension funds could not have the statutory protection of Section 659 when using such OTC instruments. The only initial change in the Inland Revenue approach was to indicate that, in certain cases, they were willing to consider Schedule D, Case I, treatment for trading companies. This was based on such taxpayers being able to demonstrate that the instrument related to short-term borrowings that were trade related, and so prima facie, fell easily within the Section 74 "wholly and exclusively" test.

Such a fiscal solution again produced a situation where the tax treatment did not interface with the commercial objectives. In part, the Inland Revenue approach reflected the old dichotomy of capital versus revenue, in that the approach was based on the instrument being used to hedge an underlying borrowing that did not itself form part of circulating capital. This suggested a tax solution that bore little relationship to how bankers and treasurers view their interest exposure management, which is to look to the total funding expense of the business, and conceptually does not create or recognize such a fiscal distinction. Indeed, the attraction of the various new treasury instruments to management is that they can now separate the financing decision (mix type and sources of indebtedness and repayment maturity profiles?) from the funding decision (what is the cost of finance and, based on market expectations, what can they do to protect against volatility?).

Second, and of more relevance to the tax situation, is that, while it may be correct to look to the actual borrowings when considering currency exchange gains and losses in respect of interest treasury instruments, it is the interest cost and not the borrowings that is the relevant tax transaction. If this approach is accepted, it is clearly correct to accord revenue and not capital gains treatment to such instruments. On the basis that such interest expense is tax deductible under the detailed rules previously outlined (either in computing Schedule D, Case I, profits or as a charge on income), it should be possible to justify and obtain symmetry and relate payments and receipts (where the option or futures contract generates a profit) to this specific tax item. Payments and receipts under this analysis would therefore be regarded as part of the total interest cost, even though, under U.K. tax law, such payments and receipts are clearly not interest and so do not automatically fall under these provisions of the Taxes Acts in obtaining relief.

It is understood that, in respect of trading companies, the Inland Revenue is now willing to follow such an approach, accepting that payments and receipts in respect of underlying borrowings will be included within the computation of the Schedule D, Case I, position. The only issue on which the Inland Revenue still considers the situation should differ is where the borrowing is directly related to funding a capital asset. In such a situation, the U.K. Inland Revenue's capital versus revenue approach still results in Schedule D, Case VI, treatment, although, on the above analysis of the instrument relating to interest not loan principal, it is submitted this approach is questionable and, in the authors' view, incorrect.

The Inland Revenue went some considerable way to addressing this issue under Section 81, Finance (No. 2) Act 1987. Using the regulatory framework established by the Financial Services Act (FSA) 1986, the capital gains tax treatment of financial futures and financial options under Section 72, Finance Act 1985 (now Section 128) was extended to include transactions where one of the counterparties is an "authorized person" or "listed institution" under the FSA. The legislation is operative from April 29, 1988 so coinciding with implementation of the relevant parts of the FSA. This removes one of the major obstacles to the development of an OTC market, although it should be noted that this is in a U.K. context. The carrying out of transactions with entities outside the United Kingdom, including exchanges not yet recognized by the U.K. Inland Revenue will, unless the U.K. taxpayer is carrying on a finance business or can demonstrate a connected capital transaction, still be exposed to the above tax approach and Case VI treatment.

While the 1987 legislation refers to futures and options, it should be appreciated that the Inland Revenue extended what was a qualifying option beyond options quoted on a recognized stock exchange or recognized futures exchange ("quoted option" and "traded option") to include the concept of a "financial option" dealt with on the OTC. This definition potentially encompasses instruments other than those in a form comparable to quoted or traded options. The definition of "financial option" includes:

1. an option relating to currency, shares, securities or an interest rate *granted by* an authorized person or listed institution;
2. an option *granted to* an authorized person or listed institution, concurrently and in association with an option falling under (1) with the same person; or
3. an option relating to shares or securities dealt in on a recognized stock exchange *granted by or to* a member of that exchange, and this encompasses that member acting as an agent.

Since most customized treasury instruments (such as FRAs, caps, collars) have the elements of relating to either an interest rate or a currency, then subject to being transacted with one of the approved counterparties, an argument for falling under this legislation would appear to apply. The legislation also contains provisions to allow the Revenue to extend the definition of "financial option" by the easily implemented expedient of statutory instruments, in widening the scope of this legislation.

Open tax issues. The changes in tax legislation and Inland Revenue approach still leave a number of problem areas which users of the market will need to consider:

1. For taxpayers who cannot demonstrate a finance trade or an underlying capital transaction, the use of treasury instruments where the counterparty is not on a recognized stock exchange or futures exchange or an approved person under the FSA, leaves the original dilemma of potential Case VI and wasting asset treatment if a capital transaction involves options.

2. While the above comments have largely centered on the position for trading companies on liabilities—the hedging of their funding obligations—where non-finnance trading companies use such instruments to hedge their assets—typically interest bearing investments and equities—the same rules will not automatically apply. U.K. tax law does not allow any deductions in computing the taxable income under Schedule D, Case III, IV or V, so preventing any automatic application of that tax legislation.

   This issue has probably been resolved by a mixture of the 1987 amendments (where a qualifying item is either Case I trading or capital gains) and more importantly a recent Inland Revenue Statement of Practice on "Tax Treatment of Transactions in Financial Futures and Options" (SP 4/88—see Appendix VII for full text). This Statement arose out of a number of representations by various investment bodies for clarification of when the Revenue would accept a future or option contract as qualifying for capital treatment. The main parties concerned were largely tax exempt bodies such as pension funds and also entities such as unit trusts and investment trusts where capital treatment meant non-taxability for that taxpayer. In addition, the area was of interest to other taxpayers with portfolio investments, especially in relation to U.K. government stocks and corporate bonds where an exemption from U.K. tax for futures or option contracts involving such securities had been introduced in 1986 (now included in Section 67, CGTA 1979).

   In covering this whole issue the Statement of Practice expands considerably on Paragraph 2 of the original LIFFE guidelines (see Appendix III). The Statement reaffirms the Inland Revenue's previously expressed view (see Appendix IV) that a company cannot speculate in futures and options. However, it confirms that where a futures or option contract has been entered into to 'hedge' an underlying asset or transaction which would itself give rise to a capital item, it will be regarded as capital and not trading.

What is helpful in the Statement is the clarification given as to how this will be determined and applied to both exchange and non-exchange contracts. To demonstrate "hedging" will require two tests to be met:

(a) The transaction is economically matched, based on value, assets, currency, etc.
(b) The futures or option contract's fluctuations in price mirror those of the underlying transaction, asset or portfolio of investments.

The Statement also contains some important concessions by the Inland Revenue in applying these tests:

(a) The tax position is determined based on the facts at the time the hedging transaction is initiated. The subsequent closing out of the futures or option contract before maturity should not alter this situation.
(b) A transaction undertaken as a capital hedge but where the underlying transaction ceases to exist (for example, the relevant investment portfolio is sold) will not give rise in practice to trading treatment on the futures or option contract if it is not closed out immediately after that event.
(c) Where the futures or option contract is entered into based on a *prospective* transaction, while no underlying capital transaction exists at the outset, capital treatment may still apply based on the facts. The Inland Revenue's intention in this area appears to be that as long as the intended transaction will be of a capital nature and the futures or option contract is hedging against or reducing risk and not being used to provide exposure to a market, then capital gains treatment will follow.

It is arguable that one of the examples used in the Statement (paragaph 9 (1)) should be trading and not capital since the hedging against interest rate risk, as opposed to changes in value of the intended underlying loan principal (as for example in taking out a futures or option contract on changes in currency rates on a non-sterling bond issue, or hedging the possible decline in value of a portfolio of U.K. Government bonds), woud appear to be more revenue than capital based. As covered previously, Statements of Practice are no more than a suggested Inland Revenue approach and it is open to the taxpayer to argue otherwise if it is beneficial to him.

The Statement in total is, however, very helpful in clarifying this area and as a result should enable most investment asset hedges to be treated as capital even where dealt in on non-recognized exchanges. What the Statement does underline is the need for careful documenting of the taxpayer's intention at the time the contract is entered into so evidence will exist to support this position in filing subsequent tax returns.

3. The Inland Revenue treatment of investment management companies still leaves them at a potential disadvantage. Since the payments under treasury instruments do not constitute "interest" or "expenses of management" no general tax relief is available to such entities. Following the FA 1987 amendments and the Statement of Practice, it should be possible by using the right exchange or counterparty to ensure all futures or option contracts for qualifying treasury instruments receive either capital gains or trading treatment. In addition to using the proper counterparties, care would also need to be exercised where a considerable number of revenue transactions were being entered into which qualify for trading treatment. This is because the quantum of such amounts could impact the tax status of the investment management company and losses carried forward as surplus expenses of management. Faced with such a situation, the practical solution is to ensure that where appropriate, transactions that will not qualify for capital treatment are carried out directly by a trading subsidiary in providing a basis for claiming a tax deduction.

While the Finance (No. 2) Act 1987 amendments and the subsequent Statement of Practice are welcome developments, it would seem that the nub of the problem is the limited U.K. tax law in granting deductions for finance costs, restricting deductions to the strict definition of "interest" or other specific allowables. Again, a contrast between the United Kingdom and many other countries can be drawn. In other countries, as long as it can be shown the expense relates to "finance costs" rather than just "interest", a tax deduction is due. It is perhaps regrettable that the various amendments over the years could not be consolidated into formal legislation to grant a deduction in computing Case I profits (for a trading company) or as a management expense (for investment management companies) as long as the taxpayer could demonstrate a specific hedge against the cost of borrowings or revenues to his business. While capital gains treatment as opposed to Case I treatment can have drawbacks especially in its more limited use of losses, the real benefit under the changes in tax law and Inland Revenue approach is that, approached correctly, taxpayers should at least be able to avoid the rather questionable benefit of Case VI!

Accounting versus taxation. There are a number of tax issues arising out of the reconciliation of the accounting treatment with U.K. tax law on interest treasury instruments. These issues apply equally to exchange-traded and OTC instruments.

The accounting treatment for the issuer is that they would not normally recognize any receipt at inception, but, instead, over the life of the transaction. This could be either on a "mark-to-market" basis or a straight-line amortization. The open tax issue is that, on the basis revenue has been received, this should be recognized subject to appropriate provision for any known future liability. United Kingdon tax law does not allow general provisions (Section 74). Case law has held that as long as a sufficiently accurate estimate can be made, then such trading-related contingent obligations are deductible (refer to *Owen v. Southern Railway of Peru Ltd.* (1956) 36 TC 602, and *Titaghur Jute Mills Ltd. v. IRC* (1978) STC 166). This clearly presents a problem for treasury instruments with future expectations not being known with any final certainty. It appears that the Inland Revenue, in appropriate circumstances, would be willing to accept a valuation of the instrument based on accepted volatility pricing models, subject to the basis being applied consistently. Where an open market exists, providing regularly quoted exchange prices, then marketing to this market should be accepted.

For the user, the situation does not automatically follow that of the issuer. Normal accounting for a hedge premium would be to amortize over the life of the hedge. Current indications are that this will be acceptable to the Inland Revenue when granting a Case I deduction for trading companies, in following the accounts treatment for tax purposes, even though any premium is normally paid in full at the outset. In cases where the user "marks-to-market," it is considered that the same criteria and principles will apply for issuers as stated above.

The potential problem in reconciling accounting and tax treatment was recognized by the U.K. Inland Revenue in the original LIFFE guidelines (see Appendix III, paragraph 6). Where a contract has been closed (and so no open position exists) the Inland Revenue guidelines confirmed that realization had occurred for tax purposes and so the user should recognize any gain or loss for tax purposes. Again, a dichotomy between tax and accounting could arise where the contract has been identified as an anticipatory hedge for accounting purposes. In such a situation the gain/loss on realization is recognized in the financial statements over the future interest period. For tax purposes, a mismatch will occur since there is no basis for deferring the tax recognition of the realized gain or loss.

Swaps (interest and currency)

General aspects of swaps

Although currency swaps historically preceded interest swaps, it is proposed to consider them together. This is because the U.K. Inland Revenue has agreed guidelines as to how they are both to be treated, and the specific tax issues arising out of currency swaps on the exchange gains and losses aspect will be considered subsequently. In looking at the tax issues common to both types of swaps, it is possible to identify two being, first, the commencement of the swap and, second, the periodic payments between swap counterparties over the duration of the swap.

Commencement of swap-arrangement fees

Swaps, by their nature, require the finding of appropriate counterparties in addition to the structuring and pricing of the transaction.

While, with the growth in the international use of swaps, this has become less of a problem, a particular tax difficulty arose on the payment of arrangement fees to the relevant counterparty for services performed in structuring the transactions.

For banks and other financial institutions, such fees should be deductible under Section 74. The problem arose for nonfinance trade taxpayers to whom the fees represented nondeductible "nothings." The amendments introduced in 1980 did not help, since a swap involves either a sale and right to repurchase of currency, or the swapping of interest rates. Under either swap structure, there is no raising of a "qualifying loan," and so no basis for taking a tax deduction. This potential pitfall, if it arises, can be overcome in the two following ways:

1. Where the arranger is also making a separate loan to the payer—for example, provision of funds to enter into the swap subsequently—for that transaction to be priced accordingly and no charges for the swap to be levied.
2. Where the arranger is the swap counterparty, instead of levying a separate arrangement fee, to instead price, at a higher level, the periodic payments (for which specific tax rules on deductibility exist) such that the counterparty is remunerated at a slightly higher level than originally priced.

The benefit of both the above is that they provide the payer with a basis for claiming a tax deduction.

Periodic payments under swap

The structure of cash flows under most swaps is as follows:

1. *Currency swap*—Initial sale of currency with a forward contract to resell back at the end of the swap, with payments at specified intervals over the swap compensating the other counterparty for loss of income on his currency sold.
2. *Interest swap*—Settling of the counterparty's interest obligations at specified payment dates and under an agreed formula.

Chapter 8

While in many swaps the periodic payments over the life of the swap are "netted" such that there is only one "net" payment at the specified settlement dates, the underlying "gross" calculations and principles remain the same.

With the development of currency swaps in the mid-to-late 1970s, the U.K. Inland Revenue took the initial view that such periodic payments were not "interest" since they did not satisfy the test of an interest expense on an underlying debt obligation to the original creditor. While under the structure of most swaps this is clearly correct, it does not seem that the Inland Revenue's alternative proposition was correct. This was to treat such amounts as being "annual payments" which, in turn, generated a basic rate tax withholding (currently 25%) under Section 349. The necessary characteristics for an amount to be treated as an "annual payment" are that:

1. It relates to a period capable of extending over one year.
2. It represents payments on a regular basis.
3. It is "pure income profit" to the recipient.

While points (1) and (2) are satisfied for most swaps, it seems arguable that point (3) is present. The requirement of "pure income profit" is that the recipient receives such amounts free and clear of any conditions, contractual obligations, or counterstipulations. In the context of a swap with each counterparty undertaking binding obligations to the other, it seems difficult to support such an approach.

The potential adverse impact of a withholding tax on the development of a swaps market led to a formal Inland Revenue response to the Banker's Association. While the technical basis of the Inland Revenue's opening position on annual payments may be open to question as outlined above, this informal concession removed the potential tax issue. The agreement, which has since been extended, albeit informally on almost the same lines, to interest swaps has probably been accepted without further taxpayer litigation or lobbying for the two following reasons:

1. It laid down guidelines as to avoiding withholding tax and ensuring tax deduction of periodic swap payments.

2. By providing a central role to U.K. banking businesses in granting this tax treatment, it was largely reflecting the market need for bank intermediation on swaps in providing credit risk control.

The relevant text of the Inland Revenue's agreement, as contained in the British Banker's Association letter of October 2, 1979, is reproduced in Appendix V. The main practical points arising are as follows:

1. Where a U.K. banking business (which can include the U.K. branch of an overseas bank recognized as a bank for Section 349 of the Taxes Act by the Board of the Inland Revenue) is a principal counterparty in a swap, and not merely a paying agent, it can receive from U.K. counterparties and make swap payments gross, regardless of the tax residence of the recipient.
2. A trading company can deduct swap payments as part of its trading results.
3. An investment company can deduct swap payments as a charge on income.
4. Withholding tax will still be accountable where the swap is between two U.K. counterparties, either of whom is a U.K. banking business (say, between two U.K. companies that do not constitute a corporate group for tax purposes). Also, a withholding will arise between a U.K. counterparty and a nonresident, though the latter is however subject to the possible existence of a double tax treaty mitigating this.
5. The U.K. banking business will treat payments and receipts under swaps as part of its normal banking business.
6. Nonbanks will be taxed on swap receipts as investment income under D-III if a U.K. counterparty and D-IV if a nonresident counterparty.

The double tax treaty relief under point (4) is dependent on the country of residence of the nonresident counterparty, and the specific terms of the treaty concluded with the United Kingdom. As the swap payments are not interest under U.K. tax law, plus the royalty article of most double tax treaties does not specify "annual payments," this leads to a situation where reliance has to be placed on the business profits article, with the swap not being connected with any branch or agency in the United Kingdom of the nonresident. This situation is strengthened where the treaty also has an "other income" article. This will typically state that income not specifically covered under other articles of the treaty is exempted from taxation in the country of source by virtue of this article.

As a result, it would not seem necessary for the normal treaty exemption claim procedures to be followed subject to adequate evidence of the tax residence of the overseas counterparty being held. It is understood, however, that, if formal application is made, the U.K. Inspector of Foreign Dividends will process and, when approved, issue an exemption certificate to the nonresident.

The above rules, while issued in connection with currency swaps, have been extended to interest-rate swaps, although the Inland Revenue has not issued any formal notice on the same basis. The main distinction is that trading companies, as well as investment companies, must take tax relief for interest-swap payments on a charge on income (i.e., payments not accruals) basis.

The only recent change that has occurred in the Inland Revenue's approach to swap payments arose, it is understood, out of a Revenue Commissioner's decision. The United Kingdom has seen the growth of financial houses and securities dealers who do not have banking status under Section 349 for U.K. tax purposes, but who are heavily involved in swap transactions as part of their overall business. They therefore fall outside the scope of the above guidelines. The Inland Revenue now accepts that such entities can pay swap payments without treatment as annual payments (and therefore not withhold tax) although, unless it receives swap payments from a U.K. banking business, the current Inland Revenue approach is that the U.K. counterparty must still deduct withholding tax.

Currency swaps—exchange gains and losses

For banks and financial institutions that are entering into currency dealing in carrying on business, revenue treatment as part of trading profits should normally follow for any currency gains, both on annual revaluations and buying/selling of currencies. This is subject to one possible exception, which is where the bank (either U.K. company or branch) has raised funds that have the character of a capital liability (e.g., subordinated loans or borrowings contributing to the capital base). In such circumstances, the profit/loss on annual revaluation would be excluded from the computation of trading results unless an argument for "matching" under Marine Midland and the subsequent Statement of Practice exists.

For other U.K. taxpayers, the raising of a primary currency obligation, which is then swapped with an agreement to buy/sell at the agreed spot rates at a future point, should, in most cases, fall to be treated as transactions on the capital account. Foreign currency is a chargeable asset for U.K. capital gains tax (Section 19(1)(b), CGTA 1979). The sale of foreign currency (whether outright or by forward contract) will therefore be a chargeable disposal for capital gains tax and the purchase of foreign currency to settle an obligation will also involve an acquisition and disposal of a chargeable asset for CGT purposes.

Applying the previously outlined U.K. tax principles to the various steps of a currency swap would appear to produce the following results:

1. On initial selling of a currency to the other counterparty, (a) for a bank or financial institution, a trading profit or loss and (b) for others, a disposal of a chargeable asset for CGT, the gain is computed by reference to the sterling acquisition cost of those funds. Where this is by simultaneous raising of a similar level of currency funding, no gain/loss should arise.

2. Where a bank is acting as an intermediate principal, the transactions with the two counterparties, in respect of different currencies, should be fully matched. Any movements in the currencies, as revalued at spot at the balance sheet dates and on repayment, should be completely offsetting, leaving the bank with no currency gain/loss. This position is recognized under Paragraph 23 of the Inland Revenue Statement of Practice (see Appendix II).

3. Where a bank or other taxpayer is a principal counterparty in a currency swap, the situation will be that it has undertaken an exchange of assets at the outset that it will revalue at year-end spot rates, along with the funding liability. This should be matched and offset by a comparable profit/loss on the reexchange contracts and so

result again in a no gain/no loss position for accounts and therefore also tax purposes.

In the case of a nonfinance trade, it is possible that the currency assets acquired will not be retained in that form, but converted into other assets or other currencies, either of a trading nature or as capital assets. To the extent this occurs, a disposal arises that will produce a capital gain/loss and, if it is in a different currency, an annual mismatching will arise. To the extent the asset is capital, any annual revaluation falls to be excluded from trading results (although, for accounts purposes, this may be partially offset by the annual revaluation of a further forward contract entered into for purchase of the relevant currency at the date of the swap terminating).

4. The periodic payments over the life of a swap may be payable in currencies other than sterling. Where an interest swap is denominated in the same currency and merely involves the exchange of interest rates, no currency exchange considerations should arise since the loan principles of each counterparty remain their own obligations. The meeting of the counterparty's interest obligations in a foreign currency should form part of the trading results of the U.K. taxpayer, translated at the relevant spot exchange rate. A similar approach and tax treatment would apply on a currency swap, for both trading and investment companies.

5. On termination and repayment of sums under the currency swap, for a bank acting as counterparty, the exchange gains and losses (to the extent any arise) will form part of its trading results.

For other taxpayers, it is necessary to break down the elements of the swap into their component parts. While swaps economically have to be looked at as a composite transaction, there is nothing in U.K. tax legislation that supports such a fiscal approach. Also, because capital transactions are being considered, they fall outside the scope of the Inland Revenue Statement of Practice. It is therefore necessary to apply the previously outlined U.K. tax principles, as follows:

(a) Repayment of its own funding obligation. This is outside the scope of U.K. tax since it represents payment of a capital liability and therefore, to the extent there is any gain or loss arising, it should not be a taxable event.

(b) The acquisition of currency other than sterling from the other swap party will be the acquisition of a chargeable asset for CGT purposes. While arguable that as the currency acquired is immediately used to clear the obligation under (a), no gain/loss should arise, an alternative argument seems more technically correct. That is that the acquisition price (specified under the swap) has to be compared with the disposal price (spot rate ruling when proceeds used to repay the capital liability) and any capital gain or loss computed."

(c) Allied with (b) is the concern that the Inland Revenue could, however, try to attribute any chargeable gain to the obligation of the swap counterparty on the basis that the currency to be received by the U.K. taxpayer has appreciated against sterling over the life of the swap. While it would seem, for U.K. tax purposes, that a debt exists, no chargeable gain can accrue to the original creditor (in this case the U.K. counterparty) unless the debt constitutes a "debt on security" (Section 134, CGTA 1979). Possible methods of planning against this exposure are covered more fully below.

(d) The realization of the assets originally received under the swap, if these were retained as currency in a separate "pool," should produce no gain/no loss, since the original acquisition price will equal the selling price to the counterparty. Difficulties, however, arise where these have been converted into other assets. Where currency received has been converted into other chargeable capital assets (e.g., investments) then the selling of those assets will produce a chargeable event for capital gains tax and the onward selling of the currency (if not simultaneously) will also produce a need to compute any gain/loss arising.

(e) Where the obligation to meet the selling of currency to the swap counterparty has been covered by a separate forward contract, then the receipt of that currency under the purchase contract will be the acquisition of a chargeable capital asset, and the computation of any capital gain/loss will be required by comparing the acquisition cost with the agreed selling price under the swap.

While, technically, the disposal of the currency under the swap occurs at the outset by entering into a contract for disposal at the point in time (by virtue of Section 27(1) CGTA 1979), the practical difficulty of computing any gain/loss is usually overcome by making the contract conditional, and disposal only occurs when the conditions are fulfilled at the end of the swap (Section 27(2) CGTA 1979).

Tax planning for currency swaps. The difficulties for nonfinance trades is that, under the above analysis of a currency swap, the U.K. counterparty, where he has taken out a nonsterling loan liability or "swapped" for a nonsterling currency, will face a mismatch in tax treatment. What was a perfect hedge for treasury and accounts purposes, will end up being taxed in different forms, plus the possibility that, in respect of capital liabilities, no taxation will be levied. In the case of a profit, this may well be acceptable but, in the case of a loss, this clearly denies any tax relief, even though the corresponding offsetting gain on assets *will* be taxable.

The following are some possible methods of planning that may in appropriate cases overcome this fiscal mismatch.

1. *Debt on security.* The exemptions on assets for capital tax purposes are limited. As covered earlier, capital assets for CGT purposes would include foreign currency held as a debt in a bank account or a forward contract for foreign currency. It would, however, exclude a debt that is *not* a "debt on security."

   What constitutes a "debt on security" is not defined in the tax legislation, and is an issue on which the courts have had to provide an answer. Based on the cases of *Aberdeen Construction Group Ltd. v. CIR* (1978) STC 127, and *W.I. Ramsey Ltd. v. CIR* (1981) STC 174, the following tests were applied:

   (a) The debt must be marketable, in that it can be freely traded.
   (b) In addition, the debt must be able to be traded at a profit or gain.
   (c) It need not be a secured debt, but it must be "similar" to loan stock and held as an investment.

   The problem for CGT purposes is that, as a forward currency contract constitutes a chargeable asset, the realization by disposal of the currency acquired under the Contract will be a capital gains event. Where the amounts are major in the context of the taxpayer's activities, it may be appropriate to consider whether purchase and sale of currency can be structured as a debt that does not meet the above tests, and is so not a chargeable asset. In essence, the taxpayer is trying to establish the same nontaxable status on the currency asset that U.K. tax law imposes on his currency liability, so tax symmetry is achieved in the situation outline in (b) and (c) on page 229.

The necessary requisites are making the swap counterparty's obligation nonassignable, such that the contractual rights could not be freely traded or at a profit. Where the gain arises because foreign currency is being sold forward against sterling, and appreciation through currency rate movements has arisen, it may be possible to refine this approach. One possibility is to acquire the appropriate foreign currency and, through depositing with a financial institution that is not a bank, then to meet the obligations under the swap, by assigning that foreign currency debt. As long as that debt has not been established as a "debt on security," the assignment should not be the realization of a gain on a chargeable asset and subject to capital gains tax.

The final variation in this area has been a revival of parallel loans while still obtaining the pricing benefits of the swap. Such structures involve splitting the swap into two loans (a matching loan out in one currency against a loan in, in the other currency) with an appropriate counterparty, rather than an outright swap and forward contract for repurchase of currencies. The loan to the counterparty would be structured as a nonassignable debt on security, so that repayment of such sums would be a nontaxable event and be granted symmetry with repayment of the capital liability. Again, care would be needed that such loans were not entered into with a bank counterparty and so brought within the ambit of U.K. capital gains tax.

Difficulties can arise in certain jurisdictions in trying to get the swap counterparty to accept such an approach. Since its balance sheet will reflect the two loans unlike under a swap, this may result in increased costs because of regulatory requirements.

In such a situation, the parallel loan could be entered into with an associate in an appropriate tax jurisdiction who will, in turn, enter into the currency swap with the third party. The requirements of such a jurisdiction are that it has a comprehensive tax treaty covering interest withholding tax with the United Kingdom and a more favorable treatment of currency gains and losses. The use of offshore entities in the context of swaps is covered more fully below.

2. *U.K. finance subsidiary.* The basic dilemma faced by U.K. companies arises out of the fact that, when not carrying on a backing/finance trade, it is considerably harder to argue any items of medium- to long-term finance as constituting circulating capital.

Within such a constraint, one approach to extend the parameters of what constitutes circulating capital is to establish a finance subsidiary. Where sufficient volumes and frequency of currency and finance transactions are carried out in a corporate group, the centralizing of such a treasury activity in a separate U.K. group company may, in appropriate circumstances, provide a basis for arguing a Schedule D, Case I, trade that is with certain limitations a quasi-bank activity. Such an activity will not overcome all tax issues—for example, withholding tax on loan interest and swap payments paid or received from non-U.K. group members—since it cannot be an Inland Revenue recognized bank under Section 349. It is, however, considered that, as long as a Case I trade can be shown, an argument would exist for extending the tests for loans undertaken and lent as constituting trading compared with capital treatment. The tax treatment of the resulting currency gains and losses would follow such an approach.

It is understood that the Inland Revenue has indicated in such cases that, where the majority of transactions are with other group companies, this cannot constitute a Case I trade. It is submitted that this is not the correct test. Whether the transactions are with fellow group companies or with external parties should not alter the tax position of whether the trade has all the necessary criteria to justify Case I treatment. This will always be a question of fact. It is, however, likely that to demonstrate a sufficient volume of business to support Case I treatment would, in practice, involve a mix of both intergroup and external transactions.

3. *Offshore vehicle.* As commented earlier, the U.K. tax treatment of currency gains and losses is not reflected in many other countries' tax systems. One alternative may therefore be to effectively "export" the tax problem to another fiscal jurisdiction. For currency swaps, in

United Kingdom Taxation

addition to being granted a more beneficial treatment of currency gains and losses, there is also a requirement that it is in a territory that has concluded a comprehensive tax treaty with the United Kingdom. This will avoid any withholding taxes and problems on deductibility of the funding costs of advances to the U.K. group. Such requirements have resulted in The Netherlands as being the optimum location. This has been assisted by the ability to obtain advance tax rulings so fixing the Dutch tax cost on such transactions. The possible structure in using a Netherlands finance company could be as that shown in Figure 8.1.

Figure 8.1 Offshore swap structure

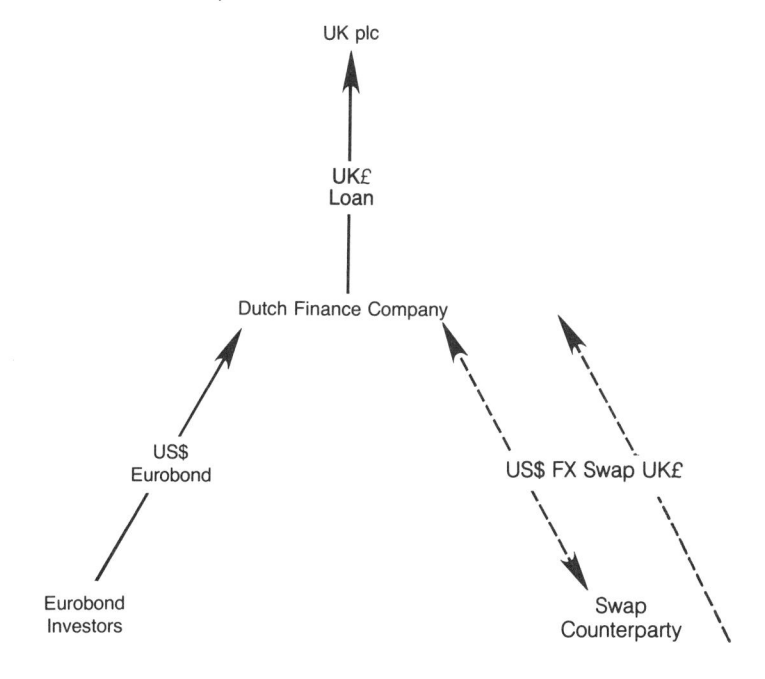

```
                        UK plc
                          ▲
                          │
                        UK£
                        Loan
                          │
                  Dutch Finance Company
                  ▲            ▲        ▲
                 /             ╲       ╲
               US$          US$ FX Swap UK£
             Eurobond              ╲       ╲
              /                     ▼       ╲
        Eurobond                  Swap
        Investors              Counterparty
```

The end result is as follows:

(a) The U.K. group is able to obtain sterling funding and not face any currency exposure for tax purposes, although, on a treasury basis, this exists for the group.

(b) The Dutch company is able to offset currency gains and losses with no asymmetry treatment as would have existed if the U.K. parent had entered into the swap directly.
(c) Payments of interest can be made gross to the Dutch company (owing to the terms of the U.K./Dutch double tax treaty) and no withholding arises in respect of payments by the Dutch company to nonresidents under its domestic tax legislation.

Currency options

In many respects, the use of currency options and consideration of their tax consequences can be seen as a return of the same issues as arose on currency swaps. These center around the two basic themes of the tax status of the user and the underlying transaction behind the use of the options.

Banks/other financial concerns

By virtue of carrying on a bona fide trade in financial instruments, Case I trading treatment should normally apply regardless of whether exchange or OTC options are used. It should be noted that, in its final form, the Inland Revenue Statement of Practice on currency gains and losses drew a distinction between futures and options (see Appendix II, paragraphs 22 and 24). In the context of trading transactions carried out by financial trades, it remains to be seen whether in practical terms this is of any impact since the valuation of, and dealing in, such options would normally fall under Case I treatment. It should also be remembered that the case of Marine Midland did not have to address the issue of currency options and this statement merely reflects the Inland Revenue view.

Commercial users

The underlying purpose of such users will be paramount. Where a trading transaction—for example, covering the cost of a sales trading contract or purchasing goods—the option premium will be a Case I deduction and profits/losses on the exercising of any option will fall under the same treatment.

Where the transaction involves speculation without any nexus with a trading transaction, the question of trading or capital treatment will follow the same U.K. tax guidelines as covered earlier on interest-related treasury instruments. The use of currency option contracts (either on recognized exchanges or OTC) following the Finance (No. 2) Act 1987 and subsequent Statement of Practice on "hedging" (see Appendix VII), should enable determination as to whether trading or capital treatment will apply. Where non-recognized counterparties are used, the issue will be determined based on the underlying transaction and therefore trading or capital treatment should still be arguable, though the spectres of potential Case VI treatment by the Revenue or wasting asset treatment on capital options will still exist.

The above comments on taxation of speculative and capital transactions would also apply to investment management companies, as well as trading companies.

Finally, it should be noted that the same ancillary issues that exist on interest options, being the point of tax recognition of gains/losses and wasting asset treatment where there is no capital gains protection under the tax legislation, would also exist for currency options.

U.K. value added tax

Value added tax (VAT) is an indirect tax which affects nearly all business transactions including treasury products. It is administered by the Commissioners of Customs and Excise, who are quite separate from the Inland Revenue. It is a transaction based tax and can be charged at 15% on gross income or expenditure.

The principal VAT statute is the Value Added Tax Act 1983 (VATA 1983) and this is supported by numerous Statutory Instruments, Customs and Excise Notices and other leaflets. The VAT net catches transactions under one of three headings: "taxable" at either the "standard" rate, currently 15%, or at the "zero" rate, or "exempt" from VAT. All other transactions are "non-taxable" since they are deemed to be outside the scope of VAT. The distinction between "taxable" and "exempt" revenue ("supplies") or "non-taxable" revenue is important because it affects the amount of recoverable VAT which is suffered on purchases and overhead expenses by many businesses, particularly in the financial sector with a large value of supplies that fall under the exempt or non-taxable categories.

Transactions in treasury products are usually exempt supplies. However, as with direct taxes, the pace of development of treasury instruments has meant that such products do not fit easily into existing VAT rules. There are numerous "grey" areas in which the treatment of particular transactions remains to be agreed with Customs and Excise, and this occurs often on a product-by-product basis. The principal criteria used to determine the VAT classification of individual financial instruments are:

1. Has a "supply" been made?
2. What is the "value" of the supply?
3. Where is the "buyer" resident?
4. What is the place of supply?
5. Has the business acted as "principal" (dealer) or "agent" (broker)?

The general approach of Customs and Excise is that most supplies of treasury products are exempt supplies falling within Item 1 of Group 5, Schedule 6, VATA 1983. It should be noted that the residence of the buyer in a non-EEC country can however render such exempt transactions as zero-rated by virtue of Item 6 of Group 9, Schedule 5, VATA 1983. For the purposes of this legislation, the Isle of Man is regarded as part of the United Kingdom.

While specific guidelines have not been published by Customs and Excise on treasury products it is understood that the following are the general principles applying to interest hedging agreements outside the framework of a recognized exchange such as LIFFE:

1. For brokerage and other arrangement fees or commissions charged in connection with the instrument, the treatment is as exempt supplies being consideration or the making of arrangements in dealing with money. Zero rating would apply where the service is supplied to a person belonging outside the EEC.

2. Initially the view of Customs and Excise was that "interest" receipts under agreements such as FRAs, caps, and so on, fell outside the scope of VAT since they did not relate to moneys lent and thus an exempt finance service. This view has now changed with the supply being treated as exempt where the counterparty is in the UK/EEC and zero rated where outside that area.

For interest rate and currency rate swaps the position is understood to be as follows:

1. The initial arrangement fees and annual administration fees (if charged separately) would be exempt where the counterparty belongs in the United Kingdom and EEC, and zero rated if not.
2. As with other interest related treasury products, the initial view of Customs and Excise that the annual swap payments were outside the scope of VAT has subsequently changed so that they are now regarded as exempt supplies where the payer is UK/EEC resident and zero rated where outside the EEC. The value of the supply where the two periodic swap payments are "netted" is the single net sum which passes between the counterparties. It is understood that Customs and Excise are currently reviewing this point but at the time of writing no change in practice has been announced.
3. Customs and Excise consider the buying and selling of foreign currency is a supply outside the scope of VAT and this should apply to the purchase and sale of currencies under a currency swap.

For transactions carried out by non-members via LIFFE and other Customs and Excise recognized exchanges, slightly different rules apply and the above guidelines are adapted as follows:

1. A LIFFE members' supply on the sale of contracts is one half of his dealing turn (and not the full consideration on sale) for currency and "short" interest rate contracts.
2. For other contracts, e.g., "long" interest rate contracts, the supply is the full dealing turn, except where the contract leads to actual delivery. In that case, the full market value of the security is the value of the supply.

Chapter 8

3. The precise nature of the security concerned is important because, under Item 1 of Group 5, Schedule 6, "the issue, transfer or receipt of, or any dealing with, money, any security for money or any note or order for the payment of money" is exempt. Item 5 exempts the making of arrangements for such supplies. However, the making of arrangements for Item 6 supplies, which is widely defined to include most interest or equity linked securities is *not* exempt. It is, therefore, essential to distinguish between "security for money" (Item 5) and "security" or "secondary security" (Item 6). Of the newer instruments, LIFFE's FT-SE 100 futures contract and The Stock Exchange's currency options are "money" items because these are always settled in cash. The gilt option contracts on LIFFE and the International Stock Exchange are "securities" because the settlement procedure (if proceeded with) envisages delivery of the relevant security. An option to acquire a "security" is an example of a "secondary security."

Customs and Excise's special treatment of LIFFE transactions as outlined above applies to financial options as well as to futures transactions. As for futures, if an option contract leads to the delivery of a security, the consideration for the supply is taken to be the full value of the security delivered. However, the excercise of a foreign currency or interest rate option or the abandonment of any option are outside the scope of VAT.

CHAPTER 9

United States taxation*

*This chapter has been added to the original text. It was written by David F. Windish.

Introduction

Tax advisers sometimes are accused of overestimating the importance of tax effects on commercial transactions. In many cases, the critics are correct. However, in the area of the treasury instruments, the difference between profit or loss often turns on a matter of a few basis points, and failure to consider potential tax effects can prove costly. Unfortunately, the rapid proliferation of treasury instruments and the almost daily variations and modifications to meet the challenges of the commercial financial world generally far outpace the development of clear and concise tax rules applicable to specific instruments.

Against the backdrop of a fast-paced commercial environment, tax advisers have had to struggle with major changes to the U.S. Internal Revenue Code, especially those introduced by the Tax Reform Act of 1986. These changes, as they affect treasury instruments, have been twofold. First, there have been far-reaching broad-based changes affecting tax rules of general application, including those applicable to capital gains, the reporting of interest income and expense, and transactions involving foreign currency. Second, more narrowly drawn rules affect specific transactions involving options, futures contracts, and hedging transactions.

Chapter 9

With these limitations in mind, this chapter provides an outline of the tax rules with which the users of the various treasury instruments must cope. The reader must keep in mind that this cannot be the complete and final story on U.S. taxation. Rather, it can be and is only a starting point.

The chapter is divided into three parts.

- The first provides an overview of those general principles of U.S. taxation that affect treasury instruments.
- The second part reviews how tax rules may differ based on the nature of the entity making use of the various treasury instruments, including banks and financial institutions, regulated investment companies or mutual funds, and tax-exempt entities.
- Finally, the third part explores tax rules as they apply to specific types of treasury instruments.

In regard to this last point, it would be convenient if the tax law was written so that one specific set of tax rules applied to each type of instrument. Unfortunately, this is not the case, since the tax law attempts to define the tax consequences of the various treasury instruments based on their function rather than their form. For instance, an interest-rate future contract may be subject to different rules depending on whether the contract is written in terms of the dollar or is based on a foreign currency. Difference in tax treatment may also depend on whether the contract qualifies as a regulated futures contract marked-to-market, is part of a straddle position, or is speculative or part of a bona fide hedging transaction. Accordingly, the discussion of tax rules as applied to specific treasury instruments in the final part of this chapter generally is based on the tax classification of these instruments rather than on their commercial classification.

General principles of U.S. taxation

Obviously, any outline of the U.S. tax system is open to the criticism that it is incomplete and does not provide coverage of all aspects of what is often a bewildering array of complex and overlapping rules and regulations. But again the attempt here is not to provide the complete story. The broad principles of U.S. taxation set out below and the brief discussion of the tax classification of various potential users of treasury products are presented merely to provide a conceptual framework for the discussion of the tax treatment of specific treasury instruments that follows.

Note that references to IRC contained in this chapter are to the Internal Revenue Code of 1986 unless otherwise indicated.

The ordinary income/capital gain distinction

The U.S. income tax code, almost from its inception, has drawn a distinction between ordinary income and capital gain. The distinction also has carried over to the treatment of expenses or losses. In general, gains or income classified as capital in nature have received preferential tax treatment, while the deduction for capital losses has been limited. Capital gains and losses are those that result from the sale or exchange of capital assets.

The Internal Revenue Code takes a negative approach to the definition of capital assets. Rather than telling us what a capital asset is, it tells us what a capital asset is not (IRC Section 1221). A "capital asset" is any property held by a taxpayer, whether or not that property is connected with the taxpayer's trade or business, except the following:

1. Stock in trade or other property that would properly be included in inventory at the close of the year.
2. Property held primarily for sale to customers in the ordinary course of a trade or business.
3. Depreciable property or real property used in the taxpayer's trade or business.
4. Copyrights, or literary, musical, or artistic compositions, or similar property when held by the creator of the property or by a taxpayer who acquired the property by gift or in trust.
5. Accounts or notes receivable acquired in the ordinary course of trade or business for services rendered or from the sale of stock in trade or inventory.
6. Certain U.S. government publications.

Without more, the treasury instruments which are the subject of this book would be classified as capital assets under the definition set out above, with the exception of those instruments held by a dealer in securities for sale in the ordinary course of business. Of course, there is more. Early on in the development of the capital asset concept, a judicial exception to the principle was made that a capital asset is any property other than property of a type specifically enumerated by the Internal Revenue Code. Under what is known as the *Corn Products Doctrine*, assets that are an integral part of day-to-day business operations are classified as ordinary assets giving rise to ordinary income or loss even though they may be technically capital assets since they are not excluded from the capital asset category by IRC Section 1221.

The *Corn Products Doctrine* arose in a decision handed down by the United States Supreme Court. The case involved a manufacturer of corn products that routinely purchased corn futures in order to assure its supply of raw materials. The Internal Revenue Service argued that losses sustained by the manufacturer from its dealings in corn futures were subject to the limitations on deductions for capital losses. The Supreme Court, however, ruled that since the corn futures were actually an integral part of the manufacturer's business, the losses were ordinary in nature and could be deducted in full.

Today, the *Corn Products Doctrine* remains a valid judicially established principle. Securities acquired solely for business purposes rather than investment may be classified as ordinary assets under the doctrine. In many cases, however, resort to the doctrine has been rendered unnecessary by various statutory rules added to the Internal Revenue Code since the *Corn Products* case was decided. These rules, of course, are discussed in connection with the discussion of the tax treatment of specific treasury instruments below. Nevertheless, the doctrine may retain some vitality for those situations that "fall between the cracks" of the present statutory framework and it offers insight into the development of special rules covering transactions in financial instruments acquired as bona fide hedges.

Tax treatment of capital gain or loss

Gain from the sale or exchange of capital assets held for more than six months was given special tax advantages before 1987 as a means of encouraging capital formation and economic growth. In the case of capital gain realized by an individual or noncorporate taxpayer, only 40% of long-term capital gain was subject to tax. In effect, this resulted in a top tax rate for an individual's capital gain of 20%, as compared to the then top rate of 50% on an individual's ordinary income. In the case of a corporate taxpayer prior to 1987, the tax on long-term capital gain was limited to 28%, as compared to the then top corporate tax rate of 46% on ordinary income.

As part of the Tax Reform Act of 1986, Congress substantially lowered the tax rates on ordinary income, but also decided that with these lower rates the special tax rates for long-term capital gain were no longer necessary. After 1987, capital gain realized by both individuals and corporations is subject to the same tax rates as ordinary income realized by these taxpayers. This translates to a top rate of 28% (with a marginal rate of 33% within a prescribed range) for individuals and 34% for corporations under the appropriate tax rate schedules.

In repealing the special advantages for long-term capital gain, however, Congress did not repeal the special limitations that apply to the deductions for capital losses. Essentially, capital losses may be deducted only to the extent of capital gains and, in the case of individuals, up to $3,000 of ordinary income. In addition, the distinctions between capital gains and losses and ordinary gains and losses for all other purposes found in the Internal Revenue Code of 1954 remain in the Internal Revenue Code of 1986. Congress also specifically stated that one of the reasons most of the distinctions between capital gain and ordinary income would remain in the Internal Revenue Code was to facilitate a return to preferential tax treatment for long-term capital gain in the future in the event tax increases or economic conditions warranted such a change.

The Tax Reform Act of 1986 obviously has lessened the significance of the ordinary/capital distinction on the income side. Nevertheless, the limitations on the deduction of capital losses to capital gain plus, in the case of an individual, $3,000, means that the distinction in certain cases can be of critical importance, especially in light of the carryover provisions for capital losses that cannot be used in the current tax year.

For individuals, unused capital losses may be carried over indefinitely. That is, unused capital losses can be carried from year to year until completely offset by future capital gain or (subject to the $3,000 annual limit) future ordinary income. Corporations, however, are subject to much more limited carryover provisions. Any unused capital loss may be carried back up to three years to offset earlier capital gain and, if unused under the carryback provision, carried forward for up to five years to offset future capital gain. Once the carryforward period expires, however, capital losses that have not been taken as a deduction against capital gain are lost and cannot be used to reduce income and taxes. These rules make both the realization and timing of capital gains and losses of critical importance despite the elimination of the preferential tax rates for capital gain.

Interest and discount

The Internal Revenue Code contains specific tax rules governing the deductibility of interest by the payor and the inclusion of interest in income by the recipient as well as the timing of the deductions and inclusions. These rules, which have evolved and expanded in scope over time, may seem unnecessarily complicated to the nontax specialist. It is, however, necessary to attempt a general understanding of these complex rules considering their interplay with the tax treatment of treasury instruments.

The Internal Revenue Code does not specifically define the term interest, although case law has established the general proposition that interest represents the payment over time for the use of money or for the forebearance on a creditor's part in demanding payment of a debt. Furthermore, an interest deduction is not allowed unless the interest is paid because of a valid obligation of the payor to pay a fixed or determinable amount of money.

As a general proposition, interest is ordinary income to the recipient (IRC Section 61(a)(4)), and a deductible expense for the payor (IRC Section 163) subject to the following limitations:

1. Personal interest paid by individual taxpayers is not deductible after 1990 and is subject to a percentage disallowance prior to 1991. (This is not a matter of concern in relation to treasury instruments.)
2. Investment interest paid by an individual taxpayer is subject to a limitation on its deductibility based on the taxpayer's investment

income. Investment interest is interest paid or accrued on indebtedness incurred or continued to purchase or carry property held for investment.
3. Interest on debt incurred to purchase or carry obligations on which the income is exempt from tax under the Internal Revenue Code is not deductible.

Original issue discount and unstated interest. Even before 1984, the issuer and holder of a publicly traded debt instrument or a debt instrument issued for publicly traded property that was issued at a discount were required to report the interest represented by the discount annually, regardless of whether they used the cash or accrual method of accounting. Also, parties to deferred payment sales could be subject to unstated interest rules that converted what was nominally principal into interest unless their contract provided for a statutorily set minimum interest rate.

In 1984, the original issue discount rules (now contained in IRC Section 1271 through Section 1275) and the unstated interest rules (IRC Section 483) were greatly expanded and rules governing market discount (separately discussed below) were added to the Internal Revenue Code. These rules are often complex and encompass such a mass of material that any in-depth treatment is impossible. Regulations in proposed form issued by the Internal Revenue Service in 1986 and dealing with imputed interest on deferred payment sales or exchanges of property, debt instruments with original issue discount, and safe haven interest rates for commonly controlled taxpayers alone encompass over 400 pages and contain additions or amendments to the income tax regulations under IRC Sections 163(e), 446, 482, 483, 1271, 1272, 1273, 1274, and 1275.

The general thrust of all of these rules, of course, is to see that the economic equivalent of interest income and expense is properly reported by both recipient and payor over the time period to which the interest relates. Essentially, the original issue discount rules that already applied to publicly traded instruments were expanded in 1984 to include debt instruments that are not publicly traded or that are issued for nontraded property, obligations issued by individuals, cash-basis holders of obligations that are not held as capital assets, and debt instruments issued for services or the use of property.

Original issue discount is determined by rates announced by the Secretary of the Treasury every month and are based on the rate of U.S. government obligations of similar duration. Original issue discount generally must be reported on an accrual basis, although cash accounting may be used in very limited circumstances. Deferred payment sales that are not subject to the original issue discount rules of IRC Sections 1271–1275 are subject to the unstated interest rules of IRC Section 483 and the regulations thereunder. The interest rates used to determine if there is unstated interest are, for the most part, the same as the interest rates used to determine original issue discount. Under IRC Section 483, however, interest income or expense is reported or deducted when payment is made in the case of a cash-method taxpayer or when it is due in the case of an accrual-method taxpayer.

Market discount. As with the original issue discount rules, the thrust of the market discount rules (IRC Sections 1276 through 1278) is to see that the economic equivalent of interest income is reported as interest income rather than some other type of income, for instance, capital gain. Market discount is a bond's stated redemption price at maturity in excess of the taxpayer's tax basis for the bond immediately after its acquisition.

On the disposition of any market discount bond that was issued after July 18, 1984, accrued market discount is treated as ordinary income and, except for limited purposes, as interest income. Accrued market discount is computed under a "ratable accrual" method or, at the election of the taxpayer, a "constant interest-rate" method. Also, at the election of the taxpayer, market discount may be included in gross income for the years to which it is attributable under the ratable accrual or constant interest-rate method rather than in full on the disposition of the bond. Of course, any gain on the disposition of the bond in excess of market discount would be capital gain, provided the bond is a capital asset in the taxpayer's hands.

Any partial principal payment on a market discount bond acquired after October 22, 1986 is included in gross income as ordinary income to the extent the payment does not exceed the accrued market discount on the bond. If a partial payment on a market discount bond is included in income, the amount of accrued market discount treated as ordinary income on disposition of the bond is reduced by the amount of the partial principal payment previously included in income. (Note that there is an election available whereby a taxpayer can report current market discount income.

If a taxpayer borrows money to purchase a market discount bond, that taxpayer's deduction for interest attributable to the debt to purchase or carry the market discount bond is limited. The net direct interest expense is deductible for the year only to the extent the interest expense exceeds the portion of market discount attributable to the year. Net direct interest expense is interest paid or accrued on debt incurred or continued to purchase or carry a market discount bond in excess of the interest, including original issue discount, includible in income as a result of holding the bond.

Short-term obligations. Under rules contained in IRC Sections 1281 through 1283, certain taxpayers must include discount on the acquisition of short-term (one year or less) taxable obligations in income based on the number of days the obligation is held during the year. The rule applies on the acquisition of both government obligations and nongovernment obligations. Taxpayers affected by this rule are accrual-method taxpayers, holders of the obligations for sale in the ordinary course of business, banks, regulated investment companies, common trust funds, taxpayers when the short-term obligations are identified as part of a hedging transaction, or taxpayers holding a stripped bond or coupon if they stripped the bond.

Rules similar to those applicable to market discount bonds apply to limit an interest expense deduction if a taxpayer borrows to purchase or carry short-term obligations with acquisition or original issue discount.

Loan fees. Any expense other than interest incurred to borrow funds and any other finance costs are capital expenditures that must be amortized over the life of the loan to which they relate and may not be deducted currently as incurred (IRC Section 263). Examples of such expenses would include commissions and similar fees incurred in order to obtain a loan, legal fees, printing costs, registration fees and other similar costs of issuing bonds, and finder's fees and commissions paid by lenders to locate borrowers.

Chapter 9

Currency gains and losses

Prior to the Tax Reform Act of 1986, U.S. tax law was unclear regarding the character, the timing of recognition, and the source of gain or loss due to fluctuations in the exchange rate of foreign currency. Furthermore, the law contained no rules for determining when the results of a foreign operation could be recorded in a foreign currency and taxpayers would translate foreign currency results into U.S. dollars in a manner inconsistent with general U.S. income tax principles.

Because the law before the 1986 Act provided no clear rules, there was often uncertainty regarding the tax treatment of many legitimate business transactions and opportunities for purely tax-motivated transactions. For instance, the U.S. tax consequences of a transaction that was undertaken to hedge foreign-exchange exposure turned, in large part, on the nature of the financial product used to effect the hedge and whether the hedging transaction related to the taxpayer's own business operations or the business operations of an affiliate. In addition, different tax rates could apply to the positions included in a hedging transaction, with the result that a transaction that produced no economic gain or loss could result in an after-tax profit or loss.

As a result of this state of affairs, Congress decided to try to establish a comprehensive set of rules to govern the U.S. tax treatment of transactions involving foreign currency. The results of this effort were incorporated into the Tax Reform Act of 1986 and are currently contained in Subpart J of the Internal Revenue Code of 1986 (Sections 985 through 989).

Functional currency. Current law reflects the principle that income or loss should be measured in the currency of a taxpayer's primary economic environment and generally adopts the financial accounting concept of functional currency as the basis for determining the amount and timing of recognition of exchange gain or loss. (The financial accounting concept is reflected in FASB Statement Number 52.) Accordingly, the U.S. dollar is the functional currency of most U.S. persons. The law, however, also provides for circumstances in which it is appropriate to measure results of a foreign operation in a foreign currency so that a taxpayer is not required to recognize exchange gain or loss on currency that is not repatriated but is used to pay ordinary and necessary expenses.

Foreign currency transactions. The lack of coherent rules for the treatment of foreign currency transactions resulted in uncertainty over the proper U.S. tax treatment of many treasury instruments. The courts addressed several issues by referring to general U.S. income tax rules that produced anomalous results when applied to exchange gain or loss. For instance, it was held that exchange gain on the repayment of a loan could be treated as income from the discharge of an indebtedness that could be deferred under tax rules applying to a loan forgiveness or settlement at less than the face amount of the debt.

Other issues were treated by old cases that were inconsistent with later case law, but that had not been expressly overruled. For example, precedent existed for both sides of the question of whether exchange gain or loss should be integrated with gain or loss from an underlying transaction. In still other situations, IRS and the courts took contrary positions, such as whether a debtor's exchange gain or loss on repayment of a loan is capital or ordinary in nature.

The new rules adopted by Congress in the Tax Reform Act of 1986 attempt to address these issues and provide uniform rules. Because of their particular importance to the proper tax treatment of the treasury instruments discussed in this work, these rules are considered in some detail in connection with the discussion of the tax treatment of specific treasury instruments under the general heading of "Section 988 Transactions."

Characterizing exchange gain or loss. A loan denominated in a foreign currency may reflect a "true" U.S.-dollar interest rate plus an anticipated annual exchange gain or loss. For example, a U.S. taxpayer who borrows a currency that is considered strong in relation to the dollar would pay less nominal interest than if the taxpayer had borrowed dollars because the lender would expect to be repaid with appreciated currency. Conversely, if the taxpayer borrows currency of a country with a high rate of inflation so that the currency is weak in relation to the dollar, the taxpayer would pay more nominal interest than if dollars had been borrowed. In these situations, at least to the extent expectations on currency movement prove correct or the parties hedge their positions, it is arguable that nominal interest is being either understated or overstated.

This relationship between the dollar price of foreign currency in the forward market and the market interest rate for the currency relative to the dollar supports the idea that exchange gain or loss should be treated as interest income or expense.

On the other hand, there are other factors that affect the stated rate of interest on a foreign currency debt that make it difficult to separate the portion of exchange gain or loss that is equivalent to interest. For instance, in addition to the relative strength of the foreign currency in relation to the dollar, the creditworthiness of the borrower remains a factor in establishing the interest rate on a loan denominated in a foreign currency. What's more, although expectations regarding a currency's future value are material in setting the rate of return on a financial asset or liability, exchange gain or loss could be more or less than expected.

Congress ultimately decided not to adopt the interest equivalency approach in its entirety, but adopted the pragmatic approach of characterizing exchange gain or loss as ordinary income or loss for most purposes. The Secretary of Treasury is authorized to treat exchange gain or loss as interest income or expense in appropriate circumstances, such as in the case of hedging transactions in which a taxpayer's expectations about future exchange rates are locked in.

In one of the first actions under this regulatory authority, the Internal Revenue Service announced that regulations to be prescribed under IRC Sections 988(a)(2) and 989(c) would provide that any foreign currency loss as defined in Section 988(b)(2) attributable to a debt obligation on which interest is excluded from gross income would be treated either as an adjustment to interest income derived from the obligation or as an interest expense subject to IRC Section 265. Accordingly, unless otherwise provided in regulations, any such foreign currency loss is not treated as a loss deductible in determining taxable income. The Internal Revenue Service also announced that for purposes of determining taxable income, regulations will limit the deductibility of foreign currency losses attributable to transactions used to hedge tax-exempt debt obligations. See Announcement 87-57.

Congress also considered whether unanticipated exchange gain or loss on a financial asset or liability should be characterized as capital gain or loss. This approach was not followed because of the difficulty in distinguishing anticipated exchange gain or loss from unanticipated exchange gain or loss. Anticipated exchange gain or loss could be measured with reference to the premium or discount element in a forward contract if one were obtained, but forward contracts are not available in all currencies and do not trade at all maturities. Even when anticipated exchange gain or loss can be determined, current law simply treats all such gain or loss as ordinary income or loss to reduce discontinuities in the law. Obviously, the elimination of the preferential rates for capital gain that was also part of the 1986 Tax Reform Act played a part in this decision since this reduced the importance of capital gain characterization, as discussed above.

Of course, no rule, especially a tax rule, is complete without its exception and the rule characterizing exchange gain or loss as ordinary is no exception. A limited exception to the ordinary income or loss characterization is provided for certain contracts that constitute capital assets in the hands of the taxpayer and are properly identified as speculative investments.

Summary. The brief discussion here, of course, in no way represents a full discussion of the comprehensive rules regarding foreign currency transactions enacted as part of the Tax Reform Act of 1986. Rather, the effort merely represents a presentation of the more salient points of the law as it affects treasury instruments. The reader also is cautioned that the law as it now stands does not represent a complete body of law, but merely a statutory outline that will take years to flesh out through the regulatory and judicial processes.

In summary, then, new Subpart J of the Internal Revenue Code provides a consistent set of rules for the treatment of all foreign currency denominated transactions and not simply those represented by certain treasury instruments. The tax treatment of any foreign currency denominated transaction turns on the identity of the taxpayer's functional currency. Exchange gain or loss is recognized on a transaction-by-transaction basis only in the case of transactions involving certain financial assets or liabilities that are denominated in a nonfunctional currency. These are referred to as "Section 988 Transactions" and are more fully discussed below.

In the case of Section 988 transactions, exchange gain or loss generally is treated as ordinary income or loss. To the extent provided in regulations, exchange gain or loss on certain hedging instruments is characterized and sourced in a manner that is consistent with the related exposure, and a portion of the unrealized exchange gain or loss on Section 988 transactions is accrued currently. Section 988 hedging transactions also are more fully explored in connection with the discussion of specific treasury instruments presented below in this chapter.

In addition to the foregoing, Subpart J provides a uniform set of criteria for determining the currency in which the results of a foreign operation should be recorded. Business entities using a functional currency other than the U.S. dollar generally must use a profit-and-loss translation method. Exchange gain or loss on a remittance from a branch is treated as ordinary income or loss, and sourced or allocated by reference to the income giving rise to post-1986 accumulated earnings. A consistent set of rules applies to the translation of foreign taxes and related adjustments.

Users of treasury instruments

The U.S. tax code, for the most part, does not distinguish between taxpayers based on their taxable activities. Generally, the same corporate tax rules apply to all corporations subject to U.S. taxation, and the same individual tax rules apply to all individuals subject to U.S. taxation. Nevertheless, there are some taxpayers for which special tax rules are provided that vary or alter the usual treatment. Special tax treatment for certain categories of users of treasury instruments is outlined in the following brief discussion.

Banks and financial institutions

For the most part, banks, mutual or stock savings associations, and other financial institutions are taxed in the same fashion as regular business corporations, subject to some special rules contained in IRC Sections 581 through 596.

Commercial banks and trust companies. The sale or exchange of a bond, debenture, note, or certificate or other evidence of indebtedness is not considered the sale or exchange of a capital asset. Accordingly, all gains and losses resulting from the sale or exchange of these instruments are considered ordinary income and loss.

No deduction is allowed for interest paid or accrued by a bank that is allocable to tax-exempt obligations acquired after August 7, 1986. In the case of tax-exempt obligations acquired before August 8, 1986, a bank, unlike other taxpayers, is permitted to deduct interest on debt attributable to the purchase or carrying of obligations on which interest is exempt from U.S. tax. The interest deduction is reduced by 20%, however, to the extent it is attributable to tax-exempt obligations acquired after 1982.

Mutual savings banks. The same ordinary income and loss rule that applies to commercial banks applies to mutual banks and savings associations on the sale or exchange of bonds and other debt instruments.

Mutual savings banks and similar institutions are entitled to deduct amounts paid or credited to depositors or holders of accounts either as dividends or interest on their deposits or withdrawable accounts. No deduction is allowed, however, for interest paid to the extent it is allocable to tax-exempt obligations.

Common trust funds. Common trust funds maintained by banks and trust companies in order to hold money in the capacity of trustee, executor, administrator, guardian, or custodian are not subject to tax. Rather, the amount of income or loss attributable to each participant is taxed as if received directly by each participant. Capital gains and losses must be segregated and reported separately to each participant.

Regulated investment companies (mutual funds)

Regulated investment companies, commonly called mutual funds, are those companies that meet the definition contained in IRC Section 851. Special tax rules are provided in Sections 852 through 855.

Generally, a regulated investment company is taxed only on its undistributed income. The undistributed portion of its ordinary net income is taxed at the regular corporate rates. To qualify for this limited tax, a regulated investment company must distribute as dividends at least 90% of its "investment company taxable income" and 90% of its "net income from tax-exempt obligations." Keep in mind, though, that an RIC will be subject to regular corporate income taxes to the extent that it does not distribute 100% of its income, including net long-term capital gains.

After 1986, a 4% excise tax is imposed on any excess of the required distribution for the year over the distributed amount for the year (IRC Section 4982). The required distribution of a regulated investment company under this provision is the sum of 97% of the regulated investment company's ordinary income for the calendar year, plus 98% of the regulated investment company's capital gain net income for the one-year period ending on October 31 of that calendar year.

Tax-exempt organizations

Organizations that are exempt from U.S. tax, such as charitable, educational, and religious organizations, and various pension funds and other employee trusts, are not usually concerned with the tax treatment of income and expenses. The main concern of these organizations in the use of treasury instruments is that the use does not produce "unrelated business income" or "debt financed income" on which regular taxes are imposed. The rules relating to the taxation of otherwise tax-exempt organizations are contained in IRC Sections 511 through 515.

All exempt organizations are taxed on their income from any unrelated business activity. A trade or business is unrelated if it is not related to the exercise or performance of the purpose or function that is the basis of the organization's tax exemption. Specifically excluded from income subject to tax under the unrelated business income rule are all dividends, interest, payments with respect to securities loans, and annuities. Also excluded are all gains and losses from the sale, exchange, or other disposition of property other than inventory and property held for sale to customers in the ordinary course of business. Also excluded are gains on the lapse or termination of options, written by the organization in connection with its investment activities, to buy or sell securities.

Taxation of specific treasury instruments

As has been previously noted, the tax classification of specific treasury instruments does not necessarily follow the common commercial divisions of these instruments. Rather, the tax classification and treatment generally follow the function that a specific instrument is serving. For instance, the tax classification and treatment of a currency contract can differ depending on whether the contract is entered into as a matter of speculation or in order to hedge an exposed position. Also, as noted in the discussion of general tax principles, a special set of rules applies in the case of transactions involving foreign currencies. Accordingly, the discussion of the tax consequences of specific treasury instruments is divided into the following categories:

1. Interest-rate swaps.
2. Options, straddles, and Section 1092.
3. Section 1256 contracts.
4. Section 988 transactions.
5. Qualified Section 988 hedges.

Interest-rate swaps

In an interest-rate swap, two parties agree to service each others' debt obligations to third parties. For example, one borrower may incur fixed-rate debt and another floating-rate debt, then each will pay the other periodic amounts determined by reference to the other's liability to its lender. Interest-rate swaps generally are used to match interest-rate exposures on the financial asset and financial liability sides of a balance sheet. Cross-currency interest rate swaps, that is, mutual agreements to service equivalent amounts of debt denominated in different currencies, may be used to match both interest and currency exposures when a taxpayer's balance sheet contains foreign currency denominated financial assets or liabilities.

Although swap payments in an interest-rate swap are measured by interest payments, they are not treated as interest because they are not paid as compensation for the use or forebearance of money. In *Revenue Ruling 87-5*, the Internal Revenue Service held that, in a cross-border U.S.-dollar denominated interest-rate swap between a U.S. person and a Netherlands bank, the payments received by the bank resulted in industrial and commercial profits exempt from U.S. tax under the U.S.–Netherlands Income Tax Convention, and not interest income.

Notice 87-4 contains source rules for U.S. income tax purposes of income and expense attributable to U.S.-dollar denominated interest-rate swaps when one party has its residence in the United States and has the U.S.-dollar as its functional currency.

Generally, swap income is sourced by reference to the residence of the recipient of the swap income. However, all swap income attributable to a U.S. trade or business is sourced in the United States and effectively connected to the U.S. trade or business. A taxpayer's swap expense attributable to a swap agreement is directly related to the class of gross income from the swap agreement. For example, in the case of a swap agreement that would generate U.S. source swap income, swap expense attributable to that transaction is allocated to the class of gross swap income from that agreement and apportioned to U.S. source income.

The Internal Revenue Service, in issuing *Notice 87-4*, took no position on whether swap income is "other fixed or determinable annual or periodical income" for purposes of withholding on cross-border interest-rate swap agreements. Accordingly, the Internal Revenue Service may assert that swap income is "fixed or determinable annual or periodical."

The preceding discussion applies to "swap income" and "swap payments." In the case of a cross-currency interest-rate swap agreement, there may be currency gain or loss as well as swap income or expense. Currency gain or loss, of course, is treated separately under the rules of Section 988 discussed below.

Options, straddles, and Section 1092

Options. For the most part, the tax treatment of option contracts is the same regardless of whether the particular option contract is a listed option (one traded on an established exchange) or an unlisted option. Options produce a direct tax effect only if they are sold, allowed to lapse, or terminated in a closing transaction through the purchase of an offsetting position. See IRC Section 1234.

Generally, the purchaser of an option realizes gain or loss on the sale of the option and the character of that gain or loss (capital or ordinary) is determined by the character of the underlying property. An option that is allowed to expire by its purchaser is treated as if it were sold on the date of expiration. If the purchaser of an option exercises the option, the amount paid for the option is treated as an adjustment to the price of the underlying property. The amount paid for a call option is considered part of the purchase price of the property on exercise, and the amount paid for a put option is considered a reduction in the amount received from the purchaser of the underlying property on exercise.

The writer of an option is not taxed on the receipt of any payment for granting the option. Rather, tax consequences are deferred until the option is exercised, terminated, or allowed to lapse by the holder of the option. Generally, the writer of an option recognizes a short-term capital gain if the option expires without being exercised. If the writer terminates a listed call through the purchase of an identical call in a closing transaction, the difference between the amount received and the amount paid to close the transaction is treated as a short-term capital gain or loss.

The writer of a put option who purchases the underlying property on the exercise of the put reduces the purchase price of the property for tax purposes by the amount received for writing the put option. The writer of a call option who sells the underlying property on the exercise of the call is treated as if he received both the option price and the amount received for the call option in exchange for the underlying property.

Straddles. Specific statutory rules contained in IRC Section 1092 prevent the use of "straddles" to defer income or to convert ordinary income or short-term capital gain into long-term capital gain.

In general, a tax straddle is defined as offsetting positions with respect to personal property. A "position" is defined to include any interest, including a futures or forward contract or option, in personal property of a type that is actively traded. An obligor's interest in a nonfunctional currency denominated debt obligation is treated as a position in the nonfunctional currency. A foreign currency for which there is an active interbank market is presumed to be actively traded. Positions are offsetting if there is a substantial diminution in the risk of loss from holding one position by reason of holding one or more other positions in personal property.

If a taxpayer realizes a loss on the disposition of one or more positions in a straddle, the amount of the loss that can be deducted is limited to the excess of the loss over any unrecognized gain in offsetting positions as of the end of the tax year. In addition, taxpayers generally must capitalize expenditures incurred to purchase or carry property that is part of a straddle. A current deduction for these expenditures is permitted only to the extent of income received with respect to the property (the capitalization rule is in IRC Section 263(g)).

Example

X, a taxpayer with a tax year ending July 31, establishes offsetting positions in Treasury bills and interest-rate futures in June of the current year. X disposes of its loss position in July at a loss of $1,000. At year's end, the offsetting gain position is open and X would realize a gain of $600 on this position if it were sold on July 31. X may take into account only $400 of its realized $1,000 loss on the position offset by the gain position that remains open. Recognition of the remaining $600 loss is deferred until the offsetting gain position is disposed of. If X continues to hold its gain position throughout the following year, additional deferred loss may be taken into account if the amount of unrecognized gain is less than $600 at that time.

Mixed straddles. In general, the loss deferral rule of Section 1092 discussed above applies to a straddle composed of both Section 1256 contracts (usually subject to the marked-to-market rules as discussed below) and positions that are not marked-to-market. The Section 1256 contracts in a mixed straddle are excluded from the mark-to-market treatment if the taxpayer designates the positions as a mixed straddle by the close of the day on which the first Section 1256 contract is acquired. A taxpayer can elect to treat gains and losses from mixed straddles using either straddle-by-straddle identification or mixed straddle accounts.

If a taxpayer elects straddle-by-straddle identification, by clearly identifying each position that is part of the identified mixed straddle before the end of the day on which the straddle is established, special rules are used to net gains and losses from the offsetting positions. These special rules may be summarized as follows:

1. When all positions of an identified mixed straddle are disposed of on the same day, net gain or loss for Section 1256 contracts and net gain or loss for non-Section 1256 contracts are determined separately. The net gain or loss from the Section 1256 contracts is then used to offset net gain or loss from the non-Section 1256 contracts to arrive at a net gain or loss figure for the identified straddle. This net gain or

loss from the straddle is treated as 60% long-term and 40% short-term gain or loss if the magnitude of the gain or loss from the Section 1256 contracts exceeds the magnitude of the gain or loss from the non-Section 1256 contracts. The net gain or loss from the straddle is treated as a short-term capital gain or loss if the magnitude of the gain or loss from the non-Section 1256 contracts exceeds the magnitude of the gain or loss from Section 1256 contracts.

2. If all non-Section 1256 contracts in a mixed straddle are disposed of on the same day, net gain or loss from the straddle is determined as above in (1), but unrealized gains or losses on the Section 1256 contracts are taken into account as well as the recognized gains or losses. The net gain or loss on the straddle attributable to the non-Section 1256 contracts is treated as short-term capital gain or loss on that day. Net gain or loss attributable to realized gain or loss on Section 1256 contracts is recognized and treated as 60% long-term and 40% short-term capital gain or loss. Gain or loss subsequently realized on the Section 1256 contracts is adjusted to reflect the extent to which gain or loss on non-Section 1256 positions was offset by unrealized gain or loss on the Section 1256 contracts.

3. If all Section 1256 contracts in an identified mixed straddle are disposed of on the same day, net gain or loss is computed as above including both realized and unrealized gains and losses on that day from the non-Section 1256 positions. Net gain or loss from the Section 1256 contracts is treated as short-term capital gain or loss to the extent of net realized and unrealized gain or loss on the non-Section 1256 positions on that day. Any excess gain or loss on the Section 1256 contracts is characterized by the 60%-40% rule.

4. If one or more but not all positions of an identified mixed straddle are disposed of in one day, either rule (2) or (3) above will apply based on the net gain or loss from the positions actually disposed of. If net gain or loss is attributable to Section 1256 contracts, rule (3) applies; and if net gain or loss is attributable to non-Section 1256 positions, rule (2) applies.

Special rules contained in Temporary Income Tax Regulations 1.1092(b)-3T(b)(2)-(7) further define the proper tax treatment of mixed straddles under the straddle-by-straddle identification method.

A mixed straddle account is merely an account for determining gains and losses from all positions held as capital assets in a designated class of activities. Use of a mixed straddle account is based on an election that is effective for the entire tax year. A separate account must be established for each class of activities.

Gains and losses in a mixed straddle account are determined each day by marking the positions in the account to market. Both realized and unrealized gains and losses are treated in a fashion similar to gains and losses from identified mixed straddles under rule (1) above, but special rules are provided if both Section 1256 contracts and non-Section 1256 positions yield net gains or losses (see Temporary Income Tax Regulations 1.1092(b)-4T(b)). Generally, the annual net gain or loss for each account is determined by netting the gains and losses for each business day of the year. No more than 50% of total annual account net gain may be treated as long-term capital gain (the balance of net gain is treated as short-term gain). If the annual net result is a loss, no more than 40% of the total annual account net loss may be treated as short-term capital loss (the balance is treated as a long-term loss).

Hedges. Certain hedging transactions are exempt from the loss deferral rule of Section 1092 and the capitalization requirement of Section 263(g), as well as the mark-to-market rules of Section 1256 discussed below. These hedging transactions are those transactions that are executed in the normal course of a trade or business primarily to reduce the risk of (1) price changes or foreign currency exchange rate fluctuations with respect to property held or to be held by the taxpayer, or (2) interest-rate or price changes, or foreign currency exchange rate fluctuations with respect to borrowings or obligations of the taxpayer.

Hedging transactions must be clearly identified before the close of the day the transactions are entered into. Gain or loss from these bona fide hedging transactions is treated only as ordinary income or loss.

Section 1256 contracts

Contracts that are classified as Section 1256 contracts by the Internal Revenue Code are treated as if they are sold on the last business day of the year (marked-to-market). Any gain or loss on a Section 1256 contract marked-to-market is treated as 40% short-term capital gain or loss and 60% long-term capital gain or loss. A Section 1256 contract is:

1. Any regulated futures contract.
2. Any foreign currency contract.
3. Any nonequity options.
4. Any dealer equity option.

Each of these terms has a special definition and these are set out below. Note that forward contracts with maturities longer than the maturities for regulated futures contracts constitute Section 1256 contracts if all the other requirements of Section 1256 are satisfied. All other forward contracts are taxed under the normal ordinary/capital gain or loss rules.

A regulated futures contract is a contract on which the amount required to be deposited and the amount that may be withdrawn depend on a system of marking-to-market and which is traded on or subject to the rules of a qualified board or exchange. A qualified board or exchange is one registered with the Securities Exchange Commission, designated as a contract market by the Commodities Futures Trading Commission, or any other exchange, board of trade, or other market that the Treasury Secretary determines has rules adequate to carry out the purposes of Section 1256.

A foreign currency contract is a contract that:

1. requires delivery of, or the settlement of which depends on the value of, a foreign currency which is a currency in which positions are also traded through regulated futures contracts;
2. is traded in the interbank market; and
3. is entered into at arm's length at a price determined by reference to the price in the interbank market.

Nonequity options are any listed options on commodities, debt instruments and broad-based stock indexes which are designated by the CFTC or determined to be qualified for CFTC designation. (See also IRC Section 1256(g) 6(A) and (B).

A dealer equity option is, with respect to an options dealer, an option to buy or sell stock (or an option on which value is determined by reference to stock or a stock index), which is purchased or granted by an options dealer in the normal course of his activity of dealing in options and is listed on the qualified board or exchange on which the option dealer is registered.

Exceptions. Contracts that otherwise meet the definition of Section 1256 contracts are not subject to the marked-to-market rules if they are part of a bona fide hedge. Gain or loss on a bona fide hedging transaction is treated as ordinary income or loss when realized. This hedging exception applies to a transaction if it is entered into by the taxpayer in the normal course of the taxpayer's trade or business primarily (1) to reduce the risk of price change or currency fluctuations with respect to property that is held by the taxpayer, or (2) to reduce risk of interest-rate or price changes or currency fluctuations with respect to borrowings made or to be made, or obligations incurred or to be incurred, by the taxpayer. A bona fide hedge must be identified before the close of the day on which the transaction is entered into.

If a Section 1256 contract is part of a mixed straddle, as discussed above in connection with straddles and Section 1092, the Section 1256 contract is treated according to the mixed straddle rules at the election of the taxpayer.

Mutual Offset System. In *Revenue Ruling 87-43*, the Internal Revenue Service considered whether contracts that are established under the Mutual Offset System between the Chicago Mercantile Exchange and the Singapore International Monetary Exchange Limited are considered traded on or subject to the rules of the exchange that assumes the contract for purposes of Section 1256 of the Internal Revenue Code.

The Chicago Mercantile Exchange (CME) is a qualified board or exchange so that contracts traded on the exchange are subject to the mark-to-market rules of Section 1256. The Singapore International Monetary Exchange Limited (SIMEX) is a foreign board of trade that is not a qualified board or exchange under Section 1256.

The Mutual Offset System between the CME and the SIMEX provides an interexchange clearing process by which customers can establish new positions or offset existing positions on one exchange, during hours in which that exchange is closed for trading, by the execution of a contract on the other exchange. The System was designed to provide investors with the economic benefits of extended trading hours while reducing the price risks and transaction costs inherent in trading on two autonomous exchanges.

Under the System, a customer initially places an order to execute a futures or option contract with a clearing member of the exchange to which the contract will ultimately be transferred (Origination Exchange). The clearing member for the Origination Exchange then transfers the order to a clearing member of the exchange where the trade will be executed (Execution Exchange). After the contract is cleared on the Execution Exchange, the contract is transferred to the Origination Exchange through an interexchange clearing process. The Origination Exchange automatically assumes the transferred contract, usually before the next trading day of the Execution Exchange. Thereafter, the contract is subject to and treated under the rules of the Origination Exchange as if it had been originally executed on that exchange without using the System. Once an order to execute a futures or option contract is placed in the System, it cannot be removed from the System except in situations when the contract cannot be cleared successfully.

The Internal Revenue Service ruled that futures contracts or option contracts established under the System are treated as traded on or subject to the rules of the Origination Exchange for purposes of Section 1256 of the Internal Revenue Code. Thus, contracts executed on the SIMEX and assumed by the CME under the System are treated as traded on or subject to the rules of a qualified board or exchange and are Section 1256 contracts. By contrast, contracts executed on the CME and assumed by the SIMEX under the System are not treated as traded on or subject to the rules of a qualified board or exchange and are not Section 1256 contracts.

Section 988 transactions

Internal Revenue Code Section 988, which was enacted as part of the Tax Reform Act of 1986, prescribes rules for the treatment of exchange gain or loss from transactions denominated in a currency other than a taxpayer's functional currency. For taxpayers using the U.S.

dollar as a functional currency, the new law retained the pre-1986 Act principles under which the disposition of foreign currency results in the recognition of gain or loss and partially retained principles treating exchange gain or loss separately from any gain or loss attributable to the underlying transaction.

The Tax Reform Act of 1986 also introduced a new category of gain or loss, called "foreign currency gain or loss" that governs the extent to which exchange gains or losses are recognized. In addition, pre-1986 Act law was modified regarding the character, source, and, in limited circumstances, the timing of recognition or exchange gain or loss. Under current law, foreign currency denominated items are translated into U.S. dollars using the exchange rate that most properly reflects income, which is generally the free market rate.

Section 988 transactions defined. Section 988 transactions are certain transactions in which the amount required to be paid or entitled to be received is denominated in a nonfunctional currency, or is determined by reference to the value of one or more nonfunctional currencies. Section 988 transactions are:

1. The acquisition of, or becoming the obligor under, a debt instrument
2. Accruing or otherwise taking into account any item of expense or gross income or receipt that is to be paid or received on a later date
3. Entering into or acquiring any forward contract, option, or similar financial instrument, such as a currency swap, *unless* the instrument is subject to the mark-to-market rules of Section 1256
4. The disposition of nonfunctional currency

A Section 988 transaction does not have to require or even permit repayment with a nonfunctional currency, as long as the amount paid or received is determined by reference to the value of a nonfunctional currency. Regulations are expected that will exclude certain transactions from the scope of Section 988 that do not have to be included in order to carry out the purposes of Section 988. Examples of items that may be excluded are trade receivables and payables that have a maturity of 120 days or less, and any other receivable or payable with a maturity of six months or less that would be eligible for exclusion under the

Original Issue Discount rules (Internal Revenue Code Section 1274). When regulations are issued, they will prescribe rules for determining the character, source, and timing of exchange gain or loss on excluded transactions.

Ordinary income or loss. In general, foreign currency gain or loss attributable to a Section 988 transaction is computed separately and treated as ordinary income or loss. Except as otherwise provided in regulations that may be issued, capital gain or loss treatment may be elected for forward contracts, futures contracts, and options that are capital assets in the hands of the taxpayer, are not marked-to-market under Section 1256, are not parts of a tax straddle, and meet certain identification requirements. In circumstances to be identified in regulations, foreign currency gain or loss may be treated as interest income or expense. Qualified Section 988 hedges, separately discussed below, fall into this last category.

Foreign currency gain or loss is defined as gain or loss on a Section 988 transaction, but only to the extent the gain or loss is realized because of a change in exchange rates between the date an asset or liability is taken into account for tax purposes (the ''booking date'') and the date it is paid or otherwise disposed of, and only to the extent there is gain or loss derived from the transaction as a whole. This definition applies to gain or loss attributable to exchange rate movements affecting the value of forward contracts or similar instruments, regardless of the particular transaction in which the gain or loss is realized. Accordingly, although a taxpayer may have a net gain on a Section 988 transaction, there is no foreign currency gain if none of the gain is due to changes in the exchange rate between the functional and nonfunctional currencies. On the other hand, if the transaction involves acquisition of an asset denominated in a currency that subsequently appreciates, there is no foreign currency gain if the asset is sold at an overall loss.

Example

Assume a taxpayer whose functional currency is the U.S. dollar acquires a pound sterling debt instrument that is not part of a Section 988 hedging transaction for £100 when the exchange rate is £1 = $1. If the taxpayer sells the obligation for £200 when the exchange rate is £1 =

$2, $100 of the taxpayer's $300 gain ($400 sales price less $100 basis) is foreign currency gain. This is calculated by multiplying the difference in exchange rates expressed in dollars per pound between the booking date and the payment date ($1 per pound) by the original sterling price of the instrument (£100). If the exchange rate at the time of sale were £1 = $.50, the taxpayer would have no gain or loss on the Section 988 transaction and thus no foreign currency gain or loss because there would be no gain or loss from the transaction as a whole. If the exchange rate were £1 = $.75, the taxpayer would have a $50 gain on the Section 988 transaction but still no "foreign currency gain" because none of the gain would be realized from changes in the exchange rate. Rather, the gain would be realized despite the unfavorable change in the exchange rate. If the exchange rate were £1 = $.25, the taxpayer would have a $50 loss, all of which would be a foreign currency loss.

Income from discharge of indebtedness. In *Kentucky & Indiana Terminal Railroad* (CA-6, 330 F. 2d 520, 1964), the court held that exchange gain realized by virtue of repayment of a foreign currency borrowing with depreciated currency should be characterized as income from the discharge of an indebtedness. The rules of Section 988 eliminate this type of treatment. Gain realized on repayment of a borrowing is attributed first to foreign currency gain by calculating the difference between the U.S.-dollar value of the loan proceeds when borrowed and when discharged, and only the balance is treated as income from discharge of indebtedness. This result is just one example of the general rule that, to the extent that gain or loss is derived from a transaction, it is attributed first to the effect of movements in exchange rates on the value of the units of nonfunctional currency originally booked by the taxpayer.

Example

Assume a taxpayer whose functional currency is the U.S. dollar borrows £100 sterling, on a note for that amount, when the pound is worth $1. The taxpayer later buys back the note for £80 after the pound has fallen to $.50. The gain from the transaction is $60. The change in the U.S.-dollar value of the pounds borrowed, measured from the date of issuance to the date of discharge of the note, is $50. Thus, $10 of the gain is income from the discharge of indebtedness.

Calculation of original issue discount. Although a taxpayer is generally required to make U.S. income tax determinations in its functional currency, regulations are expected to provide an exception to this rule for the determination of original issue discount (OID) on an obligation. Pending issuance of regulations, however, OID on an obligation denominated in a nonfunctional currency for any accrual period will be determined in that nonfunctional currency, and translated into the taxpayer's functional currency based on the average exchange rate in effect during the accrual period. The functional currency amount of the OID deducted for any accrual period is treated as the amount of functional currency added to the borrowing on account of the OID (to determine the adjusted issue price), for purposes of determining the amount of gain or loss realized when the borrowing is repaid. Similar rules will be prescribed for the calculation of bond premium.

Example

On December 31, 1988, a taxpayer using the U.S. dollar as its functional currency issues for 85.82 Deutsche marks (DM) a bond that provides for semiannual coupons of DM1 and a final payment at maturity, on December 31, 1990, of DM100.00. The exchange rate on the date of issuance is $.25/DM, so the amount of the borrowing in the taxpayer's functional currency initially is $21.45. The yield to maturity of the obligation, in terms of DM, is 5% semiannually.

The accrual period is six months, commencing with the date of issuance. At the end of the first accrual period, on June 30, 1989, the first DM1 coupon is paid. Stated interest payments are translated at the exchange rate in effect on the payment date. If the DM appreciates to $.35 at the end of the first accrual period, the dollar amount of stated interest is $.35. Accrued OID is DM3.29 (5% of DM85.82, less stated interest of DM1). This amount is translated into dollars using the average exchange rate during the accrual period. If the average value of the DM during the first accrual period is $.30, then the dollar amount of OID accrued on June 30, 1989 is $.99 (DM3.29 times $.30/DM). The taxpayer deducts the dollar amount of accrued OID (in addition to interest paid translated at the payment date) and increases its dollar basis in the bond by the same amount (from $21.45 to $22.44).

As a result of the appreciation of the DM, the taxpayer has an unrecognized currency loss of $8.75, the difference between the dollar basis of the bond, $22.44, and the DM basis translated at the current exchange rate, $31.19 (DM89.11 times $.35/DM). This currency loss is not recognized until the taxpayer discharges its indebtedness. The currency loss is treated as an ordinary loss, and is sourced by reference to the issuer's residence.

Special rule for certain investments. Except for a transaction that is part of a Section 988 hedging transaction as discussed below, Section 988 did not change the treatment of bank forward contracts or regulated futures contracts that are marked-to-market under Section 1256. (Note that the Technical and Miscellaneous Revenue Act of 1988 (TAMRA) provides certain taxpayers with an election to treat certain Section 1256 contracts as 988 transactions. The election applies to foreign currency-related regulated futures contracts and nonequity options which would otherwise be marked-to-market under Section 1256.) Section 988 does provide a special rule for certain financial instruments that are not marked-to-market (because, for example, they are traded on a foreign board or exchange that is not a qualified board or exchange under the rules of Section 1256) but are held for speculation. These instruments are given capital gain or loss treatment if:

1. They constitute capital assets.
2. Are not parts of a tax straddle (Section 1092(c)), without regard to the exception for qualified covered calls.
3. The taxpayer properly identifies them and elects capital treatment.

Identification must be made before the close of the day the transaction is entered into or some earlier time if required by regulations. TAMRA 1988 provides special rules for transactions in forward contracts options and similar instruments held by certain partnerships with "qualified funds."

Qualified Section 988 hedges

Section 988 authorizes the issuance of regulations that address the treatment of transactions that are part of a Section 988 hedging transaction. Congress included this regulatory authority to provide certainty of tax treatment for foreign currency hedging transactions, such as fully hedged foreign currency borrowing, and to ensure that such a transaction is taxed in accordance with its economic substance.

Although actual regulations under this authority have not been issued as of this writing, the Internal Revenue Service has announced (in *Notice 87-11*) that it will issue regulations that will set forth the consequences of integrating and treating as a single transaction all transactions that comprise a fully hedged Section 988 hedging transaction that is an integrated economic package. The regulations, when issued, generally will follow the provisions announced in *Notice 87-11* and will integrate a Section 988 hedging transaction only with respect to the taxpayer that enters into the transaction. Until regulations actually are issued, taxpayers are entitled to rely on *Notice 87-11*, which is summarized in the following discussion.

In general, if a transaction constitutes a qualified Section 988 hedging transaction, the qualifying transaction and the hedge are integrated and treated as a single transaction with respect to the taxpayer that has entered into the qualified hedging transaction. Neither the qualifying transaction nor the hedge that make up the qualified hedging transaction are subject to the capitalization rules of Section 263(g), the loss deferral rules of Section 1092, or the mark-to-market rules of Section 1256.

In the following discussion, *trade date* is the one calendar day on which both the interest rate on a qualifying transaction that is a borrowing under a debt instrument or the rate of return on a qualifying transaction that is the purchase of a debt instrument is set, and all exchange rates on the hedge are fixed. *Settlement date* is the first calendar day on which (1) with respect to a qualifying transaction that is a borrowing, proceeds of the borrowing are credited to the taxpayer's account, otherwise made available so that the taxpayer may draw upon such proceeds at any time, or actually received by the taxpayer, or (2) with respect to a qualifying transaction that is the purchase of a debt instrument, the debt instrument is available for delivery to the taxpayer or is credited to the taxpayer's account.

Qualified hedging transactions. A qualified hedging transaction is an integrated economic package, consisting of a qualifying transaction and a Section 988 hedge, if:

1. The interest rate on the qualifying transaction is set and all exchange rates on the Section 988 hedge are fixed on the same calendar day (the trade date) such that the cost or return with respect to the qualified hedging transaction is not affected by movements in exchange rates after the trade date
2. All transactions that comprise the qualified hedging transaction are entered into on or before the settlement date.

A *qualifying transaction* that makes up part of a qualifying hedging transaction is a borrowing under a debt instrument or the purchase of a debt instrument if the entire amount that the taxpayer is required to pay or is entitled to receive as a result of the transaction is either:

1. Denominated in terms of a functional currency.
2. Denominated in terms of a nonfunctional currency.

A qualifying transaction does not include a borrowing under a debt instrument if the payment or receipt of interest and principal is denominated in more than one currency.

A *Section 988 hedge* that makes up the second part of a qualifying hedging transaction is a spot contract, a swap agreement or agreements, forward contract, series of forward contracts, or combination thereof that fixes the cost or return with respect to a qualifying transaction or transactions in terms of a currency other than the currency in which the qualifying transaction is denominated such that the cost or return is not affected by movements in exchange rates after the trade date.

A qualifying transaction and a hedge are an *integrated economic package* so that there is a qualifying hedging transaction if:

1. The qualifying transaction and the hedge are a package as defined below
2. The qualifying transaction and the hedge make up one of the economically integrated transactions specifically enumerated in *Notice 87-11*. (These economically integrated transactions are set out below along with their particular income tax effects.)

A qualifying transaction and a hedge are a *package* if all of the following requirements are met:

1. The interest rate on a qualifying transaction that is a borrowing under a debt instrument or the rate of return on a qualifying transaction that is the purchase or a debt instrument is set, and the exchange rates on the hedge are fixed, on the trade date.
2. None of the parties to the qualifying transaction or hedge are related.
3. The requirements for identifying the qualifying hedging transaction on the taxpayer's books and records contained in Section 3 of *Notice 87-11* are met.
4. Except in the case of a qualified hedging transaction that effectively converts the purchase of a functional currency denominated debt instrument into a nonfunctional currency denominated debt instrument, the total initial amount borrowed under a debt instrument or the total initial amount paid to acquire a debt instrument that is the qualifying transaction is hedged at an exchange rate determined on the trade date.
5. All subsequent interest and principal amounts paid with respect to a qualifying transaction that is a borrowing or all subsequent interest and principal amounts received with respect to a qualifying transaction that is the purchase of a debt instrument are hedged throughout the term of the qualifying transaction at an exchange rate determined on the trade date.
6. The qualifying transaction matures on the same day the hedge expires. (A hedge expires on the last day a payment is made or received under the terms of the hedge.)
7. In the case of a qualified business unit with a residence (as defined in Internal Revenue Code Section 988(a)(3)(B)), outside of the United States, or a qualified business unit resident in the United States with a functional currency other than the dollar, both the qualifying transaction and the hedge are entered into by the same qualified business unit and the interest income or expense from the qualified hedging transaction is properly reflected on the books of such qualified business unit throughout the term of the qualified hedging transaction.
8. Subject to the limitations in (7), both the qualifying transaction and the hedge are entered into by the same individual, partnership, trust, estate, or corporation. With respect to a corporation, the same

corporation must enter into both the qualifying transaction and the hedge whether or not the corporation is a member of an affiliated group of corporations that files a consolidated return.

9. With respect to a foreign person engaged in a U.S. trade or business that enters into a qualifying transaction or hedge through such trade or business, all items of income and expense associated with the qualifying transaction and the hedge, would have been effectively connected with the U.S. trade or business throughout the term of the qualified hedging transaction had the provisions of *Notice 87-11* not applied.

The economically integrated transactions and the tax effects of integration. The following are the economically integrated transactions enumerated in *Notice 87-11* and the tax effects of integrating and treating a transaction as a single transaction.

I. QUALIFIED HEDGING TRANSACTION THAT EFFECTIVELY CONVERTS A NON-FUNCTIONAL CURRENCY BORROWING INTO A FUNCTIONAL CURRENCY BORROWING. A nonfunctional currency borrowing is effectively converted into a functional currency borrowing if:

1. The entire principal amount of nonfunctional currency received from the borrowing is sold or exchanged for functional currency on the settlement date at a rate fixed on the trade date
2. The terms of the hedge provide for the acquisition of the borrowed nonfunctional currency, in exchange for functional currency, on the calendar day when interest and principal payments are due on the borrowing and in an amount that equals such interest and principal payments.

The **tax effects** are as follows:

1. *Deemed functional currency borrowing.* The integration of the non-functional currency denominated borrowing and the hedge results in a deemed functional currency borrowing with respect to the borrower. The amount deemed to be borrowed equals the total amount of

functional currency received under the terms of the hedge in exchange for the total amount of the nonfunctional currency borrowed. The total amount of interest and principal deemed to be paid equals the total amount of functional currency paid under the terms of the hedge to acquire the nonfunctional currency necessary to make interest and principal payments on the nonfunctional currency borrowing.

2. *Determination of interest expense of the borrower.* The interest expense deductible by the borrower is determined as follows:

   (a) The issue price and stated redemption price at maturity of the deemed functional currency borrowing is determined under the provisions of Section 1273 and the regulations thereunder in units of the functional currency.

   (b) If the deemed functional currency borrowing has OID, then the rules of Section 163(e) govern the manner in which the discount is deductible by the borrower.

   (c) Any interest expense other than OID with respect to the deemed functional currency borrowing is deductible from gross income under Section 163(a) (subject to any limitations on deductibility contained in other sections of the Internal Revenue Code) in accordance with the borrower's regular method of accounting.

3. *Allocation and apportionment of interest expense.* The interest expense determined under (2) above is allocated and apportioned under Sections 1.861-8 and 1.882-5 of the regulations, subject to Section 864(e) of the Internal Revenue Code.

II. QUALIFIED HEDGING TRANSACTION THAT EFFECTIVELY CONVERTS A BORROWING IN ONE NONFUNCTIONAL CURRENCY INTO A BORROWING IN A SECOND NONFUNCTIONAL CURRENCY. A borrowing in one nonfunctional currency is effectively converted into a borrowing in a second nonfunctional currency if:

1. The entire principal amount of the first nonfunctional currency received from the borrowing is sold or exchanged for a second nonfunctional currency on the settlement date at a rate fixed on the trade date

2. The terms of the hedge provide for the acquisition of the borrowed nonfunctional currency (i.e., the first), in exchange for the second nonfunctional currency, on the calendar day when interest and principal payments are due on the borrowing and in an amount that equals such interest and principal payments.

The **tax effects** are as follows:

1. *Deemed borrowing in the second nonfunctional currency.* The intregration of the nonfunctional currency borrowing (i.e., the first) and the hedge results in a deemed borrowing in the second nonfunctional currency. The amount deemed to be borrowed equals the total amount of the second nonfunctional currency received under the terms of the hedge in exchange for the total amount of the first nonfunctional currency borrowed. The total amount of interest and principal deemed to be paid equals the total amount of the second nonfunctional currency paid under the terms of the hedge to acquire the first nonfunctional currency necessary to make interest and principal payments on the first nonfunctional currency borrowing.
2. *Determination of interest expense of the borrower.* The interest expense deductible by the borrower is determined as follows:
   (a) The issue price and stated redemption price at maturity of the deemed borrowing in the second nonfunctional currency are determined by applying Section 1273 directly to the units of the second nonfunctional currency used to make the interest and principal payments under the deemed borrowing.
   (b) If the deemed borrowing in the second nonfunctional currency has OID, then the rules of Section 163(e) govern the manner in which the amount of the discount denominated in units of the second nonfunctional currency is determined. The amount of discount deductible by the borrower in his functional currency is the amount determined in the manner described in the preceding sentence, translated into the borrower's functional currency using the weighted average exchange rate for the accrual period. Any amount of qualified periodic interest is translated into the borrower's functional currency at the spot rate on the date of

payment and deducted from gross income in accordance with the borrower's regular method of accounting.

(c) Any interest expense other than OID with respect to the deemed second nonfunctional currency borrowing is determined under Section 163(a) in units of the second nonfunctional currency (subject to normal limitations on interest deductions). The interest expense deductible by the borrower in his functional currency is the amount determined in the manner described in the preceding sentence, translated into the borrower's functional currency at the spot rate on the date of payment and deducted in accordance with the taxpayer's regular method of accounting.

3. *Allocation and apportionment.* The interest expense determined under (2) is allocated and apportioned under Sections 1.861-8 and 1.882-5 of the regulations, subject to Section 864(e).

4. *Deemed borrowing in the second nonfunctional currency is a position under Section 1092.* The deemed borrowing in the second nonfunctional currency is a position as defined in Section 1092(d)(2) for purposes of the loss deferral rules.

III. QUALIFIED HEDGING TRANSACTION THAT EFFECTIVELY CONVERTS A FUNCTIONAL CURRENCY BORROWING INTO A NONFUNCTIONAL CURRENCY BORROWING. A functional currency borrowing is effectively converted into a nonfunctional currency borrowing if:

1. The entire principal amount of functional currency received from the borrowing is sold or exchanged for nonfunctional currency on the settlement date at a rate fixed on the trade date.

2. The terms of the hedge provide for the acquisition of the borrowed functional currency, in exchange for that nonfunctional currency on the calendar day when interest and principal payments are due on the borrowing and in an amount that equals the interest and principal payments.

The **tax effects** are as follows:

1. *Deemed nonfunctional currency borrowing.* The integration of the functional currency borrowing and the hedge results in a deemed

nonfunctional currency borrowing. The amount deemed to be borrowed equals the total amount of nonfunctional currency received under the terms of the hedge in exchange for the total amount of functional currency borrowed. The total amount of interest and principal deemed to be paid equals the total amount of nonfunctional currency paid under the terms of the hedge to acquire the functional currency necessary to make interest and principal payments on the functional currency borrowing.

2. *Determination of interest expense of the borrower.* Interest expense deductible by the borrower is determined in the manner described above in connection with a qualified hedging transaction that effectively converts a borrowing in one nonfunctional currency into a borrowing in a second nonfunctional currency, except "nonfunctional currency" is substituted for the phrase "second nonfunctional currency."

3. *Allocation and apportionment.* The interest expense determined in (2) above is allocated and apportioned under Sections 1.861-8 and 1.882-5 of the regulations, subject to Section 864(e).

4. *Deemed nonfunctional currency borrowing is a position under Section 1092.*

IV. QUALIFIED HEDGING TRANSACTION THAT EFFECTIVELY CONVERTS THE PURCHASE OF A NONFUNCTIONAL CURRENCY DENOMINATED DEBT INSTRUMENT INTO A FUNCTIONAL CURRENCY DENOMINATED DEBT INSTRUMENT. The purchase of a nonfunctional currency denominated debt instrument is effectively converted into the purchase of a functional currency denominated debt instrument if:

1. In exchange for functional currency, the purchaser acquires on the trade date (at a rate set on that date), for delivery on the settlement date, an amount of nonfunctional currency equal to the purchase price of the debt instrument and exchanges such nonfunctional currency for the debt instrument on the settlement date.

2. The terms of the hedge provide for the sale or exchange of the nonfunctional currency denominated interest and principal payments received under the debt instrument for functional currency, at a rate

fixed on the trade date, on the calendar day when the payments are received.

The **tax effects** are as follows:

1. *Deemed functional currency denominated debt instrument.* The integration of the nonfunctional currency denominated debt instrument and the hedge results in a deemed functional currency denominated debt instrument with respect to the holder. The purchase price of the deemed functional currency denominated debt instrument is the amount of the functional currency paid to acquire the nonfunctional currency used for the purchase of the nonfunctional currency denominated debt instrument. The total amount of interest and principal deemed received by the holder equals the total amount of functional currency received under the terms of the hedge in exchange for the nonfunctional currency interest and principal payments received pursuant to the terms of the nonfunctional currency denominated debt instrument.
2. *Determination of interest income.* The interest income of the holder is determined as follows:
    (a) The issue price and stated redemption price at maturity of the deemed functional currency denominated debt instrument are determined under Section 1273 in units of the functional currency.
    (b) If the deemed functional currency denominated debt instrument has OID, then the interest income includible by the holder is determined under Section 1272.
    (c) If the deemed functional currency denominated debt does not have OID, then the interest is includible in gross income under Section 61 in accordance with the holder's regular method of accounting.
3. *Source.* The source of the deemed interest income is determined by reference to the source, as determined under Sections 861(a)(1) and 862(a)(1), of the interest income that would have been received under the terms of the qualifying transaction had such transaction not been integrated as a qualifying hedging transaction.

Chapter 9

V. QUALIFIED HEDGING TRANSACTION THAT EFFECTIVELY CONVERTS THE PURCHASE OF A DEBT INSTRUMENT DENOMINATED IN ONE NONFUNCTIONAL CURRENCY INTO THE PURCHASE OF A DEBT INSTRUMENT DENOMINATED IN A SECOND NONFUNCTIONAL CURRENCY. The purchase of a debt instrument denominated in one nonfunctional currency (first nonfunctional currency) is effectively converted into a debt instrument denominated in a second nonfunctional currency if:

1. In exchange for functional currency, the purchaser acquires on the trade date (at a rate set on that date), for delivery on the settlement date, an amount of the first nonfunctional currency equal to the purchase price of the debt instrument and exchanges that nonfunctional currency for the debt instrument on the settlement date.
2. The terms of the hedge provide for the exchange of the first nonfunctional currency denominated interest and principal payments received under the debt instrument for a second nonfunctional currency, at a rate fixed on the trade date, on the calendar day such payments are received.

The **tax effects** are as follows:

1. *Deemed purchase of a debt instrument denominated in the second nonfunctional currency.* The integration of the debt instrument denominated in the first nonfunctional currency and the hedge results in a deemed debt instrument denominated in the second nonfunctional currency (referred to as deemed second nonfunctional currency denominated debt instrument) with respect to the holder. The purchase price of the deemed second nonfunctional currency denominated debt instrument is the amount of the first nonfunctional currency used to purchase the first nonfunctional currency denominated debt instrument on the settlement date translated into the second nonfunctional currency at the forward exchange rate between the two currencies (as determined on the trade date) with respect to the period between the trade date and the settlement date. The total amount of interest and principal received by the holder of the deemed second nonfunctional currency denominated debt instrument equals the total amount of the second nonfunctional currency received under the hedge in exchange for the first nonfunctional currency interest and principal payments.

2. *Determination of interest income.* The interest income of the holder is determined as follows:

   (a) The issue price and stated redemption price at maturity of the deemed second nonfunctional currency denominated debt instrument are determined by applying Section 1273 directly to the units of the second nonfunctional currency to be received in exchange for the interest and principal payments to be received under the debt instrument.

   (b) If the deemed second nonfunctional currency denominated debt instrument has OID, then the rules of Section 1272 govern the manner in which the amount of such discount denominated in units of the second nonfunctional currency is determined. The amount of discount includible by the holder in his functional currency under Section 1272 is the amount determined in the manner described in the preceding sentence, translated into the holder's functional currency at the weighted average exchange rate for the accrual period. Any amount of qualified period interest is translated into the holder's functional currency at the spot rate on the date of payment and included in gross income in accordance with the holder's regular method of accounting.

   (c) Any interest income other than OID with respect to the deemed second nonfunctional currency denominated debt instrument is determined in units of the second nonfunctional currency. The interest income includible by the holder in his functional currency is the amount determined in the manner described in the preceding sentence, translated into the holder's functional currency at the spot rate on the date of payment.

3. *Source.* The source of the deemed interest income is determined by reference to the source, as determined under Sections 861(a)(1) and 862(a)(1), of the interest income that would have been received under the terms of the qualifying transaction had such transaction not been integrated as a qualifying hedging transaction.

VI. QUALIFIED HEDGING TRANSACTION THAT EFFECTIVELY CONVERTS THE PURCHASE OF A FUNCTIONAL CURRENCY DENOMINATED DEBT INSTRUMENT INTO A NONFUNCTIONAL CURRENCY DENOMINATED DEBT INSTRUMENT. The purchase of a functional currency denominated debt instrument is effec-

Chapter 9

tively converted into the purchase of a nonfunctional currency denominated debt instrument if:

1. The purchaser acquires the functional currency denominated debt instrument for functional currency.
2. The terms of the hedge provide for the sale or exchange of the functional currency denominated interest and principal payments received under the debt instrument for nonfunctional currency, at a rate fixed on the trade date, on the calendar day when such payments are received.

The **tax effects** are as follows:

1. *Deemed purchase of a nonfunctional currency denominated debt instrument.* The integration of the functional currency denominated debt instrument and the hedge results in a deemed nonfunctional currency denominated debt instrument. The purchase price of the deemed nonfunctional currency denominated debt instrument is the amount of functional currency used to purchase the functional currency denominated debt instrument on the settlement date translated into nonfunctional currency at the forward exchange rate between the two currencies (as determined on the trade date) with respect to the period between the trade date and the settlement date. The total amount of interest and principal received by the holder equals the total amount of nonfunctional currency received under the terms of the hedge in exchange for the functional currency interest and principal payments.
2. *Determination of interest income.* Interest income is determined in the manner described in connection with a qualified hedging transaction that effectively converts the purchase of a debt instrument denominated in one nonfunctional currency into the purchase of a debt instrument denominated in a second nonfunctional currency, except the phrase "nonfunctional currency" is substituted for the phrase "second nonfunctional currency."
3. *Source.* The source of the deemed interest income is determined by reference to the source, as determined under Sections 861(a)(1) and 862(a)(1), of the interest income that would have been received

under the terms of the qualifying transaction had such transaction not been integrated as a qualifying hedging transaction.

4. *Deemed nonfunctional currency debt instrument is a position under Section 1092.*

Examples: Illustrations of the application of the qualified Section 988 hedging transaction rules

I. *Synthetic functional currency liability (nonfunctional currency borrowing hedged with a swap).*

X, a U.S. corporation, has currency A as its functional currency. (The term "currency A" is used to designate a functional currency which, subject to the limitations of Section 985, can be the U.S. dollar or any other currency.) On December 24, 1987 (the trade date), X agrees to close the following transaction on December 31, 1987 (settlement date). X will borrow from an unrelated party on December 31, 1987, 100 units of currency B for three years at a 10% rate of interest, payable annually, with no principal payment due until the final installment. X will also enter into a swap agreement with an unrelated counterparty under the terms of which—(1) X will swap, on December 31, 1987, the 100 units of currency B obtained from the borrowing for 100 units of currency A, and (2) X will exchange currency A for currency B pursuant to the following table in order to obtain the units of currency B necessary to make payments on the currency B borrowing:

Date	Currency A	Currency B
December 31, 1988	8	10
December 31, 1989	8	10
December 31, 1990	108	110

The interest rate on the borrowing is set and the exchange rates on the swap are fixed on December 24, 1987.

On December 31, 1987, X borrows the 100 currency B units and swaps such units for 100 currency A units. Assume X has satisfied the identification and verification requirements of section 3 of this notice.

The currency B borrowing (which constitutes a qualifying transaction under section 2(b) of this announcement) and the swap agreement (which constitutes a hedge under section 2(c)) are a qualified hedging transaction as defined in Section 2(a). Accordingly, the currency B borrowing and the swap are integrated and treated as one transaction with the following consequences:

1. The integration of the currency B borrowing and the swap results in a deemed currency A borrowing in an amount equal to the 100 currency A units received on December 31, 1987 in exchange for the 100 units of currency B. Accordingly, the issue price under Section 1273(b)(2) is 100 currency A units.
2. The total amount of interest and principal paid by X with respect to the deemed currency A borrowing is equal to the currency A payments made by X under the swap agreement (i.e., 8 currency A units in 1988, 8 currency A units in 1989, and 108 currency A units in 1990).
3. The stated redemption price at maturity (defined in Section 1273(a)(2) and §1.1273-1(b)(1) of the proposed regulations as the amount payable at maturity other than a payment of qualified periodic interest) is 100 currency A units. Since the stated redemption price equals the issue price, there is no OID on the deemed currency A borrowing.
4. X may deduct the annual interest payments of 8 currency A units under Section 163(a) (subject to any limitations on deductibility imposed by other provisions of the code) according to its regular method of accounting. X has also paid 100 currency A units as a return of principal in 1990.
5. X must allocate and apportion its interest expense under Section 1.861-8 of the regulations (subject to Section 864(e) of the code).

II. *Synthetic functional currency liability (nonfunctional currency borrowing hedged with forward contracts)—higher-interest-rate currency.*

X, a U.S. corporation, has currency A as its functional currency. (The term "currency A" is used to designate a functional currency which, subject to the limitations of Section 985, can be the U.S. dollar or any other currency.) On December 24, 1987 (the trade date), when the spot rate is one unit of currency A equals one unit of currency B, X agrees to close the following transaction on December 31, 1987 (settlement date). X will borrow 100 units of currency B from an unrelated party on December 31, 1987 for three years at 10% interest, payable annually, with no principal payment due until the final installment. X also enters into a series of contracts with a bank to: (1) sell forward the 100 units of currency B for 99.96 units of currency A on December 31, 1987, and (2) buy forward for currency A, the amount of currency B required to make the interest and principal payments due under the currency B borrowing according to the following schedule:

Date	Currency A	Currency B
December 31, 1988	9.81	10
December 31, 1989	9.64	10
December 31, 1990	104.07	110

The interest rate on the borrowing is set and the exchange rates on the forward contracts are fixed on December 24, 1987.

On December 31, 1987, X borrows 100 currency B units and exchanges such units for 99.96 currency A units. Assume X satisfies the identification and verification requirements of Section 3 of this notice.

The currency B borrowing (which constitutes a qualifying transaction under Section 2(b) of this announcement) and the series of forward contracts (which constitutes a hedge under Section 2(c)) are a qualified hedging transaction under Section 2(a). Accordingly, the currency B borrowing and the forward contracts are integrated and treated as one transaction with the following consequences:

1. The integration of the currency B borrowing and the forward contracts results in a deemed currency A borrowing in an amount equal to the 99.96 currency A units received on December 31, 1987 for the 100 units of borrowed currency B. Accordingly, the issue price under Section 1273(b)(2) is 99.96 currency A units.
2. The total amount of interest and principal paid by X with respect to the deemed currency A borrowing is equal to the currency A payments made by X under the forward purchase contracts (i.e., 9.81 currency A units in 1988, 9.64 currency A units in 1989, and 104.07 currency A units in 1990).
3. The deemed currency A borrowing is an installment obligation within the meaning of Section 1.1273-1(b)(2)(i) of the proposed regulations and its stated redemption price at maturity (defined in Section 1273(a)(2) and §1.1273-1(b)(2)(ii) of the proposed regulations as the sum of all payments to be made under the borrowing other than qualified periodic interest) is 99.96 currency A units (i.e., under

§1.1273-1(b)(1)(ii), 8.00 units of the currency A payment in 1988, 7.86 units of the currency A payment in 1989, and 7.71 units of the currency A payment in 1990 are treated as qualified periodic interest payments). Since the stated redemption price at maturity is equal to the issue price, under Section 1273(a)(1) there is no OID on the deemed currency A borrowing. (3) The yield to maturity (as defined in §1.1272-1(f) of the proposed regulations) of the deemed currency A borrowing is 8.00%, compounded annually.

4. Therefore, assuming X is a calendar year taxpayer, it may deduct as interest expense under Section 163(a) (subject to any limitations on deductibility imposed by other provisions of the code) 8.00 currency A units in 1988, 7.86 currency A units in 1989, and 7.71 currency A units in 1990. The remainder of each payment is a return of principal.

5. X must allocate and apportion its interest expense under Section 1.861-8 of the regulations (subject to Section 864(e) of the code).

III. *Synthetic functional currency liability (nonfunctional currency borrowing hedged with forward contracts)—lower-interest-rate currency.*

The facts are the same as Example II, except the interest rate on the currency B borrowing is 6%, payable annually, and the amount of currency A units received in exchange for the proceeds of the currency B borrowing pursuant to the terms of the forward contract is 100.04. X purchases currency B forward, in exchange for currency A, pursuant to the following schedule:

Date	Currency A	Currency B
December 31, 1988	6.12	6
December 31, 1989	6.23	6
December 31, 1990	112.16	106

The currency B borrowing (which constitutes a qualifying transaction under Section 2(b)) and the series of forward contracts (which constitutes a hedge under Section 2(c)) are a qualified hedging transaction under Section 2(a). Accordingly, the currency B borrowing and the forward contracts are integrated and treated as one transaction with the following consequences:

1. The integration of the currency B borrowing and the forward contracts results in a deemed currency A borrowing in an amount equal

United States Taxation

to the currency A units received on December 31, 1987 for the 100 units of borrowed currency B. Accordingly, the issue price under Section 1273(b)(2) is 100.04 currency A units.

2. The total amount of interest and principal paid by X with respect to the deemed currency A borrowing is equal to the currency A payments made by X under the forward purchase contracts (i.e., 6.12 currency A units in 1988, 6.23 currency A units in 1989, and 112.16 currency A units in 1990).

3. The deemed currency A borrowing is treated as an installment obligation within the meaning of §1.1273-1(b)(2)(i) of the proposed regulations, and its stated redemption price at maturity (defined in Section 1273(a)(2) of the code and §1.1273-1(b)(2)(ii) of the proposed regulations as the sum of all payments to be made under the borrowing other than qualified periodic interest) is 106.15 currency A units (i.e., under §1.1273-1(b)(1)(ii), 6.12 units of the currency A payments in 1988, 1989, and 1990 are qualified periodic interest payments). Since the stated redemption price at maturity exceeds the issue price, under Section 1273(a)(1) the deemed currency A borrowing has OID equal to 6.11 currency A units.

4. The yield to maturity of the deemed currency A borrowing is 8.00%, compounded annually. Assuming X is a calendar year taxpayer, it may deduct as interest expense 8.00 currency A units in 1988 (of which 1.88 currency A units constitute OID), 8.15 currency A units in 1989 (of which 2.03 currency A units constitute OID), and 8.32 currency A units in 1990 (of which 2.20 currency A units constitute OID). The amount of the final payment in excess of the total interest expense is a return of principal and a payment of previously accrued OID.

5. X must allocate and apportion its interest expense under Section 1.861-8 of the regulations (subject to Section 864(e) of the code).

IV. *Synthetic functional currency asset (nonfunctional currency denominated debt instrument hedged with forward contracts)—higher-interest-rate currency.*

X, a U.S. corporation, has currency A as its functional currency. (The term "currency A" is used to designate a functional currency which, subject to the limitations of Section 985, can be the U.S. dollar or any other currency.) On December 24, 1987 (the trade date), when the spot rate is one unit of currency A equals one unit of currency B, X enters into a forward contract to purchase 100 units of currency B forward from a bank in exchange for 99.96 units of currency A for delivery on December 31, 1987. The 100 units of currency B are to be used for the purchase of a currency B denominated debt instrument on December 31, 1987. The instrument will have a term of three years, an issue price of 100 currency B units, and will bear interest at 10%, payable annually, with no repayment of principal until the final installment. X also enters (on December 24, 1987) into a series of forward contracts to sell the currency B interest and principal payments for currency A according to the following schedule:

Date	Currency A	Currency B
December 31, 1988	9.81	10
December 31, 1989	9.64	10
December 31, 1990	104.07	110

The rate of return on the currency B denominated debt instrument and the exchange rates on the forward contracts are fixed on December 24, 1987. On December 31, 1987 (the settlement date), X takes delivery of the 100 units of currency B and purchases the currency B denominated debt instrument. Assume X satisfies the identification and verification requirements of Section 3 of this notice.

The purchase of the currency B denominated debt instrument (which constitutes a qualifying transaction under Section 2(b) of this announcement) and the series of forward contracts (which constitutes a hedge under Section 2(c)) are a qualified hedging transaction under Section 2(a). Accordingly, the currency B denominated debt instrument and the forward contracts are integrated and treated as one transaction with the following consequences:

1. The integration of the currency B denominated debt instrument and the forward contracts results in a deemed currency A denominated debt instrument in an amount equal to the currency A units exchanged under the forward contract to purchase the units of currency B necessary to acquire the currency B denominated debt instrument. Accordingly, the issue price of 99.96 currency A units (Section 1273(b)(2) of the code).

2. The total amount of interest and principal received by X with respect to the deemed currency A denominated debt instrument is equal to the currency A units received under the forward sales contracts (i.e.,

United States Taxation

9.81 currency A units in 1988, 9.64 currency A units in 1989, and 104.07 currency A units in 1990).

3. The deemed currency A denominated debt instrument is an installment obligation within the meaning of Section 1.1273-1(b)(2)(i) of the proposed regulations, and its stated redemption price at maturity (defined in Section 1273(a)(2) of the code and §1.1273-1(b)(2)(ii) of the proposed regulations as the sum of all payments to be made under the debt instrument other than qualified periodic interest) is 99.96 currency A units (i.e., under §1.1273-1(b)(1)(ii) 8.00 units of the currency A payment in 1988, 7.86 units of the currency A payment in 1989, and 7.71 units of the currency A payment in 1990 are treated as qualified periodic interest payments). Since the stated redemption price at maturity is equal to the issue price, under Section 1273(a)(1) there is no OID on the deemed currency A denominated debt instrument.

4. The yield to maturity (as defined in §1.1272-1(f) of the proposed regulations) of the deemed currency A denominated debt instrument is 8.00%, compounded annually. Assuming X is a calendar year taxpayer, it must include interest income of 8.00 currency A units in 1988, 7.86 currency A units in 1989, and 7.71 currency A units in 1990. The remainder of each payment received is a payment of principal.

5. The source of the interest income (stated in (4) above) shall be determined by applying Sections 861(a)(1) and 862(a)(1) with reference to the currency B denominated interest income that would have been received had the transaction not been integrated.

V. *Synthetic functional currency asset (nonfunctional currency denominated debt instrument hedged with forward contracts)—lower-interest-rate currency.*

The facts are the same as in Example IV, except the interest rate on the currency B denominated debt instrument is 6%, compounded annually, and on December 24, 1987 (the trade date), X enters into a forward contract to purchase 100 units of currency B in exchange for 100.04 units of currency A for delivery on December 31, 1987. X sells forward the amount of currency B that will be received under the terms of the currency B denominated debt instrument according to the following schedule:

Chapter 9

Date	Currency A	Currency B
December 31, 1988	6.12	6
December 31, 1989	6.23	6
December 31, 1990	112.16	106

The currency B denominated debt instrument (which constitutes a qualifying transaction under Section 2(b) of this announcement) and the series of forward contracts (which constitutes a hedge under Section 2(c)) are a qualified hedging transaction under Section 2(a). Accordingly, the currency B denominated debt instrument and the forward contracts are treated as one transaction with the following consequences:

1. The integration of the currency B denominated debt instrument and the forward contracts results in a deemed currency A denominated debt instrument in an amount equal to the currency A exchanged under the forward contract to purchase the units of currency B necessary to acquire the currency B denominated debt instrument. Accordingly, the issue price of the deemed currency A denominated debt instrument is 100.04 currency A units (Section 1273(b)(2) of the code).

2. The total amount of interest and principal received by X with respect to the deemed currency A denominated debt instrument is equal to the currency A units received under the forward sales contracts (i.e., 6.12 currency A units in 1988, 6.23 currency A units in 1989, and 112.16 currency A units in 1990).

3. The deemed currency A denominated debt instrument is an installment obligation within the meaning of §1.1273-1(b)(2)(i) of the proposed regulations, and its stated redemption price at maturity (defined in Section 1273(a)(2) of the code and §1.1273-1(b)(2)(ii) of the proposed regulations as the sum of all payments to be made under the debt instrument other than qualified periodic interest) is 106.15 currency A units (i.e., under §1.1273-1(b)(1)(ii) of the proposed regulations, 6.12 units of the currency A payments in 1988, 1989, and 1990 are qualified periodic interest payments). Since the stated redemption price at maturity exceeds the issue price, under Section 1273(a)(1) the deemed currency A denominated debt instrument has OID of 6.11 currency A units.

4. The yield to maturity of the deemed currency A debt instrument is 8.00%, compounded annually. Assuming X is a calendar year taxpayer, it must include interest income of 8.00 currency A units in 1988 (of which 1.88 currency A units constitute OID), 8.15 currency A units in 1989 (of which 2.03 currency A units constitute OID), and 8.32 currency A units in 1990 (of which 2.20 currency A units constitute OID). The amount of the final payment received by X in excess of the interest income includible is a return of principal and a payment of previously accrued OID.

5. The source of the interest income (stated in (4) above) shall be determined by applying Sections 861(a)(1) and 862(a)(1) with reference to the currency B denominated interest income that would have been received had the transaction not been integrated.

Glossary of terms

American-style option (also American option) An option that may be exercised at any time up to and including the expiration date.

Arbitrage Trading strategies designed to profit from price differences for the same or similar goods in different markets. Historically, the term implied little or no risk in the trade, but more recently it has come to suggest some risk of loss or uncertainty about total profits.

Assignment (swap market) The sale of a swap contract by one party to another, usually for a lump-sum payment. Swap assignments are cumbersome because they require the approval of the remaining original party.

At-the-money An option is at-the-money when the price of the underlying instrument is very close or equal to the option's exercise price.

Back-to-back loans Two parties in different countries make loans to one another, of equal value, each loan denominated in the currency of the lender and each maturing on the same date. The payment flows are identical to those of spot and forward currency transactions. Currency swaps have a similar structure except that there is not necessarily any "loan" on the balance sheet.

Basis The spread or difference between two market prices or two interest rates: for example, the spread between commercial paper and

Glossary of Terms

Eurodollar rates or the spread between a futures price and the price of the underlying asset.

Basis point One one-hundredth of one percentage point, most often used in quotation of spreads between interest rates or to describe changes in yields on securities.

Black-Scholes (also Black-Scholes model) A widely used option-pricing equation developed in 1973 by Fischer Black and Myron Scholes. Used to price OTC options, value option portfolios, or evaluate option trading on exchanges.

Break-even point The price of the underlying instrument at which an option buyer just recovers the initial outlay or premium. For a call option, the break-even point is the exercise price plus the premium; a put option's break-even point is the exercise price minus the premium.

Capped floating-rate notes A type of floating-rate note (see *Floating-rate note*) that sets an upper limit on the borrower's interest rate. The lender foregoes the possibility of obtaining a return above the cap rate, should market interest rates exceed the cap rate, but in return receives higher-than-usual spreads over LIBOR. In essence, the note issuer obtains an interest-rate cap—a form of option—from the buyer.

Cash settlement The settlement provision on some option and futures contracts that do not require delivery of the underlying instrument. For options, the difference between the settlement price on the underlying and the option's exercise price is paid to the option holder at exercise. For futures contracts, the exchange establishes a settlement price on the final day of trading and all remaining open positions are marked-to-market at that price. (See *Marking-to-market*.)

CD (Certificate of deposit) A negotiable certificate issued by a bank as evidence of an interest-bearing time deposit.

Commercial paper A short-term unsecured promise to repay a fixed amount (representing borrowed funds plus interest) on a certain future date and at a specific place. The note stands on the general creditworthiness of the issuer or on the standing of a third party that is obligated to repay if the original borrower defaults. The most active commercial-paper market is in the United States.

Commodity Futures Trading Commission (CFTC) The federal agency that regulates futures trading in the United States.

Conversion An arbitrage strategy in options involving the purchase of the underlying instrument offset by the establishment of a synthetic short position in options on the underlying (the purchase of a put and sale of a call). The overall position is unaffected by price movements in the underlying instrument. This trade would be established when small price discrepancies open up between the long position in the underlying and the synthetic short position in the options.

Country risk The risk that most or all economic agents (including the government) in a particular country will for some common reason become unable or unwilling to fulfill international financial obligations.

Coupon-stripping The process of producing single-payment (zero coupon) instruments from existing conventional bonds. It can be accomplished either by separating the coupons from the principal or by selling receipts representing the individual coupons and principal on a security held by a trustee.

Covered writing Generally refers to selling call options "covered" by an equal or larger long position in the security underlying the option. It is a strategy intended to augment overall returns by earning fee income on the options written against securities held for normal investment purposes.

Currency swap A transaction in which two counterparties exchange specific amounts of two different currencies at the outset and repay over time according to a predetermined rule that reflects interest payments and possibly amortization of principal. The payment flows in currency swaps (in which payments are based on fixed-interest rates in each currency) are generally like those of spot and forward currency transactions.

Deep discount bonds Coupon-bearing securities that sell at prices well below par. Generally refers to seasoned bonds whose prices have declined in secondary-market trading because market yields have risen well above the levels prevailing at the time they were issued. Tax consequences discourage new issuance of deep discount bonds in the United States.

Delta The change in an option's price divided by the change in the price of the underlying instrument. An option whose price changes by $1 for every $2 change in the price of the underlying instrument has a

Glossary of Terms

delta of 0.5. At-the-money options have deltas near 0.5. The delta rises toward 1.0 for options that are deep-in-the-money, and approaches 0 for deep-out-of-the-money options. (See *At-the-money, In-the-money, Out-of-the-money,* and *Delta hedging.*)

Delta hedging   A method that option writers use to hedge risk exposure of written options by purchase or sale of the underlying asset in proportion to the delta. For example, a call option writer who has sold an option with a delta of 0.5 may engage in delta hedging by purchasing an amount of the underlying instrument equal to one-half of the amount of the underlying that must be delivered upon exercise.

A delta-neutral position is established when the writer strictly delta-hedges so as to leave the combined financial position in options and underlying instruments unaffected by small changes in the price of the underlying.

End-user (swap market)   In contrast to a swap-trading institution, a counterparty that engages in a swap to change its interest rate or currency exposure. End-users may be nonfinancial corporations, financial institutions, or governments.

Euro-commercial paper (ECP)   Notes sold in London for same-day settlement in U.S. dollars in New York. The maturities are more tailored to the needs of issuer and investor than the standard Euronote tenors of one, three, and six months. This is a recent development in the Euromarket.

Euro-commercial-paper facility   Facility for issuing short-term notes without a backup line and generally with flexible maturities.

Euronote   A short-term note issued under a note issuance facility or Euro-commercial-paper facility.

European-style option (also European option)   An option that may be exercised only on the expiration date. It is an alternative to an American option, which can be exercised on any business day prior to expiration or on the expiration date.

Exercise price (also Strike price)   The fixed price at which an option holder has the right to buy, in the case of a call option, or to sell, in the case of a put option, the financial instrument covered by the option.

Expected volatility   The degree of volatility that option pricing formulas assume will prevail over the remaining life of an option.

Glossary of Terms

Expiration (also Expiration date, Expiry, and Maturity date) (1) The date at which a European-style option may be exercised at the choice of the holder. (2) The date before or at which an American-style option may be exercised.

Floating-rate note (FRN) A medium-term security carrying a floating rate of interest that is reset at regular intervals, typically quarterly or half-yearly, in relation to some predetermined reference rate, typically LIBOR. (See *LIBOR*.)

Forward-rate agreement (FRA) An agreement between two parties wishing to protect themselves against a future movement in interest rates. The two parties agree on an interest rate for a specified period from a specified future settlement date based on an agreed principal amount. No commitment is made by either party to lend or borrow the principal amount; their exposure is only the interest difference between the agreed and actual rates at settlement.

FRABBA terms Standard terms agreed by the British Banker's Association for interbank trading of FRAs. (See *Forward-rate agreements (FRA).*)

Futures contract An exchange-traded contract generally calling for delivery of a specified amount of a particular grade of commodity or financial instrument at a fixed date in the future. Contracts are highly standardized and traders need only agree on the price and number of contracts traded.

Traders' positions are maintained at the exchange's clearinghouse, which becomes a counterparty to each trader once the trade has been cleared at the end of each day's trading session. Members holding positions at the clearinghouse must post margin that is marked at market daily. Most trades are unwound before delivery. The interposition of the clearinghouse facilitates the unwinding since a trader need not find his original counterparty, but may arrange an offsetting position with any trader on the exchange. (See *Margin* and *Marking-to-market*.)

Gamma The sensitivity of an option's delta to small unit changes in the price of the underlying. Some option traders attempt to construct "gamma-neutral" positions in options (long and short) such that the delta of the overall position remains unchanged for small changes in the price of the underlying instrument. Using this method, writers can

Glossary of Terms

produce a fairly constant delta and avoid the transactions costs involved in purchasing and selling the underlying as its price changes.

Grantor See *Writer*.

Hedge To reduce risk by taking a position that offsets existing or anticipated exposure to a change in market rates.

Hedge ratio The proportion of underlying securities or options needed to hedge a written option. The hedge ratio is determined by the delta. (See *Delta* and *Delta hedging*.)

Implied volatility The degree of volatility "implied" by the market price of an option. Since all other variables used in the theoretical option pricing formulas are observable, market participants frequently solve the equation "backwards" to determine the amount of volatility built into the market. Some option traders "trade" volatility, buying options when their implied volatility is low and selling options when their implied volatility is high.

In-the-money Option contracts are in-the-money when there is a net financial benefit to be derived from exercising the option immediately. A call option is in-the-money when the price of the underlying instrument is above the exercise price and a put option is in-the-money when the price of the underlying is below the exercise price.

Interest-rate cap An option-like feature for which the buyer pays a fee or premium to obtain protection against a rise in a particular interest rate above a certain level. For example, an interest-rate cap may cover a specified principal amount of a loan over a designated time period such as a calendar quarter. If the covered interest rate rises above the rate ceiling, the seller of the rate cap pays the purchaser an amount of money equal to the average rate differential times the principal amount times one-quarter.

Interest-rate mismatch (also Interest-rate gap or Gap) The risk/opportunity that banks face, that a shift in interest rates will reduce/increase interest income. The mismatch arises out of the repricing schedule of assets and liabilities. The banks' traditional interest-rate mismatch, lending long-term and borrowing in short-term markets, exposes them, for example, to the risk that rates will rise: as interest rates rise, low-yielding short-term liabilities will be replaced and repriced more rapidly than assets. Some money-center banks manage their interest-rate mismatches actively in the hopes of taking advantage of anticipated interest-rate changes.

Interest-rate swap A transaction in which two counterparties exchange interest payment streams of differing character based on an underlying notional principal amount. The three main types are coupon swaps (fixed rate to floating rate in the same currency), basis swaps (one floating-rate index to another floating-rate index in the same currency), and cross-currency interest-rate swaps (fixed rate in one currency to floating rate in another).

Intermediary (swap market) A counterparty who enters into a swap in order to earn fees or trading profits. Most intermediaries, or swap dealers, are major U.S. money-center banks, major U.S. and U.K. investment and merchant banks, and major Japanese securities companies.

Intrinsic value The net benefit to be derived from exercising an option contract immediately. It is the difference between the price of the underlying and the option's exercise price. An option generally sells for at least its intrinsic value.

LIBID London Interbank Bid Rate—the rate that a bank is willing to pay for funds in the international interbank market.

LIBOR London Interbank Offered Rate—the rate at which banks offer to lend funds in the international interbank market.

Long option position The position of a trader who has purchased an option regardless of whether it is a put or a call. A participant with a long call option position can profit from a rise in the price of the underlying while a trader with a long put option can profit from a fall in the price of the underlying instrument.

Margin Funds or collateral posted as a good-faith performance guarantee. In repurchase agreements, lenders of funds often make borrowers post margin by requiring them to deliver securities in excess of the amount of money borrowed. Futures and options exchanges often require traders to post initial margin when they enter into new contracts. Margin accounts are debited or credited to reflect changes in the current market prices on the positions held. Members must replenish the margin

Glossary of Terms

account if margin falls below a minimum. In similar fashion, customers must post margin on positions held for them at the exchange clearinghouse by member firms. (See *Marking-to-market*.)

Market liquidity risk The possibility that a financial instrument cannot be sold quickly and at full market value.

Marking-to-market The process of recalculating the exposure in a trading position in securities, option contracts, or futures contracts. In exchange-traded contracts, the exchange clearinghouse marks members' positions to market each day using closing market prices. Members must maintain a certain minimum level of margin at the exchange clearinghouse and must post additional margin if the marking-to-market process reduces margin below the minimum. (See *Margin*.)

Note issuance facility (NIF) A medium-term arrangement enabling borrowers to issue short-term paper, typically of three or six months' maturity, in their names. Usually a group of underwriting banks guarantees the availability of funds to the borrower by purchasing any unsold notes at each rollover date or by providing a standby credit. Facilities produced by competing banks are called, variously, revolving underwriting facilities, note purchase facilities, and Euronote facilities.

Notional principal A hypothetical amount on which swap payments are based. The notional principal in an interest-rate swap is never paid or received.

Off-balance-sheet activities Banks' business, often fee-based, that does not generally involve booking assets and taking deposits. Examples are trading of swaps, options, foreign-exchange forwards, standby commitments, and letters of credit.

Option The contractual right, but not the obligation, to buy or sell a specified amount of a given financial instrument at a fixed price before or at a designated future date. A *call option* confers on the holder the right to buy the financial instrument. A *put option* involves the right to sell the financial instrument.

Options book The aggregation of all written and purchased options held by a market participant.

OTC market (Over-the-counter market) Trading in financial instruments transacted off organized exchanges. Generally the parties

Glossary of Terms

must negotiate all details of the transactions or agree to certain simplifying market conventions. In most cases, OTC market transactions are negotiated over the telephone.

OTC trading includes transactions among market-makers and between market-makers and their customers. Firms mutually determine their trading partners on a bilateral basis.

Out-of-the-money An option contract is out-of-the-money when there is no benefit to be derived from exercising the option immediately. A call option is out-of-the-money when the price of the underlying is below the option's exercise price. A put option is out-of-the-money when the price of the underlying is above the option's exercise price.

Plain-vanilla swap A U.S.-dollar interest-rate swap in which one party makes floating-rate payments based on six-month LIBOR and receives fixed-rate funds expressed as a spread over the rate on U.S. Treasury securities. The maturity is usually five to seven years and deal size is typically at least $50 to $100 million.

Premium The price paid for an option by an option holder to the option writer.

Put option See *Options*.

Repurchase agreement (PR or repo) A holder of securities sells these securities to an investor with an agreement to repurchase them at a fixed price on a fixed date. The security "buyer" in effect lends the "seller" money for the period of the agreement, and the terms of the agreement are structured to compensate him for this. Dealers use repos extensively to finance their positions.

Reverse swap One form of activity in the secondary swap market. A reverse swap offsets the interest-rate or currency exposure on an existing swap. They can be written with the original counterparty or with a new counterparty. In either case, they are typically executed to realize capital gains.

RUF See *Note issuance facility*.

Securitization The term is most often used narrowly to mean the process by which traditional bank or thrift institution assets, mainly loans or mortgages, are converted into negotiable securities that may be purchased either by depository institutions or by nonbank investors.

Glossary of Terms

More broadly, the term refers to the development of markets for a variety of new negotiable instruments, such as NIFs and FRNs in the international markets and commercial paper in the United States, which replace bank loans as a means of borrowing. Used in the latter sense, the term often suggests *disintermediation* of the banking system, as investors and borrowers bypass banks and transact business directly.

Settlement price The price of the financial instrument underlying the option contract at the time the contract is exercised. Where necessary, option contracts specify objective standards for determining the settlement price.

Settlement risk The possibility that the operational difficulties interrupt delivery of funds even where the counterparty is able to perform.

Short option position The position of a trader who has sold or written an option regardless of whether it is a put or a call. The writer's maximum potential profit is the premium received.

Short volatility position An option position designed to profit from an expected decline in the implied volatility component of the option's price. The position can take different forms. One form is to sell options and use delta-hedging techniques to protect against changes in the price level of the underlying instrument. (See also *Straddle write* for another strategy.)

Straddle An option position designed to profit from an expected increase in the price volatility of the underlying instrument. A straddle consists of the purchase of a put and a call with the same exercise data and exercise price.

Straddle write An options strategy designed to profit from an expected decline in the implied volatility component of prices. The position consists of selling a straddle.

Swap A financial transaction in which two counterparties agree to exchange streams of payments over time according to a predetermined rule. A swap is normally used to transform the market exposure associated with a loan or bond borrowing from one interest-rate base (fixed term or floating rate) or currency of denomination to another. (See *Currency swap* and *Interest-rate swap*.)

Synthetic positions Combinations of options or the underlying instrument to produce a desired risk/gain position that cannot be obtained directly. Synthetic positions can be established in the following fashion.

1. Long call: purchase put and purchase the underlying.
2. Long put: purchase call and sell the underlying.
3. Long position in the underlying instrument: purchase call and sell put with same strike price and exercise date.
4. Short position in the underlying instrument: sell call and purchase put with same strike price and exercise date.

Tender panel A method for distributing notes issued under note issuance facilities. A group of financial institutions have the right to bid for the short-term notes issued under the facility on each issue date. (See *Note issuance facility (NIF)*.)

Time value The imputed monetary value of an option reflecting the possibility that the price of the underlying will move so that the option will become more valuable. The total value of an option, or its price, comprises its intrinsic value and its time value.

Uncovered writer (also Naked writer) Option seller who does not attempt to reduce market risk by taking offsetting positions in the underlying security or other options, a biased view in option writing—that is, anticipating that the option will fall in value.

Underlying The designated financial instruments that must be delivered in completion of an option contract or a futures contract. For example, the underlying may be fixed-income securities, foreign-exchange, equities, or futures contracts (in the case of an option on a futures contract).

Volatility The price "variability" of the instrument underlying an option contract, and defined as the standard deviation in the logarithm of the price of the underlying expressed at an annual rate. Expected volatility is a variable used in pricing options.

Voluntary termination (swap market) The cancellation of a swap contract that is agreed to by both counterparties. A voluntary termination usually involves a lump-sum payment from one party to the other.

Glossary of Terms

Writer (also Grantor)   The party that sells an option. The writer is required to carry out the terms of the option at the choice of the holder.

Zero coupon bonds   Single-payment long-term securities that do not call for period interest payments. The bonds are sold at discounts from par and the investor's entire return is realized at maturity.

Source: *Recent Innovations in International Banking,* Bank for International Settlements, April 1986.

APPENDIX I

Comparative risk table

Instrument	Credit Risk	Market Risk	Settlement Risk	Market Liquidity Risk
Currency options	Writer for premium amount until paid, buyer for cost of replacement until exercised	Limited for buyer, unlimited for writer	Premium amount on payment date, principal amount for both parties if exercised (one party pays currency A, one pays currency B)	Exchange and OTC options new, liquidity of markets untested under stress. Liquidity of exchanges superior to OTC markets, also partially dependent on liquidity of market for underlying
Interest-rate options	Same as above	Same as above	Same as above except one party delivers cash, the other securities, if exercised (could be net amount if cash settled)	Same as above
Currency swaps	Default cancels future obligations. Risk limited to replacement cost. May be principal risk if agreed in original contract	Equal to rate change on principal and interest amount	Contractual amount on successive payment dates	All OTC contracts: limited liquidity
Interest-rate swaps	Default cancels future obligations, risk limited to replacement cost. No principal risk	Complex: equivalent to bond of equal maturity on fixed side. Risk to fixed payer in swap if rates have fallen, to fixed receiver if rates rise. Small on basis swap. No market risk on principal amount	Interest payment allowed only on successive payment dates	All OTC contracts: limited liquidity

Instrument	Credit Risk	Market Risk	Settlement Risk	Market Liquidity Risk
NIFs/RUFs	Principal amount for holders of paper, same as other guarantees for writers of standbys	Writers of standbys face risk that they will be called on to lend at below-market spreads if market conditions change	Principal amount on payment date for borrower	Liquidity of paper largely untested
Forward-rate agreements	Mostly cash settled, credit risk limited to amount of market risk	Equal to market risk on deposit	Limited to amount of market risk if cash settled	Small market, limited liquidity

APPENDIX II

Inland Revenue Statement of Practice on exchange rate fluctuations

Introduction

1. The Inland Revenue has been asked for its views on the treatment under current tax law of profits and losses arising from exchange rate fluctuations following the judgment of the House of Lords in Pattison v. Marine Midland Limited (1984) AC 362. This Statement of Practice attempts to deal with some aspects of this problem. It is put forward as a practical guide to facilitate the preparation and agreement of tax computations of trading taxpayers. The general rules it contains may need to be modified in the way in which they are applied in particular circumstances, for example, where the local currency (as defined in paragraph 4 below) of an overseas trade is a currency other than sterling.

Marine Midland—A summary

2. A U.K. resident bank carried on business in international commercial banking. For the purpose of making dollar loans and advances in the course of its banking business, it borrowed US$15 million in the form of subordinated loan stock, redeemable in ten years. As a result of exchange rate fluctuations, the sterling value of the loans to

Appendix II

its customers increased, as did the liability in sterling terms of the loan stock. Its general aim was to remain matched in each foreign currency and for the most part the dollar borrowings remained invested in dollar assets. After five years, the loan stock was repaid out of existing dollar funds and at no time was any of the $15 million converted into sterling.

3. Each year in the accounts, the monetary assets and liabilities denominated in a foreign currency were valued in sterling at the exchange rate at the balance sheet date but, to the extent that currency liabilities were matched by currency assets, no profit or loss was shown for accounts purposes. The Court of Appeal and the House of Lords held that, in these circumstances, no profit or loss arose for tax purposes. On the other hand, the company brought into its profit-and-loss account any increase or decrease in the sterling value of excess dollars—i.e., to the extent that it was in an *unmatched* position—and this had been accepted as a profit or loss for tax purposes. Lord Templeman said that this practice "reflected the success or failure of the company in acquiring and holding excess dollars which could be converted into sterling." He noted without disapproval the Inland Revenue's acceptance of the practice and said it was ". . . not inconsistent with the company's submission that no profit or loss was attributable to dollar assets equal in dollar terms to dollar liabilities."

Definitions

4. In this statement:
   (a) *Translation* into sterling is regarded as the valuation of a foreign currency asset or liability in terms of sterling at a particular date.
   (b) *Conversion* into sterling is the exchange of that asset or liability for sterling.
   (c) *Local currency* is the currency of the primary economic environment in which the trade is carried on and net cash flows are generated.

The recognition of exchange differences: Accounts treatment and tax consequences

5. It has long been the general practice in the case of trading companies to bring exchange translation adjustments, other than those in respect of capital items, into account for tax purposes where they have similarly been brought into account in arriving at the accounting profit or loss. By contrast, it has been the practice in some circumstances—mainly in the case of certain overseas trading activities dealt with for accounts purposes on what is now generally referred to as the "closing rate/net investment" basis—to translate the net profit or loss for tax purposes (the so-called "profit-and-loss account" basis). In the Inland Revenue's view, the decision in Marine Midland does not make it necessary to abandon either of these practices, although it may of course affect the issue of what adjustments should be made for capital items (see below).

Translation and conversion

6. Some commentators, including some of those who accepted the invitation to comment on the Provisional Statement of Practice, have suggested that judicial dicta in the Marine Midland case can be interpreted as indicating that translation profits or losses should be ignored for tax purposes on the grounds that they have not been realized or incurred, and that exchange profits and losses should be taken into account for tax only on conversion of the relevant currency into sterling.

The Inland Revenue view

7. The Inland Revenue does not subscribe to this view as a general proposition. The Marine Midland case was decided in the context of its own very special facts. In deciding whether the account should be taken of translation profits and losses in calculating the annual profits of a business for tax purposes, it is necessary to consider the wider body of case law indicating that generally the calculation of annual profits and gains for tax purposes should start with a consid-

Appendix II

eration of the accounts drawn up in accordance with the correct principles of commercial accounting.

8. In general, the Inland Revenue view is that if the accounts of a business have been compiled in accordance with the Companies Acts and generally accepted accountancy principles and have taken account of *translation* profits and losses, then those profits and losses should normally also be taken into account for tax purposes unless there are particular reasons relevant to the case in question, including whether they are in respect of capital items, for taking a different view.

9. It is clear, too, that any attempt to deal with exchange profits and losses only where there is *conversion* into sterling would in many cases present substantial problems of identification and follow-up for both taxpayers and their taxation advisers and the Inland Revenue. In deciding what is generally accepted accountancy practice for this purpose, regard will be had in particular to Statement of Standard Accounting Practice 20: Foreign Currency Translation and to published accounting practices of particular industries.

Application of conversion bases

10. Where, exceptionally, a taxpayer considers that a different basis—including a "conversion" basis—would result from the application of the relevant case law to his particular facts, it will be necessary for him to make out his case to the inspector.

Capital and current liabilities

11. In computing trading profits for tax purposes, the question whether a loss or profit on exchange on a foreign currency loan is respectively an allowable deduction or assessable receipt is determined by the nature of the loan and whether it is to be properly regarded as a capital or current liability. The distinction between capital and current liabilities is based on principles well established in tax case law. The distinction is essentially between loans providing temporary financial accommodation and loans that can be said to add to the capital of the business. The answer in any particular case must

turn on its facts and circumstances, which have to be considered in detail.

12. The Court of Appeal and the House of Lords did not find it necessary to decide whether the borrowing by Marine Midland was a capital or current liability; the House of Lords indicated that it would have needed further evidence and argument to decide the issue. The Commissioners and the High Court, however, agreed with the Inland Revenue's view that the borrowing was a capital liability. The Inland Revenue remains of the view that the liability in question in the Marine Midland case was of a capital nature.

Matched assets and liabilities

13. The Court of Appeal and House of Lords judgments in Marine Midland indicate that where the foreign currency borrowings are matched by assets in the same currency, the capital or current nature of the borrowing will no longer be relevant in determining whether adjustments are to be made for the purposes of computing trading profits or losses for tax. In these circumstances, exchange differences, whether profits or losses, arising on long-term borrowings are not to be distinguished and adjusted in computing trading profits or losses for tax.

   Same currency

14. Liabilities and assets of the same trader are regarded as matched in the way described in paragraph 13 above to the extent that foreign currency monetary assets are equalled by liabilities in the *same currency* and a translation adjustment on one would be cancelled out by a translation adjustment on the other. In general, therefore, where there are transactions in more than one foreign currency the question of matching must be considered separately for each currency (see paragraph 21 below). However, it is possible for assets and liabilities in different currencies to be regarded as effectively matched when hedging transactions, such as forward foreign currency contracts, are taken into account (see paragraphs 22–24 below).

Appendix II

Matching of capital assets in foreign currency with current liabilities

15. There may be circumstances where foreign currency *assets* which, for tax, would be treated as capital assets are matched with current liabilities in the same currency—the reverse of the situation in Marine Midland. This may arise, for example, in the case of certain monetary assets—e.g., where loans to subsidiary companies, which for tax would be treated as capital, are matched by short-term currency borrowings, which for tax may fall to be treated as current liabilities. The Inland Revenue takes the view that the Marine Midland matching principle applies in such circumstances, with the result that, again exchange differences arising on the assets or liabilities are not to be distinguished and adjusted. Cases where, exceptionally, nonmonetary capital assets are treated as foreign currency assets for accounts purposes will need to be considered by reference to their particular facts.

Assets and liabilities not matched

16. In general, an adjustment is required to the tax computation of trading profits in respect of exchange differences that have been debited or credited to the profit-and-loss account in respect of capital items. It will be for the trader to demonstrate matching of capital currency liabilities, or assets, by reference to the position both during and at the end of the accounting period; and, where such liabilities or assets are wholly or partly matched, to show the effect if any on the tax computation. Where exchange differences relating to assets or liabilities not matched, or not completely matched, are taken to reserve, the nature of the assets or liabilities will need to be considered to determine whether or not a tax adjustment is required.

17. However, in practice, the extent to which currency assets are matched with currency liabilities will, in most cases, fluctuate in the course of an accounting period, so that it would be impracticable to measure and take account of such fluctuations on a day-by-day basis in determining what adjustment is required in the tax computation to the net exchange difference debited or credited in the profit-and-loss account. Instead the practice outlined in paragraphs 20 and 21 below may be adopted, provided it is applied on a consistent basis from year to year.

Inland Revenue Statement

A practical approach

18. In essence, the practice offered at paragraphs 20 and 21 below assumes that the extent to which currency assets and liabilities are matched during an accounting period is reflected in the size of the net exchange difference debited or credited to the profit-and-loss account or, in some circumstances, to reserve. The rules suggested for determining the adjustment to be made for tax purposes in respect of the exchange difference arising on capital assets or liabilities that are unmatched, or only partly matched, are based on the premise that capital liabilities are matched primarily with capital assets in the same currency. Any capital liabilities not matched by capital assets in the same currency are regarded as matched by current assets of the same currency, only to the extent that the current assets exceed the current liabilities in that currency.

19. Where this practice is not adopted, capital liabilities and assets will be regarded as matched only to the extent that this can be demonstrated by reference to the trader's currency assets and liabilities during the accounting period.

20. Under the practice referred to in paragraph 18, the first step will be to ascertain the aggregate of exchange differences, positive and negative, on capital assets and liabilities in the profit-and-loss account figure.

(a) *If there are no such differences then no tax adjustment is necessary.*

Example 1

A company normally trading in sterling incurs a liability on a trade debt of $600,000 when $1.5 = £1. The liability is entered in the books in sterling at £400,000. By the accounting date, sterling has fallen to $1.25 = £1, so that the sterling value of the liability has increased to £480,000. The exchange loss of £80,000 is charged to the profit-and-loss account.

There were no capital exchange differences. No adjustment is required for tax purposes because the transactions are wholly on the revenue account.

(b) *If the net exchange difference on capital items is a loss and the net difference in the profit-and-loss account is also a loss, then the smaller of the two figures is the amount to be disallowed in the tax computation as relating to capital transactions.*

Example 2

A trading company borrows $600,000 on long-term capital account when $1.5 = £1, it retains $150,000 as current assets and converts the balance of $450,000 to £300,000. The books will then show the following entries:

Capital loan ($600,000)	£400,000	Current assets ($150,000)	£100,000
		Cash on hand	300,000
	£400,000		£400,000

By the accounting date, when sterling has fallen to $1.25 = £1, these become:

Capital loan ($600,000)	£480,000	Current assets ($150,000)	£120,000
		Cash on hand	300,000
		Exchange difference to P & L account	60,000
	£480,000		£480,000

The exchange difference on capital account is £80,000 (£480,000 − £400,000) but the tax adjustment is limited to the amount charged to the profit-and-loss account, so that £60,000 is disallowed. This reflects the fact that $150,000 of the liability is matched with $150,000 assets. The whole of the exchange difference £60,000 is attributable to the excess currency liability on capital account, the value of which has increased from £300,000 to £360,000.

Example 3

A trading company incurs a liability by way of overdraft on current account of $300,000 and borrows $600,000 on capital account when $1.5 = £1. It retains $150,000 as current assets and converts the balance of $750,000 to £500,000. The books will then show the following items:

Capital loan ($600,000)	£400,000	Current assets ($150,000)	£100,000
Overdraft on current account ($300,000)	200,000	Cash on hand	500,000
	£600,000		£600,000

Inland Revenue Statement

By the accounting date, sterling has fallen to $1.25 = £1 and the book entries are then:

Capital loan ($600,000)	£480,000	Current assets ($150,000)	£120,000
Overdraft on current account ($300,000)	240,000	Cash on hand	500,000
		Exchange difference to P & L account	100,000
	£720,000		£720,000

The net exchange loss of £100,000 in the profit-and-loss account is made up of £120,000 loss on the liabilities and £20,000 profit on the assets.

The exchange difference on capital account is £80,000 (£480,000 − £400,000). This is less than the profit-and-loss account figure, so the £80,000 is disallowed for tax purposes. This reflects the matching of the $150,000 current assets with $150,000 of the current liabilities. The capital liability is therefore wholly unmatched.

(c) *If the net exchange difference on capital items is a profit and the net difference in the profit-and-loss account is also a profit, then the smaller of the two figures is the amount to be deducted in the tax computation.*

Example 4

A trading company incurs a liability by way of overdraft on current account of $150,000 and borrows a further £300,000 as a capital loan when $1.5 = £1. It converts the £300,000 to $450,000 and makes a loan (not in the course of trade) of $600,000 to an associated company. The books show the following entries at this point:

Overdraft on current account ($150,000)	£100,000	Capital assets ($600,000)	£400,000
Capital loan	300,000		
	£400,000		£400,000

By the accounting date, sterling has fallen to $1.25 = £1 and the book entries are as follows:

Appendix II

Overdraft on current account ($150,000)	£120,000	Capital assets ($600,000)	£480,000
Capital loan	300,000		
Exchange difference to P & L account	60,000		
	£480,000		£480,000

The net exchange profit of £60,000 in the profit-and-loss account comprises £80,000 profit on the assets and £20,000 loss on the liability.

The net capital exchange difference is £80,000 (£480,000 − £400,000) but the adjustment for tax purposes is limited to the figure in the profit-and-loss account of £60,000. This reflects the fact that $150,000 of the assets are matched with the dollar liability. The non-taxable exchange profit is attributable to the excess capital assets, whose sterling value changed from £300,000 to £360,000.

(d) *Where the net exchange difference on capital items produces a loss, but the net difference in the profit-and-loss account is a credit entry, then no tax adjustment is required. Similarly, no adjustment is necessary where there is a profit in respect of exchange differences on capital items, but a net loss on exchange is debited to the profit-and-loss account.*

Example 5

A trading company borrows $900,000 on capital account and raises a further sterling loan of £200,000. It converts the £200,000 to $300,000 and makes a loan (not in the course of trade) of $750,000 to an associated company. At this time $1.5 = £1. The balance of $450,000 is retained as a current asset. The books show the following entries at this point:

Capital loan ($900,000)	£600,000	Capital assets ($750,000)	£500,000
Capital loan	200,000	Current assets ($450,000)	300,000
	£800,000		£800,000

By the accounting date, the exchange rate alters to $1.25 = £1 and the book entries become:

Inland Revenue Statement

Capital loan ($900,000)	£720,000	Capital assets ($750,000)	£600,000
Capital loan	200,000	Current assets ($450,000)	360,000
Exchange difference to P & L account	40,000		
	£960,000		£960,000

The profit-and-loss account entry for the net exchange profit of £40,000 is made up of £160,000 profit on the assets and £120,000 loss on the liability.

The net capital exchange difference is a debit of £20,000, i.e., (£720,000 − £600,000) − (£600,000 − £500,000), but the profit-and-loss account shows a net credit of £40,000. No adjustment is therefore required for tax purposes. This reflects the matching of the net capital liability of $150,000 with part of the dollar current assets. The taxable exchange profit of £40,000 is attributable to the balance of the dollar current assets, whose value increased from £200,000 to £240,000.

(e) *It follows that normally the amount of any tax adjustment is limited in each case to the credit or debit for net exchange differences in the profit-and-loss account.*

More than one currency

21. Where there are transactions in more than one currency, the same principles will apply, but each currency must be considered separately. In such circumstances the exchange difference in the profit-and-loss account is the aggregate of the net exchange profits and losses arising in the various currencies and the tax computation adjustment is determined by comparing the aggregate exchange difference on capital assets and liabilities in a particular currency with the exchange difference for that currency in the profit-and-loss figure (but see paragraphs 22–24 below where hedging transactions are involved).

Example 6

A trading company borrows $900,000 on long-term capital account and DM300,000 on overdraft when £1 = $1.5 = DM3.0. It makes a loan of

Appendix II

$600,000 to an associated company (not in the course of trade) and converts $300,000 into DM600,000. It loans DM500,000 to another associated company (not in the course of trade) and retains the balance of DM400,000 as a current asset.

The books show the following entries:

Capital loan ($900,000)	£600,000	Capital assets ($600,000)	£400,000
Overdraft (DM300,000)	100,000	Capital assets (DM500,000)	167,000
		Current assets (DM400,000)	133,000
	£700,000		£700,000

By the accounting date, sterling has fallen to £1 = $1.20 = DM2.5 and the book entries are as follows:

Capital loan ($900,000)	£750,000	Capital assets ($600,000)	£500,000
Overdraft (DM300,000)	120,000	Capital assets (DM500,000)	200,000
		Current assets (DM400,000)	160,000
		Exchange difference to P & L account	10,000
	£870,000		£870,000

The net exchange difference of £10,000 comprises £50,000 loss on the dollar assets and liabilities, offset by £40,000 profit on the Deutschmark assets and liabilities.

The dollar exchange loss is entirely on capital account and should be added back to the tax computation.

The Deutschmark exchange difference comprises £60,000 profit on the assets and £20,000 loss on the liability. The net capital exchange difference on Deutschmark assets and liabilities is a profit of £33,000— i.e., (£200,000 − £167,000), so the adjustment for tax purposes is limited to £33,000. This reflects the fact that the overdraft is matched with Deutschmark current assets and the Deutschmark capital assets are unmatched.

Thus the overall adjustment to the tax computation is an addition of £17,000—i.e., (£50,000 − £33,000).

Hedging transactions

22. In considering whether a trader is matched in a particular currency, *forward exchange contracts* and *currency futures* entered into for hedging purposes may be taken into account, provided the hedging is reflected in the accounts on a consistent basis from year to

Inland Revenue Statement

year and in accordance with accepted accounting practice. For example, where a trading transaction is covered by a related or matching forward contract, under SSAP 20 the transaction may be translated using the rate of exchange specified in the forward contract. Alternatively, the forward contracts open at the balance sheet date may be shown as assets or liabilities, valued on a "mark-to-market" basis or by reference to the difference between the contracted forward exchange rates and the spot rate on the balance sheet date.

23. Where a trader enters into a *currency-swap agreement* to exchange borrowed currency for an equivalent amount of another currency (including sterling) for a fixed period, the two transactions in the original currency should be treated as matched, so that the underlying liability in the first currency is effectively converted into a liability in the second currency for the duration of the swap. If, when the swap is terminated, the currencies are swapped back at the spot rate of exchange prevailing at the commencement of the swap there will be for case I purposes no exchange loss or profit in terms of the original currency (but the capital gains consequences of unwinding the swap will need to be taken into account).

24. In the Inland Revenue's view, where currency assets or liabilities are hedged by transactions in *currency options* no matching can be said to have taken place and such transactions are unaffected by the Marine Midland decision.

Example 7: Hedging

The facts are those of Example 3 above in the subsequent accounting period at the start of which the book entries are:

Capital loan ($600,000)	£480,000	Current assets ($150,000)	£120,000
Overdraft on current account ($300,000)	240,000	Cash on hand	500,000
		Exchange difference b/f	100,000
	£720,000		£720,000

Three months from the end of the accounting period (there having been no transactions in the meantime affecting the assets and liabilities referred to in the example), when $1.18 = £1, the company enters a forward contract to purchase $600,000 at $1.20 = £1 in six months' time to hedge the capital loan that is repayable on the date the forward

Appendix II

contract matures. By the accounting date, when $1.0 = £1 the books show:

either

Capital loan ($600,000)*	£500,000	Current assets ($150,000)	£150,000
Overdraft on current account ($300,000)	300,000	Cash on hand	500,000
		Exchange difference b/f	100,000
		Exchange difference to P & L account	50,000
	£800,000		£800,000

*Translated at forward rate $1.20 = £1

or

Capital loan ($600,000)	£600,000	Current assets ($150,000)	£150,000
Overdraft on current account ($300,000)	300,000	Cash on hand	500,000
		Forward contract	100,000
		Exchange difference b/f	100,000
		Exchange difference to P & L account	50,000
	£900,000		£900,000

Because the forward contract specifically hedges the capital loan, the net exchange on capital items on either basis is £20,000 (£500,000 − £480,000; or £600,000 − £480,000 less £100,000 profit on forward contract). Because this is less than the overall exchange loss of £50,000, the capital loss of £20,000 is disallowed for tax purposes.

Overseas branches and trades

25. Where a trade carried on wholly abroad, or where an overseas branch of a trade has a local currency other than sterling, accounts will normally be drawn up in the local foreign currency and translated into sterling using the "net investment/closing rate" method (SSAP 20, paragraphs 25 and 46). In such circumstances, the Inland Revenue will accept computations based on the following:

(a) Accounts prepared in the local currency, with the adjusted profit before capital allowances, etc., translated into sterling at either the average or the closing exchange rate for the accounting period.

(b) The sterling equivalent of accounts prepared in local currency, translated into sterling using the "net investment/closing rate" method.

(c) Sterling accounts produced by the "temporal method" described in paragraphs 4 to 12 of SSAP 20.

Whichever method is adopted must be applied consistently form year to year. The method adopted in a particular case will affect only the determination of the case I profit adjusted for nontaxable and nonallowable items, but before capital allowances and stock relief are taken into account. Capital allowances and other statutory reliefs and charges will be calculated in sterling in the same way under either approach.

26. The principles outlined in this Statement of Practice should be applied in considering to what extent an adjustment for tax purposes should be made to the profit figure to be translated into sterling in respect of an exchange difference in the local foreign currency accounts.

Assets held on the "realization" basis

27. Some financial concerns hold assets, the profits on the disposal of which are treated for tax purposes as receipts of their trade, but which are not stock in trade. Such profits are assessable only when the assets are disposed of (the "realization" basis). Nevertheless, it may be the practice for accounting purposes to revalue the assets to reflect exchange rate fluctuations. Where the resulting exchange differences are either taken to the profit-and-loss account or set off against exchange differences on liabilities as part of the matching process, with the result that the profits or losses on realization are recognized for accounts purposes effectively net of exchange differences, the Inland Revenue will normally be prepared to follow the accounts treatment for tax, provided that this is applied consistently. The following example shows how this works. The treatment that is appropriate in any particular case will need to be agreed with the inspector by reference to all the relevant circumstances.

Appendix II

Example 8

A financial concern borrows $600,000 on capital account and raises a further sterling loan of £200,000. It converts the £200,000 to $300,000 and buys financial assets (realization basis) for $900,000. At this time $1.5 = £1. the books then show the following entries:

Capital loan ($600,000)	£400,000	Cost of financial assets ($900,000)	£600,000
Capital loan	200,000		
	£600,000		£600,000

At the accounting date the rate of exchange is $1.25 = £1, so the entries are as follows:

Capital loan ($600,000)	£480,000	Financial assets ($900,000)	£720,000
Capital loan	200,000		
Exchange difference to P & L account	40,000		
	£720,000		£720,000

Since the capital exchange difference is a debit of £80,000 (£480,000 − £400,000) and there is a net of £40,000 overall, no tax adjustment to the £40,000 is needed.

At the end of the net accounting period the rate of exchange has altered to $1.2 = £1 and the assets are sold, so the entries become:

Capital loan ($600,000)	£500,000	Cash proceeds of sale of financial assets ($1,200,000)	£1,000,000
Capital loan	200,000		
Exchange difference for Year 2 to P & L account	£10,000		
Exchange difference for Year 1 brought forward	40,000		
*Profit on realization of assets	250,000	300,000	
		£1,000,000	£1,000,000

328

*Sale proceeds $1.2m less cost $0.9m, giving a profit on realization of $0.3m or (at $1.2 = £1) £250,000. The exchange profit from holding the $900,000 assets, while the exchange rate moved from $1.5 = £1 to $1.2 = £1, has already been taken into account in the exchange differences.

The capital exchange difference is a loss on the loan of £20,000 (£500,000 − £480,000) but there is a profit of £30,000 in respect of current assets—i.e., £750,000 ($900,000 at $1.2 = £1) − £720,000. Thus, there is no adjustment to the figure in the profit-and-loss account for the exchange difference.

Roundabout loan arrangements

28. In exchanges of views with certain representative bodies following the decision of the House of Lords in *W. T. Ramsay Ltd. v. CIR* (1982) AC 300, the Inland Revenue indicated that they would not regard that decision as applying to arrangements involving long-term borrowing in foreign currency by banks and other concerns with related short-term loan facilities (often described as exchange roundabouts). This view was subject to reconsideration when the Marine Midland case was final.

29. Since it is accepted that Marine Midland leads to the conclusion that no case I tax adjustment arises where currency assets and liabilities are matched (see paragraph 13 above) it seems much less likely that roundabout arrangements will be used in matched situations. Where roundabouts are employed, this is likely to be in respect of unmatched or partly matched transactions and, in the Inland Revenue's view, these loan arrangements may, applying the Ramsay principle, fall to be treated for tax purposes by reference to their composite effect. Whether or not a contention based on these decisions is invoked will depend on the facts of particular cases.

30. The Inland Revenue regards this amended view as applying to roundabout arrangements entered into and to existing arrangements where they are renegotiated after the date of this statement.

Nontrading companies

31. The Marine Midland decision and the practice outlined above have no application outside the trading context. In nontrading com-

Appendix II

panies, the capital gains tax rules will apply to the acquisition and disposal of foreign currency chargeable assets (except where the transactions give rise to profits assessable under case VI of Schedule D) and exchange fluctuations will generally have no tax consequences outside the capital gains field.

Groups of companies

32. The principles and working rules outlined in this Statement of Practice apply only to individual trading companies and are not applicable to a group of companies seen as a whole, or in a way which recognizes "matching" between assets and liabilities of different companies in a group.

Capital gains

33. The decision in *Bentley v. Pike* 53 TC 590 established that a gain or loss on an asset should be computed by comparing the sterling value at the date of sale of the sale consideration with the sterling value at the date of acquisition of the acquisition cost. The principle is not affected by the Marine Midland decision, which is concerned only with the computation of trading profits.

Assessments open for earlier years

34. The practice set out in this statement will normally be applicable to years of assessment/accounting periods for which the assessments have not become final and conclusive. Where, however, it involves a change from a previously agreed basis, including the practice described in the Provisional Statement of Practice SP3/85 (Provisional), the transitional arrangements will depend on the facts of the case, and will be subject to negotiation with the inspector.

APPENDIX III

The London International Financial Futures Exchange limited taxation guidelines (issued 1982)

Over recent months, the Exchange has been in contact with the Inland Revenue with a view to producing some general guidelines as to the taxation treatment of transactions on LIFFE. Such guidelines have now been produced and are set out below.

These guidelines have been agreed with the Inland Revenue, but it must be emphasized that they have been produced for guidance only. They do not have any binding force on either the Inland Revenue or the taxpayer. They do not in any way affect a taxpayer's rights of appeal on points concerning his or her liability to tax. Except where specifically stated otherwise, these guidelines deal only with transactions which do not run to delivery. Where a transaction runs to delivery, the tax treatment will follow that normally is accorded to the underlying asset in the taxpayer's tax computations.

Method of assessment

1. Banks, financial trading companies, and insurance companies, with the exception of their life funds, will in general be taxable under Schedule D, case I.
2. As regards transactions carried out by other corporate bodies or individuals, there will be a primary assumption that any profits or

losses are of a revenue nature, but each case must depend on its own facts. It may be arguable that, where a hedging transaction is specifically related to an underlying capital transaction, capital treatment should be afforded to the financial futures transaction.

3. Individuals would normally be assessed under Schedule D, case VI, but, where an individual has an existing financial trade or trades actively through his own or a leased seat on the market, then he will probably be assessed under Schedule D, case I.

4. Companies that do not have an existing financial trade could also be assessed under Schedule D, case VI. Whether or not the activities by any person amount to trading is a question of fact. That transactions in financial futures are carried out by a company, rather than an individual, may be a factor to be taken into account (see Lewis Emanuel & Son Limited v. White (1900) 42 TC 369, and also Cooper v. C. & J. Clark Limited (1900) (Tax Leaflet 2875)), but the Inland Revenue does not consider it conclusive of trading.

Timing of assessment

5. The normal rule for assessment under Schedule D, case I, is that profits or losses may not be anticipated for tax purposes. Consequently, profits or losses in financial futures transactions would normally be taxed or allowed, only when realized.

    A profit or loss could be treated as realized, either when matched contracts are acquired, which is perhaps technically more correct, or when the clearinghouse is notified of set-off. Either approach, if consistently applied, should be acceptable unless the time of set-off were to be manipulated for tax reasons.

6. Although the normal rule would not permit the taxation of unrealized profits or the deduction of unrealized losses, the accounting treatment may be acceptable for tax purposes if the treatment of unrealized profits and losses is even-handed and consistent. However, profits or losses that have been realized at the year-end, but deferred in the accounts, would need to be brought into account for tax purposes.

7. Assessments raised under Schedule D, case VI, will be on realized profits.

8. For capital gains purposes, contracts that do not run to delivery will probably be regarded as unconditional contracts to acquire the

underlying asset and would therefore be subject to the normal rules of identification. For this purpose, it is thought that assets would be identified with each other where there are dealings in the same contract for the same delivery month.

Exchange conversion

9. All dollar-based transactions will, in theory, be required to be converted into sterling at the date of the relevant contracts. This means that the trader may be exposed to exchange rate movements on the full consideration for the contract. There will, however, be a matching dollar cash transaction that will neutralize this movement and the trader should only be taxed on the sterling equivalent of the real gain.

Nonresidents

10. Membership of the exchange may not of itself constitute a permanent establishment but, if a booth is rented or other premises are available in the United Kingdom, this could well amount to a permanent establishment.
11. Where a nonresident uses an independent broker to execute his transactions then, unless he has any other links with the United Kingdom, he would probably be protected from U.K. taxation under the terms of most double taxation treaties. If, however, he does not have the protection of a double taxation treaty, income would be attributable to him.

Capital gains—Delivery

12. Although the contracts would normally be regarded as unconditional contracts to acquire the underlying asset, this may not be correct in the case of a long gilt contract that runs to delivery. Since it is only on delivery that the asset is properly identified, the Inland Revenue considers that such contracts are conditional upon identification and that, therefore, for capital gains purposes, the purchase or sale does not take place until the asset is identified.

APPENDIX IV

Inland Revenue tax treatment of transactions in futures

In reply to the following Parliamentary Question about the tax treatment of futures:

> To ask Mr. Chancellor of the Exchequer if he is satisfied with the way in which the Inland Revenue is administering the taxation provisions in relation to futures; and if he will make a statement.

the Financial Secretary to the Treasury, Mr. John Moore, MP, gave the following Written Answer on November 29, 1985:

> Yes. Section 72 of this year's Finance Act [1985]—as proposed in my Rt. Hon. Friend's Budget Speech—that profits on transactions in commodity and financial futures, previously assessed under case VI of Schedule D, should be assessed to capital gains tax. However, it made no change where the taxpayer enters into such transactions in the course of a trade, in which case any profits remain liable to income tax or corporation tax under case I.
>
> Whether in any particular instance the activities of a taxpayer amount to trading will turn on the facts of the matter as well as on the law. But, in general, a taxpayer, whether an individual or company, would not be regarded as trading in respect of transactions that were relatively infrequent or, for example, where the intention was to hedge specific investments; and an individual is

Appendix IV

unlikely to be regarded as trading as a result of purely speculative transactions in futures.

Notes:
1. The Financial Secretary's answer explains that, if a taxpayer enters into transactions in commodity or financial futures in the course of a trade, any profits from those transactions will be liable to income tax under case I of Schedule D.
2. The answer also makes clear that, when in any particular case the activities of a taxpayer amount to trading, this will depend on the facts.
3. Finally, the answer makes clear that FA 1985 S.72, which provided that profits from transactions in futures that had previously been assessed under case VI of Schedule D should be assessed to capital gains tax, made no change in the case where a taxpayer's activities amount to trading. As the Chancellor made clear in his 1987 Budget speech, it was never the intention that S.72 should apply to trading transactions.

APPENDIX V

Extract from Banker's Association letter to members of October 2, 1979

The Inland Revenue has now confirmed that, where a bank carrying on a *bona fide* banking business in the United Kingdom enters as a principal into a currency-swap agreement in the ordinary course of its business, the fees (calculated by reference to interest-rate differentials) may be treated as normal expenses or receipts of that business and may be paid by the bank or to the bank without deduction for income tax. The Inland Revenue has further confirmed that, where a swap fee is paid to such a bank by a United Kingdom trading company, it will be treated as an ordinary trading expense and, where it is paid by an investment company, relief will be allowed as a charge under Section 248 of the Income and Corporation Taxes Act of 1970, even though the fee is paid gross.

The Inland Revenues continue to regard fees paid by U.K. residents that are not covered by the foregoing as annual payments from which income tax may be deductible under the provisions of Part II of the Income and Corporation Taxes Act of 1970, but subject to any relief afforded by an applicable double tax treaty.

APPENDIX VI

U.K. Inland Revenue recognized overseas exchanges

Non-U.K. futures exchanges

The designation of non-U.K. exchanges has taken place over the last two years but the effect was not to backdate these changes to 1985.

- The Chicago Board of Trade
- The Chicago Mercantile Exchange
- The Citrus Associates of the New York Cotton Exchange Inc.
- The Coffee Sugar & Cocoa Exchange Inc. New York
- The Commodity Exchange Inc. (COMEX)
- The Hong Kong Futures Exchange Limited
- The Mid-American Commodity Exchange
- The Montreal Exchange
- The New York Mercantile Exchange
- The New York Cotton Exchange
- The Philadelphia Board of Trade

Appendix VI

Recognized stock exchanges

The following countries' stock exchanges have also been recognized under the Income and Corporation Taxes Act 1988.

Australia	Hong Kong	Portugal
Austria	Irish Republic	Singapore
Belgium	Italy	South Africa
Canada	Japan	Spain
Denmark	Luxembourg	Sri Lanka
Finland	Netherlands	Switzerland
France	New Zealand	United States
Germany	Norway	

APPENDIX VII

Inland Revenue Statement of Practice on tax treatment of transactions in financial futures and options (issued July 1988)

1. This Statement sets out the Inland Revenue's views on the tax treatment of transactions in financial futures and options carried out by investment trusts, unit trusts, pension funds, charities, and companies which either do not trade or whose principal trade is outside the financial area. The principles set out apply to all futures and options, whether traded on an exchange or otherwise.
2. Section 72 Finance Act 1985 provides, broadly, that transactions in commodity and financial futures and traded options on recognized exchanges will be treated as capital in nature unless they are regarded as profits or losses of a trade. Section 81 Finance Act 1987 extends this treatment to other transactions in futures and options. If, under normal statutory and case law principles, profits or losses fall to be treated as trading in nature then Sections 72 and 81 have no application to those profits or losses. It is therefore necessary first to determine whether or not a taxpayer is trading in futures or options without reference to the provisions of Sections 72 and 81.
3. Whether or not a taxpayer is trading is a question of fact to be determined by reference to all the facts and circumstances of the particular case. Consideration is given to the "badges of trade." Generally a person will not be regarded as trading if the transac-

Appendix VII

tions are infrequent or to hedge specific capital investments. An individual is unlikely to be regarded as trading as a result of purely speculative transactions in options or futures.

4. If the taxpayer in question is a company, which would include an investment trust or authorized unit trust, it is necessary to consider not only the normal case law defining trading but also the case of *Lewis Emanuel and Son Ltd v. White* (42 TC 369). The broad effect of the judgment in this case is that generally a company cannot speculate and that any transactions carried out by a company must either be trading or capital in nature.

5. If a transaction in financial futures or options is clearly related to an underlying asset or transaction, then the tax treatment of the futures or options contract will follow that of the underlying asset or transaction. In general, the Inland Revenue take the view that this relationship exists where a futures or options contract is entered into in order to hedge an underlying transaction, asset or portfolio by reducing the risk relating to it; and the intention of the taxpayer in entering into the transaction is of considerable importance. Where the underlying transaction is itself treated as giving rise to a capital gain or loss, the related futures or options contract will also be treated as a capital matter and not as trading.

6. The basic conditions which have to be met if the transaction is to be treated as hedging in this sense are:

    (a) the transaction must be economically appropriate to the reduction in risk of the underlying transaction, asset or portfolio; and
    (b) the price fluctuations of the options and futures must be directly and demonstrably related to the fluctuations in value or composition of the underlying transaction, asset or portfolio at the time the heding transaction is initiated.

7. This applies equally to long and short positions, and is not dependent upon the form of the eventual disposition of the position. In other words it will apply whether the futures position is closed out or held to maturity, or in the case of an options position, closed out, exercised or held to final expiry.

Examples

8. Transactions would be treated as giving rise to capital gains or losses in the following circumstances:

(a) A taxpayer who holds gilts sells gilt futures to protect the value of his capital in the event of a fall in the value of gilt-edged securities generally.
(b) A taxpayer purchases an asset in two stages by purchasing a foreign currency future in advance of the purchase of an asset denominated in that currency, or by purchasing an option in respect of an underlying asset as a first step towards the acquisition of the asset itself.
(c) A taxpayer who holds a broadly based portfolio sells index futures or purchases index put options to protect himself against the risk to the value of the portfolio from a fall in the market (provided the fall in the index futures or options is directly and demonstrably correlated to the loss on the portfolio as it was constituted at the date the hedge was initiated).

9. But even if a transaction is not a hedging transaction in the sense of paragraph 6 above, it may, nevertheless, be regarded as capital in nature, depending on all the facts and circumstances. To take two specific examples:
(a) If a taxpayer is committed to making a bond issue in the near future and enters into an interest rate future or option with a view to protecting himself against rises in interest costs before he is able to make the issue, the Revenue will regard the transaction as being of a capital nature.
(b) If a taxpayer sells or buys options or futures as an incidental and temporary part of a change in investment strategy (e.g. changing the ratio of gilts and equities), that transaction is likely to be treated as being of a capital nature, if the transaction in the assets themselves woud be a capital matter.

10. A further uncertainty may arise if a transaction is originally undertaken as a capital hedge but the underlying transaction or motive falls away. If the futures or options transaction is closed out within a reasonably short period after the underlying motive falls away then the transaction will continue to be treated as capital in nature in accordance with the principles outlined above. If however the transaction is not closed out at that time it may be arguable that any profit or loss arising subsequently is of a trading nature. In practice the Revenue would not normally take this point in view of the original intentions of the taxpayer and the practical difficulties of making the necessary calculation.

Appendix VII

11. Where a company enters into these transactions as incidental to its trading activity, for example a manufacturer entering into transactions to hedge the price of his raw materials, then the profits or losses from these transactions would be taken into account as part of the profits and losses of the trade.

Index

A

Aberdeen Construction Group Ltd. v. CIR, 226
Accountant
  corporate users, 10–11
  objectives of, 4–5
  profit-and-loss recognition, 8–9
    advantages of approach, 8–9
Accounting
  caps, 141–49
    variable-rate borrowings, 143–47
    writer of cap, 147–49
  collars, 152
  forward-rate agreements (FRAs), 49–60
    hedge accounting, 50–57
    management information, 59
    overall considerations, 50
    speculation, 57–59
  interest-rate caps, 141–49
    variable-rate borrowings, 143–47
    writer of caps, 147–49
  issues, 6–8
  options, 114–33
    accounting entries, 115–33
    background, 114–15
    basic terminology, 107–8
    dealer equity options, 264
    hedgers, 110–29
    nonequity options, 264
    options book, 300
    traded stock options, 113–14
      margining, 113–14
    trading strategies, 111–13
      sell futures contract/buy call option, 112
      sell futures contract/write put option, 112
      write put-call straddle, 112–13
    United States taxation, 258–59
    valuation of, 108, 117
Accounting entries
  options, 115–33
  purchase, 116
  recognition of profit and loss, 117–18
  sale, 116–17
  valuation, 117
Accounting records
  initial entries, 116–17
  internal controls and, 185–86
Accounting standards
  international standards, 6
  United Kingdom, 6
  United States, 6
Accounting Standards Committee, 79
Accruals, definition of, 5
Accruals approach, 9, 13
Accrued market discount treatment, 250
American depository receipts (ADRs), 114

American Institute of Certified Public Accountants, 115, 117
  Issues Paper 86-2, 115
American option, 108, 289
Annual interest, 197, 198
Anticipatory short hedges, 37
Arbitrage, definition of, 295
Arbitraging, financial futures contracts, 23, 26
Asset-based swaps, 69, 103–4
  accounting for, 69, 103–4
  acquisition of, 103–4
  for investment purposes, 103
  for trading purposes, 103
Assets, determining value of, 8
Assignment, definition of, 295
Association of Futures Brokers and Dealers (AFBD), 21
At-the-money option, 108, 295

B

Back-to-back loans, 295
Balance sheet valuation, 8
Banker's option, 107
Banks and financial institutions, special tax treatment for, 192
Bankwagons, 162
Basis
  definition of, 295–96
  as financial instrument, 23
Basis point, definition of, 296
Bentley v. Pike, 205, 330
Black-Scholes model
  definition of, 296
  valuation and, 108
Board of Inland Revenue, 197 ff.
Break-even point, definition of, 296
British Banker's Association
  extract from letter to members, 340
  FRABBA terms, 299
Bull call spreads, 111
Buying a straddle, use of term, 110

C

Call option, 107, 112
Capital assets
  Corn Products Doctrine and, 244
  definition of, 243
  exceptions to, 243–44
Capital gains, 244–45
  long-term capital gain, 245
  special tax advantages of, 244–45
  United Kingdom tax law, 193, 201–2
    chargeable assets, 201–2
    options instruments, 202
    time of disposal for, 202

355

Index

Capital Gains Tax Act (CGTA), 202
Capital losses
  United Kingdom tax law, 245–46
    carrying forward of, 245–46
Capped floating rate notes, definition of, 296
Caps
  accounting for, 141–49
    variable-rate borrowings, 143–47
    writer of cap, 147–49
  definition of, 137–38
  markets, 141
  risk control, 175–76
  uses of, 140
Cash settlement, definition of, 290
Certificates of deposit (CDs), 18
  definition of, 296
Chicago Board of Trade, 22
Chicago Mercantile Exchange (CME), Mutual Offset System, 264–65
Clearco Limited, 87–90
Clearinghouse, definition of, 22
Collars
  accounting for, 152
  definition of, 138–39
  risk control, 175–76
COMEX, 167
Commercial banks and trust companies, special tax treatment for, 255
Commercial paper, definition of, 296
Commodity Futures Trading Commission (CFTC), 296
Common trust funds, special tax treatment for, 255
Comparative risk table, 308–9
Consistency, definition of, 5
Control standards, 3
Conversion, definition of, 297
Corn Products Doctrine, 244
Corporate users
  framework for, 10–11
  swaps, 72–94
    cross-currency swaps, 68–69, 86–94
    currency swaps, 63, 67–68, 79–86
    fees, 75
    foreign currency translation, 75
    interest-rate swaps, 65–67, 72–75, 99
    termination, 78
Country risk, 167
  definition of, 297
Coupon-stripping, definition of, 297
Covered writing, definition of, 297
Credit limits, internal controls and, 183–84
Credit risk, 158–59, 163, 171
  credit extension and, 164
  identification of, 163
  monitoring exposure to, 163
  with non-credit-extending instruments, 164
  note issuance facilities (NIFs), 164
  revolving underwriting facilities (RUFs), 164
  transaction growth and technology, 166
Cross-currency swaps, 68–69, 86–94
  United States taxation, 251
Currency futures, 40
Currency gains and losses
  United Kingdom tax law, 203–6

    balance sheet approach, 204
    disparity in treatment, 203
    revenue versus capital, 203–4
    underlying transaction, 204
  United States taxation, 250–54
    exchange gain or loss, 251–53
    foreign currency transactions, 251
    functional currency, 250–51
Currency options
  risk control, 169–70
  United Kingdom taxation, 234–35
    banks and other financial concerns, 234
    commercial users, 235
Currency swaps, 63, 67–68, 79–86
  definition of, 297
  exchange gains and losses, 226–34
  periodic payments under, 223–34
  risk control, 171
  tax planning methods, 229–33
    debt of security, 229–31
    offshore vehicle, 233–34
    U.K. finance subsidiary, 232–33

D

Davies v. Shell Co. of China, 206
Dealer equity options, definition of, 264
Deductibility of interest
  Internal Revenue Code, 246
  United Kingdom taxation
    banking activities, 198
    costs of finance, 200
    critical issues for treasury instruments, 200–1
    discount versus interest, 199–200
    general concepts, 199
    investment management companies, 199
    trading companies, 198–99
    U.K. branches of nonresident companies, 199
Deep discount bonds, definition of, 297
Default, as major credit risk, 163
Delivery
  capital gains, 335
  financial futures contracts, 20
  settlement risk and, 15
Delivery risk, *See* Settlement risk.
Delta, definition of, 297–98
Delta hedging, 298
Disclosure
  financial futures contracts, 42
  forward-rate agreements (FRAs), 69
Discounts, deductibility of, 199–200

E

Economic risk analysis, swaps, 71
EDP support, internal controls and, 187
End-user, swap market, 298
Euro-commercial paper (ECP), definition of, 298
Euro-commercial paper (ECP) facility, definition of, 298
Eurocurrency, 18
Euronote, definition of, 298
European option, 108, 298
Exchange gains or losses
  currency swaps, 226–27

356

Index

interest equivalency approach, 252
treated as interest income or expense, 252
United States taxation, 251–53
Exchanges
futures market, 21
international exchanges, 22
Exchange-traded treasury instruments, United Kingdom taxation, 210–11
Execution Exchange, Mutual Offset System, 265
Exercise price, definition of, 298
Expected volatility, definition of, 298
Expiration date, definition date, 299

F

Fees
corporate users, 75
institutional users, 12
Finance Act of 1980, 200
Financial Accounting and Standards Board (FASB) statements, 3, 49
Financial futures contracts
accounting for, 26–42
currency futures, 40
disclosure, 42
hedging, 28–40
anticipatory long hedge of asset carried at cost, 35–37
anticipatory short hedge of liability, 37–40
hedges of assets carried at lower of cost or market value, 31–32
long hedge of liability carried at cost, 32–34
short hedge of asset carried at cost, 28–31
overall basis of accounting, 26–27
speculation, 40–42
stock index futures, 40
definition of, 17, 299
delivery, 20
fungibility quality, 17
key ingredient in, 17
margining, 22–23
original margin, 22
procedures, 22–23
variation margin, 22–23
markets, 20–21
types of, 17–18
foreign-exchange contracts, 19
long-term interest-rate contracts, 19
short-term interest-rate contracts, 18–19
stock index contracts, 19
uses of, 23–26
arbitraging, 26
hedging, 23–25
speculation, 25
Financial instruments
risk assessment, 169–82
risk control, 155–61, 169–82
caps, 175–76
collars, 175–76
currency options, 169–70
currency swaps, 171
floors, 175–76
forward-rate agreements, 176–78

interest-rate futures, 176
interest-rate options, 169–70
interest-rate swaps, 171–75
NIFs/RUFs, 178–79
repurchase agreements, 179–82
Financial Services Act of 1986, 21
Financial Times-Stock Exchange 100, 19
Floating-rate note (FRN), definition of, 299
Floors
accounting for, 149–52
definition of, 138
interest-rate floors
accounting for, 149–52
definition of, 138
risk control, 175–76
Floor trader, 21
Foreign currency, gain or loss, Section 988, 267–68
Foreign currency contract, definition of, 262
Foreign currency transactions, United States taxation, 251–53
Foreign-exchange futures contracts, 19
Forward-rate agreements (FRAs)
accounting for, 49–60
hedge accounting, 50–57
management information, 59
overall considerations, 50
speculation, 57–59
advantages of, 48
assets, 49
definition of, 45–46, 293
disadvantages of, 48
disclosure, 69
hedging strategies, 48–49
assets, 49
interest spreads, 49
liabilities, 49
markets, 49
risk control, 176–78
six against nine months, 46
in swap market, 98
in United Kingdom, 47
uses of, 47–49
FRABBA terms, definition of, 299
Functional currency, United States taxation, 250–51
Functional currency borrowing
conversion into nonfunctional currency borrowing, 277–78
tax effects, 277–78
Fungibility, financial futures contracts, 17
Future-rate agreements (FRAs), *See* Forward-rate agreements (FRAs).
Futures contracts, *See* Financial futures contracts.
Futures markets
clearinghouses, 22
exchanges, 21
as mechanism for hedgers, 20

G

Gamma, definition of, 299–300
Gap, definition of, 300

357

Index

Going concern, definition of, 5
Grantor, *See* Writer.

H

Hedged asset, 10
Hedged liability, 10
Hedge ratio, 300
Hedgers
  financial futures contracts, 20–21
  goals of, 21
Hedging, 8–10, 23
  accruals approach and, 9, 13
  corporate users, 10–11
    existing asset or liability, 10
    potential commitment, 11
    trade commitment, 10–11
  definition of, 294
  financial futures contracts, 20–21, 23–25, 28–40
    anticipatory long hedge of asset carried at cost, 35–37
    anticipatory short hedge of liability, 37–40
    hedges of assets carried at lower of cost or market value, 31–32
    long hedge of liability carried at cost, 32–34
    short hedge, 24–25
    short hedge of asset carried at cost, 28–31
  forward-rate agreement (FRAs) strategies, 48–49
    assets, 49
    interest spreads, 49
    liabilities, 49
  options, 119–29
    deferring unrealized differences, 120–21
    foreign currency option transaction, example of, 121–25
    hedging existing asset, liability, or transaction, 120
    income enhancer, 132–33
    interest-rate option transaction, example of, 125–29
    methods, 118
    lower of cost or market, 118
    mark-to-market, 118
    potential commitment, 120
    professional standards, 115
    qualifying option for hedge accounting, 119–20
    recommended treatment, 120–21
    speculators, 118–19
    strategies, 119
    trade commitment, 120
    trade spread transaction, example of, 129–32
  qualifying transaction, 272
  Section 988 hedge, 272
  short hedge, 24
  United States taxation, 261–62
  versus speculative approach, 8–10
Holder, options, 107

I

Implied volatility, 300
Income
  tests of income under U.K. tax law, 194–95
  characterization of asset, 194
  enduring benefit, 194
  fixed versus circulating capital, 194
  incidence, 194
Income and Corporation Taxes Act 1970, 193
Income enhancers, definition of, 111
Income tax schedules, United Kingdom, 195–96
Individual risk, versus overall risk, 159–60
Inland Revenue, tax treatment of futures transactions, 332
Inland Revenue Statement of Practice (on exchange rate fluctuations), 206–8, 313–40
  accounts treatment and tax consequences, 315–17
  conversion bases, 316
  Inland Revenue view, 315–16
  translation and conversion, 315
  assessments open for earlier years, 330
  assets held on realization basis, 327–29
  capital and current liabilities, 316–17
  capital gains, 330
  definitions, 314
  groups of companies, 330
  hedging transactions, 324–26
    example, 325–26
  introduction, 313
  matched assets and liabilities, 317–23
    assets and liabilities, 318
    examples, 319–23
    matching capital assets in foreign currency, 318
    practical approach, 319
    same currency, 317–18
  more than one currency, 323–24
    example, 323–24
  nontrading companies, 329–30
  overseas branches and trades, 326–27
  roundabout loan arrangements, 330
  summary of Marine Midland, 313–14
Institutional users
  fees/commissions, 12
  framework for, 11–12
  market-to-market approach, 11–12
Interest, limitations on, 246–47
Interest and discount
  United States taxation, 246–49
    loan fees, 249
    market discount, 248–49
    original issue discount (OID) and unstated interest, 247–48
    short term obligations, 249
Interest equivalency approach, exchange gain or loss, 252
Interest-rate caps
  accounting for, 141–49
    variable rate borrowings, 143–47
    writer of caps, 147–49
  definition of, 137–38, 294
  markets, 141
  uses of, 140
Interest-rate collars
  accounting for, 152
  definition of, 138–39
Interest-rate floors
  accounting for, 149–52

358

Index

definition of, 138
floor trader, 21
risk control, 175–76
Interest-rate futures contracts
  long-term, 18–19
  risk control, 176
  short-term, 17–18
Interest-rate mismatch, definition of, 294
Interest-rate options, risk control, 169–70
Interest rates, deregulation of, 161
Interest-rate swaps, 65–67, 72–75, 99
  definition of, 295
  risk control, 171–75
  United States taxation, 257–58
    Notice 87-4, 258
    Revenue Ruling 87-5, 257–58
Interest-rate treasury instruments, United Kingdom taxation, 210
Interest spreads, forward-rate agreements (FRAs), 49
Interest swaps, periodic payments under, 223–24
Intermediary, swap market, definition of, 301
Internal controls
  risk, 182–87
    accounting records, 185–86
    credit limits, 183–84
    EDP support, 187
    procedures and policy manuals, 183
    reporting, 186–87
    trade tickets, 185
    trading limits, 185
Internal Revenue Code
  Section 988
    calculation of original issue discount, 269–70
    income from discharge of indebtedness, 268–69
    ordinary income or loss, 267–68
    qualified hedges, 270–91
    special rule for certain investments, 270
    transactions, 270
  Section 988, 265–91
  Subpart J, 253–54
International Accounting Standards (IAS), 6
International Business Machines (IBM), 86
International Monetary Market (IMM), 20, 22
In-the-money option, 108, 300
Intrinsic value
  definition of, 301
  options, 108
Investment management companies
  deductibility of interest and, 199
  tax rules for, 193

L

Liabilities
  determining value of, 8
  forward-rate agreements (FRAs), 49
LIBID, definition of, 301
LIBOR, definition of, 301
Loan fees, United States taxation and, 249
Loans
  back-to-back loans, 295
  deductibility of interest, 197–201

  banking activities, 198
  costs of finance, 200
  discount versus interest, 199–200
  investment management companies, 199
  trading companies, 198–99
  treasury instruments, 200–1
  U.K. branches of nonresident companies, 199
London International Financial Futures Exchange (LIFFE), 19, 21, 22
  limited taxation guidelines, 333–38
    capital gains—delivery, 335
    exchange conversion, 335
    method of assessment, 333–34
    nonresidents, 335
    timing of assessment, 334–35
Long hedge, 32, 35
Long option position, definition of, 301
Long-term capital gains, 245
  special tax advantages of, 244–45
Long-term interest-rate futures contracts, 19

M

Margin, definition of, 300–02
Margining, 22–23
  financial futures contracts, 22–23
    original margin, 22
    procedures, 22–23
    variation margin, 22–23
  original margin, 22
  variation margin, 22–23
Marine Midland Ltd. v. Pattison, 206
Marked to market, 22
Market discount
  accrued market discount treatment, 248
  definition of, 248
  net direct interest expense and, 249
  partial payments on market discount bonds, 248–49
  United States taxation and, 248–49
Market liquidity risk, 167, 171
  definition of, 302
  new market trading, 167
Market risk, 158–59, 160, 162
Markets
  caps, 141
  financial futures contracts, 20–21, 20–22
  forward-rate agreements (FRAs), 49
  interest-rate caps, 141
Market-to-market approach, institutional users, 11–12
Market volatility, *See* Volatility.
Matched intermediaries, 95–97
MATIF (Paris) Exchange, 22
Maturity date, definition date, 293
Middle straddles
  United States taxation, 260–62
  gains and losses, 262
Multinational portfolios, *See* Portfolios.
Mutual Offset System
  Section 1256 contracts, 264–65
    Execution Exchange, 265
    Origination Exchange, 265
Mutual savings banks, special tax treatment for, 255

359

Index

N

Naked writer, definition of, 305
Net direct interest expense, market discount and, 248–49
New financial instruments
  effect of volatility on, 161
  risk assessment, 159
New instrument markets, 161
New market trading, market liquidity risk and, 167
New product development, effect on transaction risk, 168
New York Futures Exchange, 22
Nonequity option, definition of, 264
Nonfunctional currency borrowing
  conversion into functional currency borrowing, 274–75
    tax effects, 274–75
  conversion into second nonfunctional currency, 275–76
    tax effects, 276–77
  hedged with forward contracts, 284–86
    higher interest-rate currency, 284–86
    lower interest-rate currency, 286–87
  hedged with swap, 283–84
Nonfunctional currency denominated debt instrument
  conversion into functional currency denominated debt instrument, 278–79
    tax effects, 279
  hedged with forward contracts, 287–89
    higher interest-rate currency, 287–88
    lower interest-rate currency, 289
Note issuance facilities (NIFs), 164
  definition of, 302
  risk control, 178–79
Notice 87-11, 271–72
Notional principal, definition of, 302

O

Off-balance-sheet activities, definition of, 302
"Open outcry" market, 210
Options
  accounting for, 114–33
    accounting entries, 115–33
    background, 114–15
    hedgers, 119–29
      deferring unrealized differences, 120–21
      of existing asset, liability, or transaction, 120
      foreign currency option transaction, example of, 121–25
      interest-rate option transaction, example of, 125–29
      potential commitment, 120
      qualifying option for hedge accounting, 119–20
      recommended treatment, 120–21
      strategies, 119
      trade commitment, 120
      trade spread transaction, example of, 129–32
    income enhancer, 132–33
    methods, 118
      lower of cost or market, 118
      mark-to-market, 118
    professional standards, 115
    speculators, 118–19
  basic terminology, 107–8
    American option, 108
    banker's option, 107
    call option, 107
    European option, 108
    put option, 107
    traded option, 107
  dealer equity options, 264
  definition of, 302
  nonequity options, 264
  options book, 302
  traded stock options, 113–14
    margining, 113–14
  trading strategies, 111–13
    sell futures contract/buy call option, 112
    sell futures contract/write put option, 112
    write put-call straddle, 112–12
  United States taxation, 252–53
  uses, 109–11
    hedges, 109–10
    income enhancers, 111
    speculation, 109
    trading, 110–11
  valuation of, 108, 117
    intrinsic value, 108
    premium, 108
    time value, 108
Ordinary income/capital gain distinction, United States taxation, 243–44
Original issue discount (OID), 247–48, 269
  determination of, 248
  Internal Revenue Code rules for, 247
Original margin, 22
Origination Exchange, Mutual Offset System, 265
Out-of-money option, 108, 303
Overall risk, versus individual risk, 159–60
Over-the-counter (OTC) markets, 114–15, 302–03
Over-the-counter (OTC) treasury instruments, United Kingdom taxation, 214–22

P

Plain-vanilla swap, 303
Portfolios
  exposure to market rise, 160
  multinational growth of, 160
  new instrument markets, 161
  trend toward hedging, 160
Position, Internal Revenue Code definition, 259
Premium
  definition of, 303
  options, 108
Price risk, *See* Market risk.
Procedures manuals, internal controls and, 183
Profit-and-loss account, deferred losses taken to, 32
Prudence, definition of, 5
Pure cap, 138
Put-call straddle, 112–13
Put option, 107, 112

Index

Q

Qualifying transaction
  definition of, 272
  and hedge as integrated economic package, 272-74

R

W. I. Ramsey Ltd. v. CIR, 230, 329
Regulated futures contract, definition of, 262
Regulated investment companies, United States taxation, 255-56
Regulatory standards, 3
Reporting, internal controls and, 186-87
Repurchase agreements
  definition of, 303
  risk control, 179-82
Revaluation, advantages of, 99
Revenue Ruling 87-43, Mutual Offset System and, 264
Reverse swap, 303
Revolving underwriting facilities (RUFs), 164
  risk control, 178-79
Risk
  country risk, 167
  credit extension history, 156
  credit risk, 158-59, 163, 171
    credit extension and, 164
    identification of, 163
    monitoring exposure to, 163
    with non-credit-extending instruments, 164
    note issuance facilities (NIFs), 164
    revolving underwriting facilities (RUFs), 164
    transaction growth and technology, 166
  in financial instruments, 169-82
    caps, 175-76
    collars, 175-76
    currency options, 169-70
    currency swaps, 171
    floors, 175-76
    forward-rate agreements, 176-78
    interest-rate futures, 176
    interest-rate options, 169-70
    interest-rate swaps, 171-75
    NIFs/RUFs, 178-79
    repurchase agreements, 179-82
  financial system impact, 156-57
  internal controls, 182-87
    accounting records, 185-86
    credit limits, 183-84
    EDP support, 187
    procedures and policy manuals, 183
    reporting, 186-87
    trade tickets, 185
    trading limits, 185
  market liquidity risk, 167, 171
    new market trading, 167
  market risk, 158-59, 160, 162
  pricing in new instrument markets, 156-57
  risk assessment, 159-60
  settlement risk, 165-66
    delivery and location errors, 165
    protection in automated transactions, 166

solvency risk, 158
technology risk, 165
  importance of computer systems to, 165
transaction risk, 167-68
  effect of new product development on, 168
  effect of volume on, 167
transfer risk, 167
Risk assessment, 159-60, 169-82
  individual versus overall risk, 159-60
  of new financial instruments, 159
Risk-pricing, long-term interest rates, 157-58

S

Schedule D, United Kingdom income tax code, 195-96, 198
Section 1256 contracts
  definition of, 262
  exceptions, 263-64
  Mutual Offset System, 264-65
  United States taxation, 262-64
Section 988 transactions, 253-54
Section 988
  Internal Revenue Code, 265-91
    calculation of original issue discount, 269-70
    income from discharge of indebtedness, 268-69
    ordinary income or loss, 267-68
    qualified hedges, 270-91
    special rule for certain investments, 270
    transactions, 266-67
Securitization, 303-04
Selling a straddle, use of term, 111
Settlement date, 271
Settlement price, definition of, 304
Settlement risk, 165-66
  definition of, 304
  delivery and location errors, 165
  protection in automated transactions, 166
Short hedges, 24
  anticipatory short hedges, 37
  of asset carried at cost, 38
Short interest, 197, 198
Short option position, 304
Short-term interest-rate futures contracts, 18-19
  definition of, 18
  example of, 18
  popularity of, 19
Short-term obligations, United States taxation and, 249
Short volatility position, 304
Singapore International Monetary Exchange Limited (SIMEX), Mutual Offset System, 22, 264-65
Solvency risk, 158
Special tax treatment
  banks and financial institutions, 254
  commercial banks and trust companies, 255
  common trust funds, 255
  mutual savings banks, 255
  regulated investment companies, 255-56
  tax-exempt organizations, 256

361

Index

Speculation
  financial futures contracts, 25, 40–42
  options, 118–19
Speculative position, versus hedging approach, 8–10
Spread, establishment of, 26
Standards
  accounting standards, 3, 13
  control standards, 3
  regulatory standards, 3
Standards and Poor's 100/500 contracts, 19
Statement of Practice of Inland Revenue, 313–40
  accounts treatment and tax consequences, 315–17
    conversion bases, 316
    translation and conversion, 315
  assessments open for earlier years, 330
  assets held on realization basis, 327–29
  capital and current liabilities, 316–17
  capital gains, 330
  definitions, 314
  groups of companies, 330
  hedging transactions, 324–26
    example, 325–26
  introduction, 313
  matched assets and liabilities, 317–23
    assets and liabilities, 318
    examples, 319–23
    matching capital assets in foreign currency, 318
    practical approach, 319
    same currency, 317–18
  more than one currency, 323–24
    example, 323–24
  nontrading companies, 329–30
  overseas branches and trades, 326–27
  roundabout loan arrangements, 329
  summary of Marine Midland, 313–14
Statements of Financial Accounting Standards (SFAS), 6, 11, 16, 115, 119
Statements of Standard Accounting Practice (SSAP), 6, 79, 115
Stock index futures contracts, 19
Straddles
  buying a straddle, 110
  definition of, 298
  put-call straddle, 112–13
  selling a straddle, 111
  United States taxation, 258–59
    Section 1092, 258
Straddle write, 304
Strike price, definition of, 298
Stripped cap, 138
Subpart J, Internal Revenue Code, 253–54
Swaps
  accounting for, 70–104
    asset-based swaps, 69, 103–4
    corporate users, 72–94
      cross-currency swaps, 68–69, 86–94
      currency swaps, 63, 67–68, 79–86
      fees, 75
      foreign currency translation, 75
      interest-rate swaps, 65–67, 72–75, 99
      termination, 78
  economic risk analysis, 71
  financial institutions, 94–95
  fundamental principles underlying account preparation, 70
  matched intermediaries, 95–97
  swap traders, 98–99
  assignment, 289
  definition of, 63, 304
  intermediary, 295
  periodic payments under, 223
  revaluation of, 99–103
  swap income, 258
  types of, 63–69
    asset-based swaps, 69, 103–4
    cross currency swaps, 68–69, 86–94
    currency swaps, 63, 67–68, 79–86
    interest-rate swaps, 65–67, 72–75, 99, 301
    plain-vanilla swap, 303
    reverse swap, 303
  United Kingdom taxation, 222–34
    commencement of swap-arrangement fees, 222
    currency swaps, 222, 226
    general aspects of swaps, 222
    periodic payments under swap, 223
Swap traders, 98–99
Sydney Futures Exchange, 22
Synthetic asset, 103
Synthetic functional currency asset
  higher interest-rate currency, 287–88
  lower interest rate currency, 289
Synthetic functional currency
  liability, Section 988 hedging
  transaction rules, 283–87
Synthetic positions, definition of, 305

T

Taxation guidelines
  London International Financial Futures Exchange (LIFFE), 333–38
    capital gains—delivery, 335
    method of assessment, 333–34
    nonresidents, 335
    timing of assessment, 334–35
Tax-exempt organizations, treasury instruments and, 193, 256
Tax planning methods
  currency swaps, 230–33
  debt of security, 230–32
  offshore vehicle, 233–34
  United Kingdom finance subsidiary, 232–33
Tax Reform Act of 1986, 253
Tax straddle, definition of, 259
Technology risk, 165
  importance of computer systems to, 165
Tender panel, definition of, 305
Time value
  definition of, 305
  options, 108
Trade date, 271
Traded option, 107, 113–14
Trade-related discounts, deductibility of, 199–200

Index

Trade tickets, internal controls and, 185
Trading companies, deductibility of interest and, 198–99
Trading limits, internal controls and, 185
Trading strategies
 options, 111–13
  sell futures contract/buy call option, 112
  sell futures contract/write put option, 112
  write put-call straddle, 112
Transaction risk, 167–68
 effect of new product development on, 168
 effect of volume on, 167
Transactions, types of, 4–5
Transfer risk, 167
Treasury bonds, 19, 20, 100
Treasury instruments
 United Kingdom taxation, 210
  amendments to U.K. tax treatment, 212
  exchange-traded instruments, 210
  interest-rate treasury instruments, 210
  over-the-counter (OTC) instruments, 217–22
 United States taxation
  hedges, 262–63
  interest-rate swaps, 257–58
  middle straddles, 260–62
  options, 258–59
  straddles, 259–60
"True" U.S. dollar interest rate, 251

U

Uncovered writer, definition of, 305
Underlying, definition of, 305
United Kingdom taxation, 191–235
 capital gains tax, 201–2
 currency gains and losses, 203–5
  revenue versus capital, 203–5
 currency options, 234–35
  banks and other financial concerns, 234
  commercial users, 234
 deductibility of expenses, 196
 deductibility of interest, 197–201
  banking activities, 198
  costs of finance, 200
  critical issues for treasury instruments, 200–1
  discount versus interest, 199–200
  general concepts, 199
  investment management companies, 199
  trading companies, 198–99
  U.K. branches of nonresident companies, 199
 general tax principles, 193–97
 income tax schedules, 195–96
 income versus capital, 194–95
 Marine Midland Ltd., and Inland Revenue Statement of Practice, 206–10
 swaps, 222
  commencement of swap-arrangement fees, 222–23
  currency swaps, 223, 226–34
  general aspects of swaps, 222
  periodic payments under swap, 223
 taxation of specific treasury instruments, 210
  amendments to U.K. tax treatment, 212

 exchange-traded instruments, 211
 interest-rate treasury instruments, 210
 over-the-counter (OTC) instruments, 214–22
 types of users, 192–93
  banks and financial institutions, 192
  exempt organizations, 193
  investment activities, 193
  trading activities, 192–93
United States taxation
 capital gains, 244–45
  long-term capital gain, 245
  special tax advantages of, 244–45
 capital losses, 245–46
  carrying forward of, 245–46
 currency gains and losses, 250–52
  exchange gain or loss, 251–53
  foreign currency transactions, 251
  functional currency, 250–51
 general tax principles, 242–54
 interest and discount, 246–49
  loan fees, 249
  market discount, 248–49
  original issue discount (OID) and unstated interest, 247–48
  short-term obligations, 249
 ordinary income/capital gain distinction, 243–44
  capital assets, 243–44
  Corn Products Doctrine, 244
  Tax Reform Act of 1986 and, 245
 Section 1256 contracts, 263–65
 taxation of specific treasury instruments, 257–63
  hedges, 262–63
  interest-rate swaps, 257–58
  middle straddles, 260–62
  options, 258–59
  straddles, 259–60
 users of treasury instruments, 254–56
  banks and financial institutions, 254–55
  commercial banks and trust companies, 255
  common trust funds, 255
  mutual savings banks, 255
  regulated investment companies, 255–56
  tax-exempt organizations, 256
Unstated interest rules, 247

V

Valuation
 options, 108, 117
  intrinsic value, 108
  premium, 108
  time value, 108
Variation margin, 22–23
Volatility
 definition of, 305
 deregulation of interest rates, 161
 distribution of world information, 162
 effect of market speculators on, 161–62
 effect on new financial instruments, 161
 effect of technology on, 162
 expected volatility, 298
 implied volatility, 300
Volume, effect on transaction risk, 167
Voluntary termination, swap market, 305

Index

W

World Bank, 86
Writer
　definition of, 306
　options, 107
　uncovered writer, 305

Z

Zero coupon bonds, definition of, 306